EXTRAORDINARY

B●DIES

EXTRAORDINARY B●DIES:

FIGURING

PHYSICAL

DISABILITY

IN AMERICAN CULTURE

AND LITERATURE

ROSEMARIE GARLAND THOMSON

Columbia University Press • New York

Cover photo: Frida Kahlo, "Self-Portrait with Portrait of Doctor Farill," 1951. © Banco de México, fiduciary of the Diego Rivera and Frida Kahlo Museums. Reproduced with permission from the Instituto Nacional de Bellas Artes y Literatura (INBA), Mexico.

Columbia University Press
Publishers Since 1893
New York   Chichester, West Sussex
Copyright © 1997 Columbia University Press

Library of Congress Cataloging-in-Publication Data
Thomson, Rosemarie Garland.
Extraordinary bodies : figuring physical disability in American
culture and literature / Rosemarie Garland Thomson.
p.   cm.
Includes bibliographical references and index.
ISBN 0–231–10516–9 (cloth : acid-free paper). —
ISBN 0–231–10517–7 (paper)
1. American fiction—19th century—History and criticism.
2. American fiction—20th century—History and criticism.
3. Physically handicapped in literature.   4. Body, Human, in
literature.   5. Body, Human—Social aspects.   6. Physically
handicapped—Social aspects.   7. Women in literature.   8. Popular
culture—United States—History.   9. Sideshows—United States—
History.   10. Feminism and literature—United States.   I. Title.
PS374.P44T49   1997
813'.0093520816—dc20   96–21998

Casebound editions of Columbia University Press books are printed on permanent and durable acid-free paper.
Printed in the United States of America

c 10 9 8 7 6 5 4 3 2 1
p 10 9 8 7 6 5 4 3 2 1

Contents

· · · · ·

EXTRAORDINARY

B●DIES

PREFACE & ACKNOWLEDGMENTS

• • • • •

This book is the consequence of a coming-out process. As is often the case for people with disabilities, I had learned to see my bodily difference as a private matter, an aspect of myself that I acknowledged and negotiated in the world with a mixture of composure and embarrassment. I knew that my body made people uncomfortable to varying degrees and that it was my job to reassure them that I was going to be fine—that we were going to do fine together. I did not identify with disability culture, nor did I have any friends with disabilities. Like many women before feminist consciousness-raising or some black people before the civil rights movement, I saw my difference from the valued norm as a personal situation rather than as a political or social issue.

Nevertheless, in my work as a literary critic, I always recognized and identified with the myriad of critically unnoticed disabled characters scattered throughout the works I read. But because the idea of drawing attention to disability contradicted a lifetime of disavowing it, my critical coming out was at first quite tentative and unsettling. Without the bold feminist assertion that the personal is political and its authorization of identity politics as a critical perspective, without the recent broadening of our scope of academic inquiry, I would never have allowed myself to embark on a project such as this. I persisted because the time was ripe to introduce disability into the academy's interrogation of the politics of representation. I am indebted, then, to this moment in the history of critical thought and cultural studies. Being out about disability has enabled me both to discover and to establish a field of disability studies within the humanities and to help consolidate a community of scholars who are defining it.

This book owes its being to the encouragement of Michael Gilmore and to my introduction by the late Irv Zola to the body of scholarship and supportive group of scholars working in disability studies in the social sciences. For generous support and helpful comments on the manuscript at various stages, I am grateful to my colleagues Bob Bogdan, Mary Campbell, Lenny Cassuto,

Lenny Davis, Wai Chee Dimock, Tracy Fessenden, Skip Gates, Caroline Gebhard, Nancy Goldstein, David Gerber, Gene Goodheart, Harlan Hahn, Phil Harper, Liz Hodgson, Amy Lang, Claudia Limbert, Simi Linton, Paul Longmore, Eric Lott, Helena Michie, David Mitchell, Elisabeth Pantajja, Karen Sanchez-Eppler, and Robin Warhol and to the 1992 Commonwealth Center Postdoctoral Fellowship Committee at the College of William and Mary.

Several institutions supported this project along the way with research and writing grants. I wish to thank the National Endowment for the Humanities for a Fellowship for University Teachers in 1994–95, the Wood Institute of the College of Physicians for a research fellowship in 1995, the Massachusetts Historical Society for an Andrew W. Mellon Research Fellowship in 1995, the American Association of University Women for a dissertation fellowship in 1991–92, the Brandeis University Department of English for an Andrew W. Mellon Dissertation Fellowship in 1991–92, and the Brandeis University Women's Studies Department for their dissertation fellowship in 1991–92.

I am also grateful to the Women's Committee of the Modern Language Association for awarding the 1989 Florence Howe Award for Feminist Scholarship to my essay entitled "Speaking About the Unspeakable: The Representation of Disability as Stigma in Toni Morrison's Novels," which is an early exploration of a part of chapter 5. I appreciate as well the encouragement of the Society for Disability Studies, which awarded me its Emerging Scholar Award in 1990. Portions of chapters 2 and 5 appear in a different form in an essay on Ann Petry in *Women's Studies International,* and a version of chapter 4 is published in *American Literature.* I appreciate the editors' permission to reprint this material. I also want to thank Jennifer Crewe and Leslie Kriesel at Columbia University Press for their generous support and careful editing.

The constancy, emotional sustenance, patience, encouragement, and support of Bob, Rob, Lena, and Cara Thomson make this project and many other things possible. I also want to acknowledge my sustaining relationships with friends scattered across the country and to thank the many women who helped care for my children over the years so that I had some quiet time to write and read.

PART I

• • • • •

Politicizing Bodily Differences

Nature is only the raw material of culture, appropriated, preserved, enslaved, exalted, or otherwise made flexible for disposal by culture in the logic of capitalist colonialism.

—**Donna Haraway,** *Primate Visions*

Representation is the organization of the perception of [actual bodily differences] into comprehensibility, a comprehensibility that is always frail, coded, in other words, human.

—**Richard Dyer,** *The Matter of Images*

Anomaly appears only against the background provided by the paradigm.

—**Thomas S. Kuhn,** *The Structure of Scientific Revolutions*

O N E

· · · · ·

Disability, Identity, and Representation: An Introduction

The Disabled Figure in Culture

In its broadest sense, this book investigates how representation attaches meanings to bodies. Although much recent scholarship explores how difference and identity operate in such politicized constructions as gender, race, and sexuality, cultural and literary criticism has generally overlooked the related perceptions of corporeal otherness we think of variously as "monstrosity," "mutilation," "deformation," "crippledness,"or "physical disability."[1] Yet the physically extraordinary figure these terms describe is as essential to the cultural project of American self-making as the varied throng of gendered, racial, ethnic, and sexual figures of otherness that support the privileged norm. My purpose here is to alter the terms and expand our understanding of the cultural construction of bodies and identity by reframing "disability" as another culture-bound, physically justified difference to consider along with race, gender, class, ethnicity, and sexuality. In other words, I intend to introduce such figures as the cripple, the invalid, and the freak into the critical conversations we devote to deconstructing figures like the mulatto, the primitive, the queer, and the lady. To denaturalize the cultural encoding of these extraordinary bodies, I go beyond assailing stereotypes to interrogate the conventions of representation and unravel the complexities of identity production within social narratives of bodily differences. In accordance with postmodernism's premise that the margin constitutes the center, I probe the peripheral so as to view the whole in a fresh way. By scrutinizing the disabled figure as the paradigm of what culture calls deviant, I hope to expose the assumptions that support seemingly neutral norms. Therefore, I focus here on how disability operates in culture and on how the discourses of disability, race, gender, and sexuality intermingle to create figures of otherness from the raw materials of bodily variation, specifically at sites of representation such as the freak show, sentimental fiction, and black women's liberatory novels. Such an analysis furthers our collective understanding of the complex processes by which *all* forms of corporeal diversity acquire the cultural meanings undergirding a hierarchy of bodily traits that determines the distribution of privilege, status, and power.

One of this book's major aims is to challenge entrenched assumptions that "able-bodiedness" and its conceptual opposite, "disability," are self-evident physical conditions. My intention is to defamiliarize these identity categories by disclosing how the "physically disabled" are produced by way of legal, medical, political, cultural, and literary narratives that comprise an exclusionary discourse. Constructed as the embodiment of corporeal insufficiency and deviance, the physically disabled body becomes a repository for social anxieties about such troubling concerns as vulnerability, control, and identity. In other words, I want to move disability from the realm of medicine into that of political minorities, to recast it from a form of pathology to a form of ethnicity. By asserting that disability is a reading of bodily particularities in the context of social power relations, I intend to counter the accepted notions of physical disability as an absolute, inferior state and a personal misfortune. Instead, I show that disability is a representation, a cultural interpretation of physical transformation or configuration, and a comparison of bodies that structures social relations and institutions. Disability, then, is the attribution of corporeal deviance—not so much a property of bodies as a product of cultural rules about what bodies should be or do.

This socially contextualized view of disability is evident, for example, in the current legal definition of disability established by the Americans with Disabilities Act of 1990. This landmark civil rights legislation acknowledges that disability depends upon perception and subjective judgment rather than on objective bodily states: after identifying disability as an "impairment that substantially limits one or more of the major life activities," the law concedes that being legally disabled is also a matter of "being regarded as having such an impairment."[2] Essential but implicit to this definition is that both "impairment" and "limits" depend on comparing individual bodies with unstated but determining norms, a hypothetical set of guidelines for corporeal form and function arising from cultural expectations about how human beings should look and act. Although these expectations are partly founded on physiological facts about typical humans—such as having two legs with which to walk upright or having some capacity for sight or speech—their sociopolitical meanings and consequences are entirely culturally determined. Stairs, for example, create a functional "impairment" for wheelchair users that ramps do not. Printed information accommodates the sighted but "limits" blind persons. Deafness is not a disabling condition in a community that communicates by signing as well as speaking.[3] People who cannot lift three hundred pounds are "able-bodied," whereas those who cannot lift fifty pounds are "disabled." Moreover, such culturally generated and perpetuated standards as "beauty," "independence," "fitness," "competence," and "normalcy" exclude and disable many human bodies while validating and affirming others. Even though the law attempts to define disability in terms of function, the meanings attached to physical form and appearance constitute "limits" for many people—as evidenced, for example, by "ugly laws," some repealed as recently as 1974, that restricted visibly disabled people from public places.[4] Thus, the ways that bodies interact with the socially engineered environment and conform to social expectations determine the varying degrees of disability or able-bodiedness, of extra-ordinariness or ordinariness.

Consequently, the meanings attributed to extraordinary bodies reside not in inherent physical flaws, but in social relationships in which one group is legitimated by possessing valued physical characteristics and maintains its ascendancy and its self-identity by systematically imposing the role of cultural or corporeal inferiority on others. Representation thus simultaneously buttresses an embodied version of normative identity and shapes a narrative of corporeal difference that excludes those whose bodies or behaviors do not conform. So by focusing on how representation creates the physically disabled figure in American culture, I will also clarify the corresponding figure of the normative American self so powerfully etched into our collective cultural consciousness. We will see that the disabled figure operates as the vividly embodied, stigmatized other whose social role is to symbolically free the privileged, idealized figure of the American self from the vagaries and vulnerabilities of embodiment.

One purpose of this book, then, is to probe the relations among social identities—valued and devalued—outlined by our accepted hierarchies of embodiment. Corporeal departures from dominant expectations never go uninterpreted or unpunished, and conformities are almost always rewarded. The narrative of deviance surrounding bodies considered different is paralleled by a narrative of universality surrounding bodies that correspond to notions of the ordinary or the superlative. Cultural dichotomies do their evaluative work: this body is inferior and that one is superior; this one is beautiful or perfect and that one is grotesque or ugly. In this economy of visual difference, those bodies deemed inferior become spectacles of otherness while the unmarked are sheltered in the neutral space of normalcy. Invested with meanings that far outstrip their biological bases, figures such as the cripple, the quadroon, the queer, the outsider, the whore are taxonomical, ideological products marked by socially determined stigmata, defined through representation, and excluded from social power and status. Thus, the cultural other and the cultural self operate together as opposing twin figures that legitimate a system of social, economic, and political empowerment justified by physiological differences.[5]

As I examine the disabled figure, I will also trouble the mutually constituting figure this study coins: the normate. This neologism names the veiled subject position of cultural self, the figure outlined by the array of deviant others whose marked bodies shore up the normate's boundaries.[6] The term *normate* usefully designates the social figure through which people can represent themselves as definitive human beings. Normate, then, is the constructed identity of those who, by way of the bodily configurations and cultural capital they assume, can step into a position of authority and wield the power it grants them. If one attempts to define the normate position by peeling away all the marked traits within the social order at this historical moment, what emerges is a very narrowly defined profile that describes only a minority of actual people. Erving Goffman, whose work I discuss in greater detail later, observes the logical conclusion of this phenomenon by noting wryly that there is "only one complete unblushing male in America: a young, married, white, urban, northern, heterosexual, Protestant father of college education, fully employed, of good complexion, weight and height, and a recent record in sports."[7] Interestingly, Goffman takes for granted that femaleness has no part in his sketch of a normative human being. Yet this image's ubiquity, power, and value resonate clearly. One testimony to the power of the normate subject position is that people often try to fit its description in the same way that Cinderella's stepsisters attempted to squeeze their feet into her glass slipper. Naming the figure of the normate is one conceptual strategy that will allow us to press our analyses beyond the simple dichotomies of male/female, white/black, straight/gay, or able-bodied/disabled so that we can examine the subtle interrelations among social identities that are anchored to physical differences.

The normate subject position emerges, however, only when we scrutinize the social processes and discourses that constitute physical and cultural otherness. Because figures of otherness are highly marked in power relations, even as they are marginalized, their cultural visibility as deviant obscures and neutralizes the normative figure that they legitimate. To analyze the operation of disability, it is essential then to theorize at length—as I do in part 1—about the processes and assumptions that produce both the normate and its discordant companion figures. However, I also want to complicate any simple dichotomy of self and other, normate and deviant, by centering part 2 of the book on how representations sometimes deploy disabled figures in complex, triangulated relationships or surprising alliances, and on how these representations can be both oppressive and liberating. In part 2, my examination of the way disability is constituted by the freak show, sentimental fiction, and black women's liberatory novels focuses on female figures for two reasons: first, because the links between disability and gender otherness need investigating, and second, because the non-normate status accorded disability feminizes all disabled figures. What I uncover by closely analyzing these sites of representation suggests that disability functions as a multivalent trope, though it remains the mark of otherness. Although centering on disabled figures illuminates the processes that sort and rank physical differences into normal and abnormal, at the same time, these investigations suggest the possibility of potentially positive, complicating interpretations. In short, by examining disability as a reading of the body that is inflected by race, ethnicity, and gender, I hope to reveal possibilities for signification that go beyond a monologic interpretation of corporeal difference as deviance. Thus, by first theorizing disability and then examining several sites that construct it, I can uncover the complex ways that disability intersects with other social identities to produce the extraordinary and the ordinary figures who haunt us all.

The Disabled Figure in Literature

The discursive construct of the disabled figure, informed more by received attitudes than by people's actual experience of disability, circulates in culture and finds a home within the conventions and codes of literary representation. As Paul Robinson notes, "the disabled, like all minorities, have . . . existed not as subjects of art, but merely as its occasions." Disabled literary characters usually remain on the margins of fiction as uncomplicated figures or exotic aliens whose bodily configurations operate as spectacles, eliciting responses from other characters or producing rhetorical effects that depend on disability's cultural resonance. Indeed, main characters almost never have physical disabilities. Even though mainstream critics have long discussed, for example, the implications of Twain's Jim for blacks, when literary critics look at disabled characters, they often interpret them metaphorically or aesthetically, reading them without political awareness as conventional elements of the sentimental, romantic, Gothic, or grotesque traditions.[8]

The disparity between "disabled" as an attributed, decontextualizing identity and the perceptions and experiences of real people living with disabilities suggests that this figure of otherness emerges from positioning, interpreting, and conferring meaning upon bodies. Representation yields cultural identities and categories, the given paradigms Alfred Schutz calls "recipes," with which we communally organize raw experience and routinize the world.[9] Literary conventions even further mediate experience that the wider cultural matrix, including literature itself, has already informed. If we accept the convention that fiction has some mimetic relation to life, we grant it power to further shape our perceptions of the world, especially regarding situations about which we have little direct knowledge. Because disability is so strongly stigmatized and is countered by so few mitigating narratives, the literary traffic in metaphors often misrepresents or flattens the experience real people have of their own or others' disabilities.

I therefore want to explicitly open up the gap between disabled people and their representations by exploring how disability operates in texts. The rhetorical effect of representing disability derives from social relations between people who assume the normate position and those who are assigned the disabled position. From folktales and classical myths to modern and postmodern "grotesques," the disabled body is almost always a freakish spectacle presented by the mediating narrative voice. Most disabled characters are enveloped by the otherness that their disability signals in the text. Take, as a few examples, Dickens's pathetic and romanticized Tiny Tim of *A Christmas Carol*, J. M. Barrie's villainous Captain Hook from *Peter Pan*, Victor Hugo's Gothic Quasimodo in *The Hunchback of Notre Dame*, D. H. Lawrence's impotent Clifford Chatterley in *Lady Chatterley's Lover*, and Tennessee Williams's long-suffering Laura Wingfield from *The Glass Menagerie*. The very act of representing corporeal otherness places them in a frame that highlights their differences from ostensibly normate readers. Although such representations refer to actual social relations, they do not of course reproduce those relations with mimetic fullness. Characters are thus necessarily rendered by a few determining strokes that create an illusion of reality far short of the intricate, undifferentiated, and uninterpreted context in which real people exist. Like the freak shows that I will discuss in chapter 3, textual descriptions are overdetermined: they invest the traits, qualities, and behaviors of their characters with much rhetorical influence simply by omitting—and therefore erasing—other factors or traits that might mitigate or complicate the delineations. A disability functions only as visual difference that signals meanings. Consequently, literary texts necessarily make disabled characters into freaks, stripped of normalizing contexts and engulfed by a single stigmatic trait.

Not only is the relationship between text and world not exact, but representation also relies upon cultural assumptions to fill in missing details. All people construct interpretive schemata that make their worlds seem knowable and predictable, thus producing perceptual categories that may harden into stereotypes or caricatures when communally shared and culturally inculcated.[10] As Aristotle suggests in the *Poetics*, literary representation depends more on probability—what people take to be accurate—than on reality. Caricatures and stereotypical portrayals that depend more on gesture than complexity arise necessarily out of this gap between representation and life. Stereotypes in life become tropes in textual representation. For example, Marianna Torgovnick describes the trope of the primitive as a discursive construct in the broadest sense, a "world" that has been "structured by sets of images and ideas that have slipped from their original metaphoric status to control perceptions of [actual] primitives."[11] Such portrayals invoke, reiterate, and are reinforced by cultural stereotypes. A highly stigmatized characteristic like disability gains its rhetorical effectiveness from the powerful, often mixed responses that real disabled people elicit from readers who consider themselves normates. The more the literary portrayal conforms to the social stereotype, the more economical and intense is the effect; representation thus exaggerates an already highlighted physical difference. Moreover, Western tradition posits the visible world as the index of a coherent and just invisible world, encouraging us to read the material body as a sign invested with transcendent meaning. In interpreting the material world, literature tends to imbue any visual differences with significance that obscures the complexity of their bearers.

Besides stripping any normalizing context away from disability, literary representation sets up static encounters between disabled figures and normate readers, whereas real social relations are always dynamic. Focusing on a body feature to describe a character throws the reader into a confrontation with the character that is predetermined by cultural notions about disability. With the notable exception of autobiographical texts—such as Audre Lorde's *Zami*, which I address in the last chapter—representation tends to objectify disabled characters by denying them any opportunity for subjectivity or agency. The plot or the work's rhetorical potential usually benefits from the disabled figure remaining other to the reader—identifiably human but resolutely different. How could Ahab operate effectively if the reader were allowed to see him as an ordinary fellow instead of as an icon of monomaniacal revenge—if his disability lost its transcendent meaning? What would happen to the pure pity generated for Tiny Tim if he were portrayed as sometimes naughty, like a "normal" child? Thus the rhetorical function of the highly charged trait fixes relations between disabled figures and their readers. If disabled characters acted, as real people with disabilities often do, to counter their stigmatized status, the rhetorical potency of the stigma would be mitigated or lost. If Hawthorne's Chillingworth made many friends, for instance, or appeared lovable to Hester, his role in *The Scarlet Letter* would be diminished. If Flannery O'Connor's Hulga Hopewell were pretty, cheerful, and one-legged instead of ugly and bitter, "Good Country People" would fail. So, like *tableaux vivants*, beauty pageants, and freak shows—all related forms of representation grounded in the conventions of spectacle—literary narratives of disability usually depend on the objectification of the spectacle that representation has created.

The Gap Between Representation and Reality

Whether one lives with a disability or encounters someone who has one, the actual experience of disability is more complex and more dynamic than representation usually suggests. Just one example illustrates the skill disabled people often must learn in managing social encounters. Initial or casual exchanges between normate and disabled people differ markedly from the usual relations between readers and disabled characters. In a first encounter with another person, a tremendous amount of information must be organized and interpreted simultaneously: each participant probes the explicit for the implicit, determines what is significant for particular purposes, and prepares a response that is guided by many cues, both subtle and obvious. When one person has a visible disability, however, it almost always dominates and skews the normate's process of sorting out perceptions and forming a reaction.[12] The interaction is usually strained because the nondisabled person may feel fear, pity, fascination, repulsion, or merely surprise, none of which is expressible according to social protocol. Besides the discomforting dissonance between experienced and expressed reaction, a nondisabled person often does not know how to act toward a disabled person: how or whether to offer assistance; whether to acknowledge the disability; what words, gestures, or expectations to use or avoid. Perhaps most destructive to the potential for continuing relations is the normate's frequent assumption that a disability cancels out other qualities, reducing the complex person to a single attribute. This uncertainty and discord make the encounter especially stressful for the nondisabled person unaccustomed to disabled people. The disabled person may be anxious about whether the encounter will be too uncomfortable for either of them to sustain and may feel the ever-present threat of rejection. Even though disability threatens to snap the slender thread of sociability, most physically disabled people are skilled enough in these encounters to repair the fabric of the relation so that it can continue.

To be granted fully human status by normates, disabled people must learn to manage relationships from the beginning. In other words, disabled people must use charm, intimidation, ardor, deference, humor, or entertainment to relieve nondisabled people of their discomfort. Those of us with disabilities are supplicants and minstrels, striving to create valued representations of ourselves in our relations with the nondisabled majority. This is precisely what many newly disabled people can neither do nor accept; it is a subtle part of adjustment and often the most difficult.[13] If such efforts at reparation are successful, disabled people neutralize the initial stigma of disability so that relationships can be sustained and deepened. Only then can other aspects of personhood emerge and expand the initial focus so that the relationship becomes more comfortable, more broadly based, and less affected by the disability. Only then can each person emerge as multifaceted, whole. If, however, disabled people pursue normalization too much, they risk denying limitations and pain for the comfort of others and may edge into the self-betrayal associated with "passing."

This is not to suggest that all forms of disability are interchangeable or that all disabled people experience their bodies or negotiate their identities in the same ways. Indeed, it is precisely the variation among individuals that cultural categories trivialize and that representation often distorts. Disability is an overarching and in some ways artificial category that encompasses congenital and acquired physical differences, mental illness and retardation, chronic and acute illnesses, fatal and progressive diseases, temporary and permanent injuries, and a wide range of bodily characteristics considered disfiguring, such as scars, birthmarks, unusual proportions, or obesity. Even though the prototypical disabled person posited in cultural representations never leaves a wheelchair, is totally blind, or profoundly deaf, most of the approximately forty million Americans with disabilities have a much more ambiguous relationship to the label. The physical impairments that render someone "disabled" are almost never absolute or static; they are dynamic, contingent conditions affected by many external factors and usually fluctuating over time. Some conditions, like multiple sclerosis or arthritis, are progressive and chronic; others, such as epilepsy, can be acute. Even seemingly static disabilities like amputation affect activities differently, depending on the condition of the rest of the body.

Of course, everyone is subject to the gradually disabling process of aging.

The fact that we will all become disabled if we live long enough is a reality many people who consider themselves able-bodied are reluctant to admit.[14] As physical abilities change, so do individual needs, and the perception of those needs.The pain that often accompanies or causes disability also influences both the degree and the perception of impairment. According to Elaine Scarry, because pain is invisible, unverifiable and unrepresentable, it is often subject to misattribution or denial by those who are not experiencing it.[15] Disability, then, can be painful, comfortable, familiar, alienating, bonding, isolating, disturbing, endearing, challenging, infuriating, or ordinary. Embedded in the complexity of actual human relations, it is always more than the disabled figure can signify.

That anyone can become disabled at any time makes disability more fluid, and perhaps more threatening, to those who identify themselves as normates than such seemingly more stable marginal identities as femaleness, blackness, or nondominant ethnic identities.[16] In addition, the time and way in which one becomes disabled influence its perception, as do the ways one incorporates disability into one's sense of self or resists it. For instance, the gradual disablement of aging or a progressive illness may not be considered a disability at all. In contrast, a severe, sudden impairment, as from an accident, is almost always experienced as a greater loss than is a congenital or gradual disability, which does not demand adjustment so abruptly. A disability's degree of visibility also affects social relations. An invisible disability, much like a homosexual identity, always presents the dilemma of whether or when to come out or to pass. One must always anticipate the risk of tainting a new relationship by announcing an invisible impairment or the equal hazard of surprising someone by revealing a previously undisclosed disability. The distinction between formal and functional aspects of a disability affects its perception as well. People whose disability is primarily functional but not visible often are accused of malingering or of disappointing expectations about their physical capabilities. Yet those whose disabilities are largely formal often are considered incapable of things they can easily do. Furthermore, formal conditions such as facial disfigurement, scarring, birthmarks, obesity, and visual or hearing impairments corrected with mechanical aids are usually socially disabling, even though they entail almost no physical dysfunction. Moreover, as the history of the freak show that appears in chapter 3 reveals, no firm distinction exists between primarily formal disabilities and racial physical features considered atypical by dominant, white standards.

Although categories such as ethnicity, race, and gender are based on shared traits that result in community formation, disabled people seldom consider themselves a group. Little somatic commonality exists among people with different kinds of disabilities because needs and situations are so diverse. A blind person, an epileptic, a paraplegic, a deaf person, and an amputee, for example, have no shared cultural heritage, traditional activities, or common physical experience. Only the shared experience of stigmatization creates commonality. Having been acculturated similarly to everyone else, disabled people also often avoid and stereotype one another in attempting to normalize their own social identities. Moreover, many disabled people at one time considered themselves nondisabled and may have had very limited contact with disabled people before joining their group. As with all culturally imposed categories extrapolated from biological differences, the identity has a forced quality that levels intragroup variations. For example, the now crumbling institution of "special" education enacts this cultural impulse toward ghettoization by segregating people with disabilities from nondisabled students regardless of individual needs. Finally, most disabled people are surrounded by nondisabled families and communities in which disabilities are unanticipated and almost always perceived as calamitous. Unlike the ethnically grouped, but more like gays and lesbians, disabled people are sometimes fundamentally isolated from each other, existing often as aliens within their social units.[17]

Yet representation frequently obscures these complexities in favor of the rhetorical or symbolic potential of the prototypical disabled figure, who often functions as a lightning rod for the pity, fear, discomfort, guilt, or sense of normalcy of the reader or a more significant character. I intend here to shift from this usual interpretive framework of aesthetics and metaphor to the critical arena of cultural studies to denaturalize such representations. By examining the "disabled figure," rather than discussing the "grotesque" or "cripple" or "deformed," I hope to catapult this analysis out of a purely aesthetic context and into a political one. By opening up a critical gap between disabled figures as fashioned corporeal others whose bodies carry social meaning and actual people with atypical bodies in real-world social relations, I suggest that representation informs the identity—and often the fate—of real people with extraordinary bodies.

An Overview and a Manifesto

In a sense, this book is a manifesto that places disability studies within a humanities context. Although disability studies has developed as a subfield of scholarly inquiry in the academic fields of sociology, medical anthropology, special education, and rehabilitative medicine, almost no studies in the humanities explicitly situate disability within a politicized, social constructionist perspective.[18] One of my aims in this book, then, is to begin formulating what disability studies might look like as a subfield in literary criticism and cultural studies. I will therefore outline in some detail here the contents and the arguments that appear in the following chapters.

This project entails two tasks: first, theorizing the operation of disability in cultural and literary representation; and second, focusing on exemplary sites that construct disability in culture and in texts. Thus, part 1 of the book incorporates a range of theoretical work from various academic arenas, most of which does not address disability directly but instead conceptually dances around its edges. Having examined in this introduction how the disabled figure operates in literary representation and having probed as well the differences between disability in life and in representation, I explore in chapter 2 the ways that several discourses address the construction of disability. First, I detail the cultural intertwining of femininity and disability and recruit feminist theory as a related discourse of otherness that can be transferred to analyses of disability. Second, I enlist three sociocultural theories, Erving Goffman's notion of stigma, Mary Douglas's concept of dirt, and Michel Foucault's ideas on particularity and identity, in order to uncover the processes that construct disability. Third, I critique the role of the disabled figure within the ideology of liberal individualism. Finally, I analyze how the ideology of work has constructed the disabled figure over time as the means of addressing disability has shifted from a compensation to an accommodation model. These theoretical speculations lay the groundwork for the analyses that follow, each of which centers on narratives of corporeal otherness that raise broad questions of how selfhood is represented in American culture.

Part 2 shows how the ideologies of self-reliance, autonomy, progress, and work, as well as the processes of stigmatization and the formation of the modern subject, influence how the disabled figure and the cultural self are represented at specific literary and cultural sites. As I have suggested, these particular sites allow me to probe the complexities in culture's use of disabled figures. Each cultural and literary production explored here employs disabled figures in ways that sometimes reinscribe their cultural otherness but also at times exploit the disabled figure's potential for challenging the institutions and political policies that derive from and support a narrow norm. These narratives of corporeal/cultural difference thus simultaneously confirm and challenge the received definition of physical disability as bodily inadequacy.

Chapter 3 examines American freak shows as popular social rituals that constructed and disseminated a figure whose crucial cultural work was to exhibit to the American masses what they imagined themselves not to be. Such shows choreographed human variation into a spectacle of bodily otherness that united their audiences in opposition to the freaks' aberrance and assured the onlookers that they were indeed "normal." Highly structured conventions of representation sculpted exoticized "freaks" from people who have what we now call "physical disabilities," as well as from other people whose bodies could be made to visually signify absolute alienness. Giants, dwarfs, visibly physically disabled people, tribal non-Westerners, contortionists, fat people, thin people, hermaphrodites, the mentally disabled, and the very hirsute—all shared the platform equally as human oddities. Their only commonality was being physically different from their audiences. For the price of a ticket, the process of what David Hevey calls "enfreakment"[19] offered to the spectators an icon of physical otherness that reinforced the onlookers' common American identity, verified by a body that suddenly seemed by comparison ordinary, tractable, and standard.

I also suggest that freak shows at the same time offered a counternarrative of peculiarity as eminence, the kind of distinction described by Bakhtin's and Foucault's notions of the particularized pre-Enlightenment body. Straddling the ideologies of the traditional and the modern, the freak show manifested tension between an older mode that read particularity as a mark of empowering distinction and a newer mode that flattened differences to achieve equality. In such a liminal space, the domesticated freak simultaneously embodied exceptionality as marvel and exceptionality as anomaly, thus posing to the spectator the implicit political question of how to interpret differences within an egalitarian social order.

Chapter 4 centers on sentimental social protest novels written by mid-nineteenth-century middle-class white women, in which disabled figures function as discursive lightning rods for complex social tensions. I argue that Harriet Beecher Stowe's *Uncle Tom's Cabin*, Rebecca Harding Davis's *Life in the Iron Mills*, and Elizabeth Stuart Phelps's *The Silent Partner* construct gendered and racialized disabled figures as icons of corporeal vulnerability in an attempt to spotlight the conflict between social justice and individual freedom inherent in the American liberal tradition. This cluster of texts introduces what I call a compensation model, in which disability is interpreted as a lack that must be compensated for by what I term the "benevolent maternalism" of the middle-class women. Whereas freak shows literally display the disabled to confirm the "normal," these texts display disabled figures in order to mobilize and validate social reform agendas. Although the disabled figures invoke a rhetoric of sympathy to achieve sociopolitical reform, they also define and legitimize the normalized, gendered role of the maternal benefactress that these novels promote for women of the emerging middle class, who were marginalized within the changing social order. The increasingly negative portrayals of disabled women figures as the genre moves from Stowe through Phelps comprises an anxious subtext that splits the disabled women and the benefactresses, paralleling the displacement of middle-class white women from meaningful work. This escalating renunciation of the disabled figure tests the limits of domesticity's script of maternal benevolence as a solution to the problems of female roles in late-nineteenth-century America.

Chapter 5 discusses several twentieth-century, women-centered African-American liberatory novels that use the disabled figure and other extraordinary bodies to elaborate an identity that insists upon and celebrates physical difference. In these texts, the extraordinary body invokes a principle of difference over sameness that serves a postmodern politics that is nationalist rather than assimilationist. Whereas the nineteenth-century sentimental novels of the previous chapter cast the disabled figure as antithetical to the female role they sought to delineate, these black nationalist texts incorporate such a figure into their vision of oppositional identity. Ann Petry's 1946 novel *The Street* tentatively initiates this type of representation, and is followed by the post–civil rights version of black female subjectivity articulated by Toni Morrison's first five novels and by Audre Lorde's "biomythography" *Zami: A New Spelling of My Name*. I suggest that one rhetorical aim of these works is to establish a narrative of the particularized body as a site of politicized historical inscription instead of physical deviance. Disabled figures such as Morrison's Eva Peace and Baby Suggs, for example, revise a history of assigned corporeal inferiority so that bodily differences become markers of exceptionality to be claimed and honored. This ideology of identity as particularity rejects the cultural implementation of democracy that normalizes sameness and stigmatizes difference. Such a strategy of identity formation validates what I call an accommodation model of interpreting disability, as opposed to the earlier compensation model. My final point is that this appropriation of the extraordinary body rehabilitates the premodern narrative of the wondrous freaks by casting the disabled women as politicized marvelous monsters (in the medieval sense) whose singular bodies bear the etchings of individual and collective history.

Although none of these cultural or textual sites employs the politicized term "physical disability" that is at the center of this study, the freak show, this sentimental reform fiction, and these black women's liberatory novels all participate in varying ways in the cultural work of defining the disabled subject as an object of visual difference. This book thus begins what I hope will be a lively conversation within the humanities not only about the construction of disability through representation but also about the attendant political consequences.

T W O

· · · · ·

Theorizing Disability

Feminist Theory, the Body, and the Disabled Figure

The Female Body and the Disabled Body

Many parallels exist between the social meanings attributed to female bodies and those assigned to disabled bodies. Both the female and the disabled body are cast as deviant and inferior; both are excluded from full participation in public as well as economic life; both are defined in opposition to a norm that is assumed to possess natural physical superiority. Indeed, the discursive equation of femaleness with disability is common, sometimes to denigrate women and sometimes to defend them. Examples abound, from Freud's delineating femaleness in terms of castration to late-nineteenth-century physicians' defining menstruation a disabling and restricting "eternal wound" to Thorstein Veblen's describing women in 1899 as literally disabled by feminine roles and costuming. Even feminists today invoke negative images of disability to describe the oppression of women; for example, Jane Flax asserts that women are "mutilated and deformed" by sexist ideology and practices.[1]

Perhaps the founding association of femaleness with disability occurs in the fourth book of *Generation of Animals*, Aristotle's discourse of the normal and the abnormal, in which he refines the Platonic concept of antinomies so that bodily variety translates into hierarchies of the typical and the aberrant. "[A]nyone who does not take after his parents," Aristotle asserts, "is really in a way a monstrosity, since in these cases Nature has in a way strayed from the generic type. The first beginning of this deviation is when a female is formed instead of a male." Here the philosopher, whom we might consider the founding father of Western taxonomy, idealizes bodies to produce a definitive, seemingly neutral "generic type" along with its antithesis, the "monstrosity," whose departure from such a "type" is a profound "deviation." Aristotle's spatial metaphor places a certain human figure, the "generic type," at the center of his system. On the outer margin is the "monstrosity," the physical consequence of Nature's having "strayed" onto a path of deviance, the first stop along which is the female body. Aristotle thus conjoins the "monstrosity"—whom we would today term "congenitally disabled"—and the female outside the definitive norm. In Book Two, Aristotle affirms this connection of disabled and female bodies by stating that "the female is as it were a deformed male"or—as it appears in other translations—"a mutilated male."[2]

More significant than Aristotle's simple conflation of disability and femaleness is his declaration that the source of all otherness is the concept of a norm, a "generic type" against which all physical variation appears as different, derivative, inferior, and insufficient. Not only does this definition of the female as a "mutilated male" inform later depictions of woman as diminished man, but it also arranges somatic diversity into a hierarchy of value that assigns completeness to some bodies and deficiency to others. Furthermore, by defining femaleness as deviant and maleness as essential, Aristotle initiates the discursive practice of marking what is deemed aberrant while concealing what is privileged behind an assertion of normalcy. This is perhaps the original operation of the logic that has become so familiar in discussions of gender, race, or disability: male, white, or able-bodied superiority appears natural, undisputed, and unremarked, seemingly eclipsed by female, black, or disabled difference. What this passage makes clearest, however, is that without the monstrous body to demarcate the borders of the generic, without the female body to distinguish the shape of the male, and without the pathological to give form to the normal, the taxonomies of bodily value that underlie political, social, and economic arrangements would collapse.[3]

This persistent intertwining of disability with femaleness in Western discourse provides a starting point for exploring the relationship of social identity to the body. As Aristotle's pronouncement suggests, the social category of disability rests on the significance accorded bodily functioning and configuration, just as the social category of woman does. Therefore, feminist theory's recent inquiries into gender as a category, the body's role in identity and selfhood, and the complexity of social power relations can readily transfer to an analysis of disability. Moreover, applying feminist theory to disability analysis infuses it with feminism's insistence on the relationship between the meanings attributed to bodies by cultural representations and the consequences of those meanings in the world. As I bring feminism to disability studies, I will also suggest how the category of disability might be inserted into feminist theory so that the bodily configurations and functioning we call "disabled" will be included in all feminist examinations of culture and representation. This brief exploration aims then at beginning to alter the terms of both feminist and disability discourses.

Feminist Theory and Disability Discourse

Contemporary feminist theory has proved to be porous, diffuse, and—perhaps most significant—self-critical. Thus, we speak now of "feminisms," "conflicts in feminism," "hyphenated feminisms," and even "postfeminism."[4] Historically, academic feminism combines the highly political civil rights and accompanying identity politics impulses of the 1960s and 1970s with poststructuralism's theoretical critique of the liberal humanist faith in knowledge, truth, and identity, often adding an insistence on materiality gleaned from Marxist thought. The focus of feminist conversation has shifted from early debates between liberal and radical feminisms, which focused on achieving equality, to later formulations of cultural and gynocentric feminisms, which highlighted and rehabilitated female differences. Most recently, the debate between those who would minimize differences to achieve equality and those who would elaborate differences to valorize the feminine has been complicated by an interrogation of gender construction itself and a recognition of multiple axes of identity, both of which profoundly challenge the very notion of "woman" as any kind of unified identity category.[5] Feminism's insistence that standpoint shapes politics; that identity, subjectivity, and the body are cultural constructs to be questioned; and that all representation is political comprise the theoretical milieu in which I want to examine disability.

The strands of feminist thought most applicable to disability studies are those that go beyond a narrow focus on gender alone to undertake a broad sociopolitical critique of systemic, inequitable power relations based on social categories grounded in the body. Feminism thus becomes a theoretical perspective and methodology examining gender as a discursive, ideological, and material category that interacts with but does not subordinate other social identities or the particularities of embodiment, history, and location that inform subjectivity. Briefly put, feminism's often conflicting and always complex aims of politicizing the materiality of bodies and rewriting the category of woman combine exactly the methods that should be used to examine disability.[6]

I want to extend in a fresh juxtaposition, then, the association of disability and femaleness with which I began this section. But rather than simply conflating the disabled body with the female body, I want to theorize disability in the ways that feminism has theorized gender. Both feminism and my analysis of disability challenge existing social relations; both resist interpretations of certain bodily configurations and functioning as deviant; both question the ways that differences are invested with meaning; both examine the enforcement of universalizing norms; both interrogate the politics of appearance; both explore the politics of naming; both forge positive identities. Nevertheless, feminism has formulated these terms and probed these concerns much more thoroughly than disability studies has.[7]

Eve Kosofsky Sedgwick's distinction, for example, between a "minoritizing" and a "universalizing" view of difference can be applied to disability discourse. According to Sedgwick's hybrid of feminist and queer theory, one minoritizes difference by imagining its significance and concerns as limited to a narrow, specific, relatively fixed population or area of inquiry. In contrast, a universalizing view sees issues surrounding a particular difference as having "continuing, determinative importance in the lives of people across the spectrum of [identities]."[8] Disability studies should become a universalizing discourse in the way that Sedgwick imagines gay studies and feminism to be. Disability (or gender or homosexuality) would then be recognized as structuring a wide range of thought, language, and perception that might not be explicitly articulated as "disability." I am proposing, then, a universalizing view of disability by showing how the concept of disability informs such national ideologies as American liberal individualism and sentimentalism, as well as African American and lesbian identities. Such terms from feminist theory can be enlisted to challenge the persistent assumption that disability is a self-evident condition of physical inadequacy and private misfortune whose politics concern only a limited minority.

A universalized disability discourse that draws on feminism's confrontation with the gender system requires understanding the body as a cultural text that is interpreted, inscribed with meaning—indeed *made*—within social relations. Such a perspective advocates political equity by denaturalizing disability's assumed inferiority, by casting it as difference rather than lack. Although this constructionist perspective does the vital cultural work of destigmatizing the differences we call gender, race, or disability, the logic of constructionism threatens nevertheless to obscure the material and historical effects of those differences and to erase the very social categories we analyze and claim as significant. Thus, the poststructuralist logic that destabilizes identity can free marginalized people from the narrative of essential inadequacy, but at the same time it risks denying the particularity of their experiences.[9] The theoretical bind is that deconstructing oppressive categories can neutralize the effects of real differences.

A disability politics cannot at this moment, however, afford to banish the category of disability according to the poststructualist critique of identity in the way that some feminists have argued for abandoning the concept of woman as hopelessly imprisoning and abstract.[10] The kind of access to public spaces and institutions that women gained in the nineteenth century and have expanded since the 1960s was only fully mandated for disabled people by the Americans with Disabilities Act of 1990, a broad civil rights law that is only beginning to be implemented. And while in the movement toward equality, race and gender are generally accepted as differences rather than deviances, disability is still most often seen as bodily inadequacy or catastrophe to be compensated for with pity or good will, rather than accommodated by systemic changes based on civil rights. On the one hand, then, it is important to use the constructionist argument to assert that disability is not bodily insufficiency, but instead arises from the interaction of physical differences with an environment. On the other hand, the particular, historical existence of the disabled body demands both accommodation and recognition. In other words, the physical differences of using a wheelchair or being deaf, for example, should be claimed, but not cast as lack.[11]

Both constructionism and essentialism, then, are theoretical strategies—framings of the body—invoked for specific ends, such as psychologically liberating people whose bodies have been defined as defective or facilitating imagined communities from which positive identities can emerge. Strategic constructionism destigmatizes the disabled body, makes difference relative, denaturalizes so-called normalcy, and challenges appearance hierarchies. Strategic essentialism, by contrast, validates individual experience and consciousness, imagines community, authorizes history, and facilitates self-naming. The identity "disabled" operates in this mode as a pragmatic narrative, what Susan Bordo calls "a life-enhancing fiction" that places the reality of individual bodies and perspectives within specific social and historical contexts.[12]

Imagining Feminist Disability Discourse

But if the category "disabled" is a useful fiction, the disabled body set in a world structured for the privileged body is not. Disability, perhaps more than other differences, demands a reckoning with the messiness of bodily variety, with literal individuation run amok. Because disability is defined not as a set of observable, predictable traits—like racialized or gendered features—but rather as *any* departure from an unstated physical and fuctional norm, disability highlights individual differences. In other words, the concept of disability unites a highly marked, heterogeneous group whose only commonality is being considered abnormal. As the norm becomes neutral in an environment created to accommodate it, disability becomes intense, extravagant, and problematic. Disability is the unorthodox made flesh, refusing to be normalized, neutralized, or homogenized. More important, in an era governed by the abstract principle of universal equality, disability signals that the body cannot be universalized. Shaped by history, defined by particularity, and at odds with its environment, disability confounds any notion of a generalizable, stable physical subject. The cripple before the stairs, the blind person before the printed page, the deaf person before the radio, the amputee before the typewriter, and the dwarf before the counter are all proof that the myriad structures and practices of material, daily life enforce the cultural standard of a universal subject with a narrow range of corporeal variation.

Disability, as a formal identity category, can pressure feminist theory to acknowledge physical diversity more thoroughly. Perhaps feminism's most useful concept for disability studies is standpoint theory, which recognizes the immediacy and complexity of physical existence. Emphasizing the multiplicity of all women's identities, histories, and bodies, this theory asserts that individual situations structure the subjectivity from which particular women speak and perceive.[13] Incorporating postmodernism's challenge of the unsituated, objective Enlightenment viewpoint, feminist standpoint theory has reformulated gender identity as a complex, dynamic matrix of interrelated, often contradictory, experiences, strategies, styles, and attributions mediated by culture and individual history. This network cannot be separated meaningfully into discrete entities or ordered into a hierarchy. Acknowledging identity's particular, complex nature allows characteristics beyond race, class, and gender to emerge. Standpoint theory and the feminist practice of explicitly situating oneself when speaking thus allow for complicating inflections such as disability or, more broadly, body configuration—attributions such as fat, disfigured, abnormal, ugly, or deformed—to enter into our considerations of identity and subjectivity. Such a dismantling of the unitary category woman has enabled feminist theory to encompass—although not without contention—such feminist specializations as, for example, Patricia Hill Collins's "black feminist thought" or my own explorations of a "feminist disability studies."[14] So just as feminist theory can bring to disability theory strategies for analyzing the meanings of physical differences and identifying sites where those meanings influence other discourses, it can also help articulate the uniqueness and physicality of identity.

A feminist political praxis for women with disabilities needs, then, to focus at times on the singularity and perhaps the immutability of the flesh, and at the same time to interrogate the identity it supports. For example, in exploring the politics of self-naming, Nancy Mairs claims the appellation "cripple" because it demands that others acknowledge the particularity of her body. "People . . . wince at the word 'cripple'," Mairs contends. Even though she retains what has been a derogatory term, she insists on determining its significance herself: "Perhaps I want them to wince. I want them to see me as a tough customer, one to whom the fates/gods/viruses have not been kind, but who can face the brutal truth of her existence squarely. As a cripple, I swagger." Here Mairs is not simply celebrating the term of otherness or attempting to reverse its negative connotation; rather, she wants to call attention to the material reality of her crippledness, to her bodily difference and her experience of it. For Mairs, the social constructionist argument risks neutralizing the significance of her pain and her struggle with an environment built for other bodies.[15]

Disability, however, is left out of several mainstream feminist assumptions. For instance, while feminism quite legitimately decries the sexual objectification of women, disabled women often encounter what Harlan Hahn has called "asexual objectification," the assumption that sexuality is inappropriate in disabled people. One woman who uses a wheelchair, for example, and is also quite beautiful reports that people often respond to her as if this combination of traits were a remarkable and lamentable contradiction. The judgment that the disabled woman's body is asexual and unfeminine creates what Michelle Fine and Adrienne Asch term "rolelessness," a social invisibility and cancellation of femininity that can prompt disabled women to claim the female identity that the culture denies them. For example, Cheryl Marie Wade insists upon a harmony between her disability and her womanly sexuality in a poem characterizing herself as "The Woman With Juice."[16] As Mairs's exploration of self-naming and Wade's assertion of sexuality suggest, a feminist disability politics would uphold the right for women to define their physical differences and their femininity for themselves rather than conforming to received interpretations of their bodies.

Wade's poem of self-definition echoes Mairs by maintaining firmly that she is "not one of the physically challenged." Rather, she claims, "I'm the Gimp/ I'm the Cripple/I'm the Crazy Lady." Affirming her body as at once sexual and different, she asserts, "I'm a French kiss with cleft tongue." Resisting the cultural tendency not only to erase her sexuality but to depreciate and objectify her body, she characterizes herself as "a sock in the eye with gnarled fist." This image of the disabled body as a visual assault, a shocking spectacle to the normate eye, captures a defining aspect of disabled experience. Whereas feminists claim that women are objects of the evaluative male gaze, Wade's image of her body as "a sock in the eye" subtly reminds us that the disabled body is the object of the stare. If the male gaze makes the normative female a sexual spectacle, then the stare sculpts the disabled subject into a grotesque spectacle. The stare is the gaze intensified, framing her body as an icon of deviance. Indeed, as Wade's poem suggests, the stare is the gesture that creates disability as an oppressive social relationship. And as every person with a visible disability knows intimately, managing, deflecting, resisting, or renouncing that stare is part of the daily business of life.

In addition, disabled women must sometimes defend against the assessment of their bodies as unfit for motherhood or of themselves as infantilized objects who occasion other people's virtue. Whereas motherhood is often seen as compulsory for women, disabled women are often denied or discouraged from the reproductive role that some feminist thinkers find oppressive. The controversial feminist ethic of care has also been criticized by feminist disability scholars for undermining symmetrical, reciprocal relations among disabled and nondisabled women as well as for suggesting that care is the sole responsibility of women. Making disabled women the objects of care risks casting them as helpless in order to celebrate nurturing as virtuous feminine agency. Philosopher Anita Silvers explains that "far from vanquishing patriarchal systems, substituting the ethics of caring for the ethics of equality threatens an even more oppressive paternalism."[17]

Perhaps more problematic still, feminist abortion rationale seldom questions the prejudicial assumption that "defective" fetuses destined to become disabled people should be eliminated. The concerns of older women, who are often disabled, tend also to be ignored by younger feminists.[18] One of the most pervasive feminist assumptions that undermines some disabled women's struggle is the liberal ideology of autonomy and independence that fuels the broader impulse toward female empowerment. By tacitly incorporating the liberal premise that levels individual characteristics to posit an abstract, disembodied subject of democracy, feminist practice often leaves no space for the needs and accommodations that disabled women's bodies require.[19] Prominent disability rights activist Judy Heumann's angry and disappointed words reflect an alienation not unlike that between some black women and some white feminists: "When I come into a room full of feminists, all they see is a wheelchair."[20] These conflicts testify that feminists—like everyone else, including disabled people themselves—have absorbed cultural stereotypes.

Femininity and Disability

Although I insist on disabled women's identity even while questioning its sources, I also want to suggest that a firm boundary between "disabled" and "nondisabled" women cannot be meaningfully drawn—just as any absolute distinction between sex and gender is problematic. Femininity and disability are inextricably entangled in patriarchal culture, as Aristotle's equation of women with disabled men illustrates. Not only has the female body been labeled deviant, but historically the practices of femininity have configured female bodies similarly to disability. Foot binding, scarification, clitoridectomy, and corseting were (and are) socially accepted, encouraged, even compulsory cultural forms of female disablement that, ironically, are socially enabling, increasing a woman's value and status at a given moment in a particular society. Similarly, such conditions as anorexia, hysteria, and agoraphobia are in a sense standard feminine roles enlarged to disabling conditions, blurring the line between "normal" feminine behavior and pathology.[21]

The disciplinary regimes of feminine beauty often obscure the seemingly self-evident categories of the "normal" and the "pathological." For example, the nineteenth-century Euroamerican prescription for upper-class feminine beauty—pale skin, emaciated body, wide eyes—precisely paralleled the symptoms of tuberculosis, just as the cult of thinness promoted by the fashion industry today mimics the appearance of disease.[22] In a similar example, the iconography and language describing contemporary cosmetic surgery in women's magazines persistently casts the unreconstructed female body as having "abnormalities" that can be "corrected" by surgical procedures that "improve" the appearance by producing "natural looking" noses, thighs, breasts, chins, and so on.[23] This discourse terms women's unmodified bodies as unnatural and abnormal, while casting surgically altered bodies as normal and natural. Although cosmetic surgery is in one sense a logical extension of beauty practices such as using makeup, perming or relaxing hair, lightening skin, and removing hair, it differs profoundly from these basically decorative forms of self-reconstruction: like clitoridectomies and scarification, it involves the mutilation and pain that accompany many disabilities.

All of these practices cannot, of course, be equated; however, each transforms an infinitely plastic body in ways similar to the effects of disability. Beautification changes are imagined to be choices that will sculpt the female body so it conforms to a feminine ideal. Disabilities, in contrast, are imagined to be random transformations that move the body away from ideal forms. In a society in which appearance is the primary index of value for women (and increasingly for men), beautification practices normalize the female body and disabilities abnormalize it. Feminization prompts the gaze; disability prompts the stare. Feminization increases a woman's cultural capital; disability reduces it.

But as Aristotle's equation of females with mutilated males suggests, even the ideal female body is abnormal compared to the universal standard of the male body. The normative female—the figure of the beautiful woman—is the narrowly prescribed opposite of the ideal male. If he is to be strong, active, large, hirsute, hard, then she must be weak, passive, small, hairless, soft. The normative female body, then, occupies a dual and paradoxical cultural role: it is the negative term opposing the male body, but it is also simultaneously the privileged term opposing the abnormalized female body.[24] For example, the nineteenth-century obsession with scientific quantification produced a detailed description of absolute beauty, laid out by Havelock Ellis, with a Darwinian ranking determined entirely by physical characteristics and ranging from the "beautiful" European woman to what was considered to be her grotesque opposite, the African woman.[25] Moreover, scientific discourse conceived this anatomical scale of beauty as simultaneously one of pathology. The further a female body departed from absolute beauty, the more "abnormal" it became. The markers of this indubitable pathology were traits like dark skin and physical disability, or behaviors like prostitution, that were often linked to body characteristics. Within this scheme, all women are seen as deviant, but some more so than others. So the simple dichotomy of objectified feminine body and masculine subject is complicated by other oppositions. Indeed, the unfeminine, unbeautiful body defines and is defined by the ideal feminine body. This aberrant figure of woman has been identified variously in history and discourse as black, fat, lesbian, sexually voracious, disabled, or ugly. What is important here is that this figure's deviance and subsequent devaluation are always attributed to some visible characteristic that operates as an emblem of her difference, just as beauty has always been located in the body of the feminine woman.

As one manifestation of the unbeautiful woman, then, the figure of the disabled woman disrupts oppositional paradigms. This cultural figure of the disabled woman, not the actual woman with a disability, is the subject of this study. Because representation structures reality, the cultural figures that haunt us often must, like Virginia Woolf's Angel of the House, be wrestled to the floor before even modest self-definition, let alone political action, can occur. The figure of the disabled woman I focus on here is a product of a conceptual triangulation. She is a cultural third term, defined by the original pair of the masculine figure and the feminine figure. Seen as the opposite of the masculine figure, but also imagined as the antithesis of the normal woman, the figure of the disabled female is thus ambiguously positioned both inside and outside the category of woman.

Disabled Women Figures

My purpose here is to trace the complexities that arise from the presence of these ambiguous disabled women figures within cultural and literary texts in which, for the most part, they occupy marginal positions. In almost every case, the disabled woman figure functions as a symbol of otherness, either positive or negative. The presence of these often multiply marginalized figures complicates and unbalances seemingly stable narrative economies in the texts. In the account of freak shows in chapter 3, for example, exhibitions of disabled women of color introduce race, gender, and ethnicity into freak discourse, which seems initially to turn upon the simple opposition between "normal" and "abnormal" bodies. Freaks always appeared not just as monsters, but as gendered and racialized monsters.

The complication provoked by the disabled woman figure is perhaps clearest, however, in the literary texts examined here. Shifting the analytical focus from main characters and central plots to the secondary, or even incidental, disabled women reveals complex alignments and otherwise buried tensions at work in the texts. In chapter 4, for instance, the cluster of nineteenth-century sentimental fiction sets a feminine narrative voice and perspective against a masculine point of view. If, however, we recognize the triangle of the implicitly masculine cultural self, the feminine woman, and the disabled woman, fresh perspectives emerge. Examining the opposition that these social reform novels posit between the feminine woman and the disabled woman—between Elizabeth Stuart Phelps's heroine, Perley, and her deaf and mute antiheroine, Catty, for instance—reveals the texts' otherwise obscured entanglement in liberal individualist ideology. Similarly, the primary discourse in the twentieth-century African-American novels discussed in chapter 5 is one of race. Yet, as with the earlier group of texts, examining the disabled figures' rhetorical function complicates the primary opposition between black and white culture on which the novels turn. In Toni Morrison's *Tar Baby*, for example, the blind Therese's narrative empowerment must be contrasted with the beautiful Jadine's loss of power in order for the novel's social critique to be fully apprehended. Thus, the presence of the disabled woman figure challenges any simple textual reading that arranges dominant and marginal positions along a single axis of identity such as gender, race, or class.

Sociocultural Analyses of the Extraordinary Body

Erving Goffman's Stigma Theory

As I have suggested, the contemporary theory most suited to examining disability fuses identity politics with the poststructuralist interrogation of identity, truth, and knowledge, places its concerns in historical context, and forms a complex analysis of the relationship between society and the body. Although feminist theory's attention to the body and identity is useful in this regard, to satisfactorily formulate disability theory it is necessary to invoke several other theorists, though their main focus is neither gender nor disability. To clarify how representation attaches meaning to the physical differences we term disability, I discuss here the intersections of body and culture probed by Erving Goffman, Mary Douglas, and Michel Foucault, among others. Of these, only Goffman's sociological stigma theory directly addresses disability; to utilize Douglas's, Foucault's, and others' work, I have extrapolated how disability could be included in their analyses. This brief survey highlights the aspects of these theorists' ideas that pertain to the ways the disabled body emerges from culture.

Erving Goffman's definitive 1963 analysis, *Stigma: Notes on the Management of Spoiled Identity,* lays out a theory of stigmatization as a social process that attempts to account for all forms of what Simone de Beauvoir's earlier study of women called "Otherness."[26] Despite its curiously insensitive title and disturbingly hostile tone toward its subjects—perhaps in the tradition of Freud—Goffman's work underpins the nascent field of disability studies in the social sciences. Like feminist theory, stigma theory provides a useful vocabulary for placing disability in social contexts. Whereas terms such as "otherness" or "alterity" dominate literary criticism, both are limited for explaining marginalized identities because they are nouns. In contrast, the term "stigma," taken by Goffman from the Greek practice of branding or marking slaves and criminals and from Christian notions about the wounds of saints, can take many grammatical forms to match the component strands of a complex social process. The transitive verb "stigmatize," for example, suggests a process with both a subject and an object. Such semantic flexibility can call to account a "stigmatizer," identify an institution that is "stigmatizing," isolate a "stigma" as only one aspect of a whole, complex individual, or describe people or traits as "stigmatized." Some social psychologists have extended Goffman's theory by using the term "mark" to name a potentially stigmatizable physical or behavioral trait. This subtle distinction stresses the separation between actual characteristics or behavior and the processes of devaluing them.[27] Individuals are "markable" because of particular traits, and "markers" are those who interpret certain traits as deviant. Stigma theory thus provides a means of precisely tracing the production of cultural "minorities" or "others." In short, "stigmatize" describes distinctions among people, their physical traits, what is done to them, who does it, and what it means.

In essence, stigmatization is an interactive social process in which particular human traits are deemed not only different, but deviant. It is a form of social comparison apparently found in all societies, though the specific characteristics singled out vary across cultures and history. Most important is that these social devaluations are collective, part of a communal acculturation process. Stigmatization creates a shared, socially maintained and determined conception of a normal individual, what I earlier termed a normate, sculpted by a social group attempting to define its own character and boundaries. Though any human trait can be stigmatized, the dominant group has the authority and means to determine which differences are inferior and to perpetuate those judgments.[28] Thus terms like "minority," "ethnicity," and "disability" suggest infusing certain differences with negative value. Stigmatization not only reflects the tastes and opinions of the dominant group, it reinforces that group's idealized self-description as neutral, normal, legitimate, and identifiable by denigrating the characteristics of less powerful groups or those considered alien. The process of stigmatization thus legitimates the status quo, naturalizes attributions of inherent inferiority and superiority, and obscures the socially constructed quality of both categories.

Recent elaborations of stigma theory by social scientists probe the motivation for this apparently universal social process. A phenomenological account suggests that stigmatization arises from the human impulse to categorize differences and impose some kind of meaningful order on experience. All people apparently need to routinize their lives with interpretive schemata, or what Alfred Schutz calls "recipes," that make their worlds seem knowable and predictable. But stigmatizing is more than organizing experience. In this complex process, certain human traits become salient, such as the physiological characteristics we use to anchor "sex," "race," "ethnicity," and "disability." Goffman identifies three types of physical and behavioral characteristics from which stigmata are usually constructed by a given social unit: first are physical disability, deformity, or anomaly; next are individual behaviors such as addiction, dishonesty, unpredictability, lack of education or manners, or certain sexual habits; finally are race, religion, ethnicity, or gender.[29] Complex hierarchies of assigned social status are founded on such actions and characteristics.

Goffman further refines his analysis of social stigmatization by recognizing that most people in this society possess some stigmatized trait to some degree, making the group who meet the narrow criteria of the idealized norm a very small minority. The prototypical figure whom Western society constructs as its ideal and its norm is the remnant of humanity after all those bearing stigmatized traits have been peeled away. The normate figure Goffman acknowledges—the "young, married, white, urban, northern, heterosexual, Protestant father of college education, fully employed, of good complexion, weight and height, and a recent record in sports" that I mentioned earlier—is an updated version of the self-possessed individual delineated in nineteenth-century American discourse. By pointing out how few real people conform to this description, Goffman reveals the illusory, ideological nature of the normate subject position. It is an image that dominates without material substance, a phantom "majority" opposed to an overwhelming and equally illusory "minority."[30]

The implicit question underlying stigma theory is why differences within social groups are not simply perceived without assigned values. While poststructuralist theory posits that binary opposition is always hierarchical, social scientists tend to ground explanations in data about social practices. An historicist approach, for example, asserts that parents, institutional practices, and various forms of art and communications media inculcate stigmatization across generations and geographies. On the individual level, motivational or psychological explanations suggest that projecting unacceptable feelings and impulses onto members of less powerful groups establishes identity and enhances self-worth. Regardless of the cause, such a widespread, if not universal, human practice flies in the face of modernity's ideology of liberal democracy.

Stigma theory is useful, then, because it untangles the processes that construct both the normative as well as the deviant and because it reveals the parallels among all forms of cultural oppression while still allowing specific devalued identities to remain in view. It essentially resituates the "problem" of disability from the body of the disabled person to the social framing of that body. Finally, stigma theory reminds us that the problems we confront are not disability, ethnicity, race, class, homosexuality, or gender; they are instead the inequalities, negative attitudes, misrepresentations, and institutional practices that result from the process of stigmatization.

"Matter Out of Place": Mary Douglas's Concept of Dirt

Anthropologist Mary Douglas also points to cultural patterns that show how the disability category operates. In her classic study, *Purity and Danger: An Analysis of Concepts of Pollution and Taboo*, Douglas speculates about the relativity of dirt in ways that can be applied to the cultural meaning of disability. Dirt, she observes, is "matter out of place . . . the by-product of a systematic ordering and classification of matter, in so far as ordering involves rejecting inappropriate elements."[31] Hygiene and pathogenicity, Douglas points out, are relatively recent legitimations for the concept of dirt as a cultural contaminant. Dirt is an anomaly, a discordant element rejected from the schema that individuals and societies use in order to construct a stable, recognizable, and predictable world.[32] One might combine Douglas and Goffman to assert that human stigmata function as social dirt.

This cultural intolerance of anomaly is one of the most pervasive themes in Western thought. One example is Aristotle's *Poetics*, the founding document of Western literary criticism, in which the schemata we call "probability" and "rationality" delimit the tragic plot, determining which elements may be properly included and which do not fit. For the plot to be unified, which is Aristotle's essential requirement, anomalies must be excluded. Another particularly vivid instance of this antipathy toward difference occurs in Kant's aesthetic theory, "Critique of Judgment," in an exceedingly abstract discussion on beauty. Kant asserts that colors are beautiful only if they are "pure," only if they display a "uniformity [that] is troubled and interrupted by no foreign sensation." Consequently, Kant believes that simple colors are beautiful and composite colors are not. Such a definition of beauty parallels Douglas's conception of purity as the absence of dirt, the anomalous element. Such abstract value systems that structure elements into the pure and the corrupt, the legitimate and the illicit, might easily be transformed into the ideology of human racial purity that deems some people impure, unbeautiful, or unfit.[33]

Douglas's interpretation of dirt as anomaly, as the extra-ordinary, can be extended to the body we call "disabled" as well as to other forms of social marginalization. Like dirt, all disability is in some sense "matter out of place" in terms of the interpretive frameworks and physical expectations our culture shares. Visible physical disability lies outside the normative ordering system and can only be included and comprehended under Douglas's classifications of "aberrant" or "anomalous," categories that accommodate what does not fit into the space of the ordinary.[34] Douglas does not include disability in her theory, though she refers to the common infanticide of congenitally disabled newborns as an example of the way cultures deal with anomaly. Nevertheless, her speculations suggest that disability is the systematic social interpretation of some bodies as abnormal, rather than any actual physical features. Douglas acknowledges that culture mediates all individual experience, imposing systems of perception that are not easily revised. She notes further that all societies must come to terms with the anomalies that their schemata produce. Because cultures do not tolerate such affronts to their communal narratives of order, what emerges from a given cultural context as irremediable anomaly translates not as neutral difference, but as pollution, taboo, contagion. Elaborating this process, Douglas discusses five ways that cultures cope with the extraordinary. These strategies correspond generally to the manner in which our culture frames and responds to disability.

First, social groups can reduce ambiguity by assigning the anomalous element to one absolute category or the other. Similar to other dualistic systems such as gender and race, the disabled/able-bodied dichotomy sorts people by interpreting physical traits that are in fact less easily categorized than the system admits. For example, although actual impairments usually affect particular body parts or physical functions, one specific difference classifies an entire person "disabled" even though the rest of the body and its functions remain "normal." According to this totalizing "master status," the deviant characteristic overwhelms all of a person's other, unmarked aspects.[35] Categories of cultural otherness thus reduce individuals to particular identifying traits, rendering a multifaceted individual a "black," a "gay," or one of the "disabled." Institutions such as legal systems have enforced such dichotomous classifications in the name of both justice and discrimination. Indeed, so powerful is the cultural imperative to structure experience with absolute categories that figures who seemingly defy classification—such as mulattos, freaks, transvestites, bisexuals, and others hybrids—elicit anxiety, hostility, or pity and are always rigorously policed.[36] The rigidity of social order testifies to the destabilizing threat of ambiguity as well as the artificial, constructed quality of all social identities.

Douglas identifies the second cultural solution to anomaly as elimination. She notes wryly that if the necks of night-crowing cocks are "promptly wrung, they do not live to contradict the definition of a cock as a bird that crows at dawn." This principle Douglas offers so casually becomes much more troubling when it is applied to people with disabilities. Both the modern eugenics movement, which arose from the mid-nineteenth-century scientific community, and its current counterpart, reproductive technology designed to predict and eliminate "defective" fetuses, reveal a determination to eradicate disabled people. While the rhetoric claims that such procedures are aimed at

ending disability, the reality is often that people with disabilities are eliminated. Eugenics, "the science of improving the stock," was a respected field
that successfully promoted mandatory sterilization laws in the United States
as well as the Immigration Restriction Act of 1924, both of which reflected
fears that the "best" people would be outnumbered by their physical or mental "inferiors." The notion of improvement and its concomitant concept of de-
generacy depend on the values of autonomy and productivity included in
liberal individualism, as well as on the Platonic idealism that is our Western
inheritance. Indeed, Ronald Walters argues that eugenic thinking was a secular manifestation of the nineteenth-century reform effort to perfect society.
Eliminating disabled people as discordant social elements is the logical extension of an ideology that esteems national and individual progress toward
self-reliance, self-management, and self-sufficiency, a point to which I will
return.[37]

A third cultural response Douglas recognizes is "avoiding anomalous
things." Historically, disabled people have for the most part been segregated either as individuals or in groups. Much of Michel Foucault's analysis of the
modern subject reveals the way marginalized individuals—such as disabled
people—have been enclosed, excluded, and regulated. Societies encode their
collective prejudices in segregation legislation, such as the common U.S. "ugly
laws" of the nineteenth and twentieth centuries that banned visibly disabled
people from appearing in public places.[38] Similarly, asylums and almshouses
that flourished in nineteenth-century America provided custodial segregation
as limited aid for disabled people. Perhaps the most enduring form of segregation has been economic: the history of begging is virtually synonymous with the
history of disability. Much of American disability legislation has attempted to
sort out this conflation, termed by Tom Compton the "vagrant/beggar/cripple
complex."[39] Today, disabled people, especially women, tend to be ghettoized by
poverty and lack of education, those stigmatic situations that so frequently co-
incide with and reinforce marginalization based on physical traits.

Segregation, despite its disadvantages, can forge the sense of community
from which politicized consciousness and nationalism emerges. Although a
fraught debate goes on regarding the merits and dangers of racial or gender nationalism versus assimilation, the solidarity wrested from strategic separatism
often leads to political activism and challenges social attitudes. Because disabled people tend to be scattered among the nondisabled, political unity and
consciousness-raising have emerged primarily as a result of traditional segregation or the self-imposed segregation that often accompanies positive-identity
politics. The highly politicized deaf community, for example, arose from segre-

gated schools for the deaf. The independent living movement also partly owes its existence to the practice of segregated education and institutionalization.[40]

Douglas suggests that a fourth method social groups use to deal with anomaly is to label it dangerous. Both segregation and elimination are social and political practices based in part on the interpretation of physical disability as not only anomalous but dangerous, indeed contaminating, like dirt. Douglas points out that although an individual response to anomaly can be quite complex, public beliefs tend to reduce dissonance among individual responses and promote a conformity that finds expression in larger social institutions. Consequently, anomaly often becomes synonymous with danger and evil. This is nowhere clearer than in the symbolic uses of disability in literature and film. That ubiquitous icon of physical anomaly, the monster, exemplifies culture's preoccupation with the threat of the different body.[41] Disabilities do not simply mark evil, but function as menace in such prototypical villains as Shakespeare's Richard III, Dickens's Quilp, Melville's Ahab, Poe's Hop Frog, and Stanley Kubrick's Dr. Strangelove. Like the monsters who are their fantastic cousins, disabled characters with power virtually always represent a dangerous force unleashed on the social order, as attested by Flannery O'Connor's one-armed villain Tom Shiftlet in "The Life You Save May Be Your Own," Carson McCullers' hunchbacked Cousin Lymon Willis from "The Ballad of the Sad Cafe," Nathanael West's crippled Peter Doyle of *Miss Lonelyhearts*, and Hawthorne's humpbacked Roger Chillingworth of *The Scarlet Letter*.[42] Because these characters operate as embodiments of an unnamed, profound peril, the narrative resolution is almost always to contain that threat by killing or disempowering the disabled character. The logic that governs this cultural narrative, then, is that eliminating the anomaly neutralizes the danger.

The interpretation of disability as a sign of evil or sin is explained in another way by Melvin Lerner's "just world" theory. According to Lerner, the human need for order and predictability gives rise to a belief that people get what they deserve or that the way things are is the way they should be. Such a theory accounts not only for the norms that establish justice, but also for the judgment of differences. It is the logic of theodicy: if something "bad"—like having a disability—happens to someone, then there must be some "good" reason—like divine or moral justice—for its occurrence. This troubling way of thinking gained much force and legitimacy from nineteenth-century social Darwinian pseudoscience, especially Herbert Spencer and his American disciples' application of Lamarckian evolution to social relations. Although this doctrine provides a psychological safeguard against the intolerable randomness of experience, it results in victim-blaming and scapegoating of those who are different. Because disability is such a contingent condition, it may inspire the kind of anxiety that a "just world" concept is most suited to relieve. Not only can anyone become disabled at any time, but the pain, bodily damage, or impairment sometimes associated with disability make it seem an uncontained threat to those who consider themselves normal. The belief that disabled people are simply the losers in some grand competitive scheme or the once-accepted conviction that masturbation caused blindness attest to the prevalence of just-world assumptions about disability.[43] Perhaps the most unfortunate current just-world assumption is that AIDS is a moral judgment on homosexuals and intravenous drug users.

Bodies that are disabled can also seem dangerous because they are perceived as out of control. Not only do they violate physical norms, but by looking and acting unpredictable they threaten to disrupt the ritualized behavior upon which social relations turn.[44] The uncontrolled body does not perform typically the quotidian functions required by the elaborately structured codes of acceptable social behavior. Blindness, deafness, or stuttering, for instance, disturb the complex web of subtle exchanges upon which communication rituals depend. Wheelchairs or paralysis require different ambulatory choreographies. Furthermore, the disabled body transgresses individualism's codes of work and autonomy by enacting patterns that differ from the norm, another point I will discuss more fully later.

The modern secular world's method of labeling disability dangerous is to term it pathological rather than evil or immoral. Freud's essay on "The Exceptions," for example, labels disabled people psychologically pathological. Conflating the inner and outer selves, Freud concludes that "deformities of character" are the results of physical disability. Indeed, disability has been almost entirely subsumed in twentieth-century America under a medical model that pathologizes disability. Although medical interpretation rescues disability from its earlier associations with evil, pathologized difference is fraught with assumptions of deviance, patronizing relationships, and issues of control.[45]

The fifth and final cultural treatment of anomaly Douglas observes is incorporating the anomalous elements into ritual "to enrich meaning or to call attention to other levels of existence."[46] Of Douglas's five solutions, this is culture's only potentially positive or transformative interpretation of the extraordinary. I will briefly mention here two of several theorists who expand Douglas's idea by exploring anomaly's potential to alter cultural patterns, though none specifically discusses disability. In *The Structure of Scientific Revolutions*, Thomas S. Kuhn revises the narrative of incremental scientific discovery by tracing the role of anomaly in scientific understanding. What

Kuhn calls "normal science" finds coherence and unanimity by excluding the extraordinary from its paradigms, by suppressing "fundamental novelties because they are necessarily subversive of its basic commitments."[47] Kuhn defines "novelties" as phenomena that cannot be aligned with scientific expectations, and argues that when such exceptional phenomena accumulate or become so compelling that they can no longer be dismissed, their presence forces a shift in scientific paradigms so that a new set of beliefs emerges.

Kuhn's view of the extraordinary's power to unsettle the ascendant order is echoed by Mikhail Bakhtin's notion that the grotesque body as carnivalesque disrupts the status quo and inverts social hierarchies. Whereas Kuhn sees anomaly as subverting scientific classification, Bakhtin posits the carnivalesque as a ritualistic use of the extraordinary body to disturb the social order. According to Bakhtin, the carnivalesque figure—perhaps his version of the disabled figure—represents "the right to be 'other' in this world, the right not to make common cause with any single one of the existing categories that life makes available; none of these categories quite suits them, they see the underside and falseness of every situation."[48] Bakhtin's concept of the disorderly body as a challenge to the existing order suggests the radical potential that the disabled body as sign for difference might possess within representation. The Bakhtinian carnivalesque figure frequently appears in critical analyses of the grotesque as a liminal aesthetic category that enables radical representations by straddling and transgressing categories.[49] Imagining anomaly and the grotesque as agents capable of reconstituting cultural discourses suggests the possibility of interpreting both dirt and disability not as discomforting abnormalities or intolerable ambiguities, but rather as the entitled bearers of a fresh view of reality. Moreover, because the disabled figure always represents the extraordinary, such interpretations open the way for us to imagine narratives of physical disability other than deviance and abnormality. Indeed, I argue in the following chapters that at specific sites of representation, the disabled figures operate in varying degrees as challenges to the cultural status quo, introducing issues and perspectives with the potential to refigure the social order.

Historicizing the Disabled Body: Michel Foucault's "Docile Bodies"

While Goffman and Douglas offer relational analyses that help us place disability in a social context, Michel Foucault's speculations on the constitution of the modern subject bring to disability the notion of historical change that both Goffman and Douglas omit. Foucault's conception of the ways that power embedded in everyday practices structures subjects suggests how cultural classification and stigmatization—which may indeed be universal, as sociologists assert—are nevertheless complicated by history. Whereas Goffman's stigma theory illuminates the modern context of disability, Foucault's theory of the eighteenth-century shift to a modern, Enlightenment, reason-based concept of the body supports other readings and treatments of the disabled body.

Arguing that the modern subject emerged in the Neoclassical age, as discourse and institutions solidified to reproduce new social relations of domination and subordination, Foucault asserts in *Discipline and Punish* that feudal society transformed into a "disciplinary regime" that systematically controlled the body as concern for its efficient operation and its ultimate utility increased. This concept of "docile bodies" yields the rigid taxonomies so fundamental to nineteenth- and twentieth-century Western science and medicine's project of distributing human characteristics in discrete and hierarchical relations to one another.[50] Architectural, pedagogical, and medical practices manipulated the body, both generating and enforcing the Cartesian image of an individual as a separate, isolated, efficient machine whose goal was self-mastery. Such a utilitarian concept of the body, incited by economic crisis, led in the seventeenth century to what Foucault calls in *Madness and Civilization* the "Great Confinement" of beggars, the poor, and the idle in hospitals. These hospitals were, however, not medical facilities but poorhouses, institutions established by the aristocracy and the bourgeoisie to segregate, assist, and punish a great "undifferentiated mass" of economically unproductive people, the ostensible failures at self-mastery. Concern with culling out the "sick poor" from economically useful mendicants gave rise in the eighteenth century to a dominant ideology of health and physical well-being as a civic duty and political objective. Medicine, then, as administered by doctors, enforced what Foucault terms in *Power/Knowledge* a "Politics of Health," rationalized by hygiene and bent not on aid but on containment through "curing."[51] This discourse, which classified the healthy body and the pathological body, focused on disciplining all bodies in the name of improvement. This instrumental view of the body as a productive, well-operating machine produced the idea of a norm, which Foucault calls a "new law of modern society" and a "principle of coercion," used to measure, classify, and regulate human bodies.[52]

Foucault's historical explanation of the norm as a uniquely modern concept brings us to the threshold of stigma theory, to oppressive hierarchies of physical appearance. Whereas Goffman's and Douglas's transhistorical and transcultural accounts naturalize the norm, Foucault aggressively presents the norm as both coercive and punitive by connecting it not merely to devaluing social attitudes, but to social institutions legitimated by historical conceptions of deviance. Foucault, however, never mentions disabled people specifically in his analysis. Although many paupers had physically disabilities, he never makes distinctions among them.[53] We can nevertheless extrapolate from Foucault's theory that the modern social identity of "disabled" emerged from the shifts he charts and that it arose in tandem with its opposite: the abstract, self-possessed, autonomous individual.

Foucault's suggestion that the modern individual is determined by its own particularity is the most useful insight for my purposes here. Whereas in premodern society, individuating markers indicated power and privilege, in modern society, an unmarked norm is the reference point. Those who most depart from the normative standard are most subordinated. Whiteness, for example, is concealed and neutral, while blackness carries the burden of "race." These differences are marked also in the costuming of pre- and post-Enlightenment aristocratic males. Before the nineteenth century, an array of ornate particulars—crowns, scepters, insignias, badges, wigs—distinguished the powerful individuals from the undifferentiated lowly masses. Today, however, male power is costumed in indistinguishable, undistinguished business suits and ties, while otherness is elaborately visible, whether marked by the prisoner's striped suit, the Star of David arm band, or the decorative woman's ornate gown and high heels. Foucault's theory thus predicts the position of power and privilege at the heart of Goffman's stigma theory: the unmarked, prototypical subject, the "unblemished" one, the normate.[54] In its complex social codification, power is veiled by a rhetoric of neutrality that creates the illusion of meritocracy. Yet power's visible nonparticularity is its marker in the subtle economy of display that signals status in modernity.

Although disability has historically been seen as a disadvantage or a curse, in modern times markers of individuation like physical disability render one a "case" upon which power is exercised. But disability might have been more easily read in a premodern society as a distinguishing mark of power and prestige, whereas in the modern era, disempowerment is marked by visible stigmata. Indeed, Harlan Hahn offers archeological evidence suggesting that disabled people may have been held in high regard in earlier cultures. The saints' stigmatic wounds, Oedipus's and Socrates's lameness, Tiresias's and Homer's blindness, and Philoctetes's wound certainly seem to function as ennobling marks rather than signs of a diminishing abnormality like those of the modern "cripple."[55] Foucault's notion that the significance of particularity shifted in modernity, then, challenges the definition of disability as a corruption of the norm. Such speculations enable us to envision interpretations of the extraordinary human body other than deviance and inferiority.

Taken together, Goffman's analysis of disability as defined by social relations, Douglas's observations about cultural responses to anomaly, and Foucault's historical delineation of the modern norm as unmarked reveal the physically disabled figure as a culturally and historically specific social construction. Such a critical framework helps situate the disabled figure within the American ideologies of liberal individualism and the moral imperative of work, and illuminates how the disabled figure operates in literature.

The Disabled Figure and the Ideology of Liberal Individualism

Emerson's Invalid and the Doctrine of Self-Reliance

In anthropologist Robert Murphy's groundbreaking ethnography of his own disability, *The Body Silent*, he emphasizes that others' avoidance, discomfort, and devaluation of him amounted to a loss of status and a wound to his self-image as devastating as his recent paraplegia. Disability, Murphy observes, "is a social malady. . . . We are subverters of an American Ideal, just as the poor are betrayers of the American Dream."[56] Murphy goes beyond simply acknowledging the social dimensions of disability to examine the disabled figure's crucial role in establishing the boundaries of the normate American self. Like the poor, Murphy asserts, disabled people are made to signify what the rest of Americans fear they will become. Freighted with anxieties about loss of control and autonomy that the American ideal repudiates, "the disabled" become a threatening presence, seemingly compromised by the particularities and limitations of their own bodies. Shaped by a narrative of somatic inadequacy and represented as a spectacle of erratic singularity, the disabled figure delineates the corresponding abstract cultural figure of the self governing, standardized individual emerging from a society informed by consumerism and mechanization. Cast as one of society's ultimate "not me" figures, the disabled other absorbs disavowed elements of this cultural self, becoming an icon of all human vulnerability and enabling the "American Ideal" to appear as master of both destiny and self. At once familiarly human but definitively other, the disabled figure in cultural discourse assures the rest of the citzenry of who they are not while arousing their suspicions about who they could become.[57]

Witness, for instance, a brief but exemplary invocation of the disabled figure in Ralph Waldo Emerson's rhetoric of "Self-Reliance." "And now we are men . . ." writes Emerson in the 1847 version, "not minors and invalids in a protected corner, not cowards fleeing before a revolution, but guides, redeemers, and benefactors, obeying the Almighty effort, and advancing on

Chaos and the Dark." Using the disabled figure again in his later essay "Fate," Emerson disparages conservatives by characterizing them as "effeminated by nature, born halt and blind" and able "only, like invalids, [to] act on the defensive." Scholars have noted that Emerson's elaboration of liberal individualism as a neo-Platonic, disembodied form of masculinity depends upon his construction of and flight from a denigrated, oppositional femininity upon which he projects a fear not only of dependence and neediness, but also of what David Leverenz calls "the perils of the body."[58] What has gone unremarked, however, is Emerson's invocation of "invalids" as a related category of otherness that mutually constitutes his liberal self. Unlike the supposedly inviolable real "men," who act as "guides, redeemers, and benefactors" capable of "advancing," Emerson's disparaged and static "invalids" are banished "in a protected corner," along with "minors" and, presumably, women. The "blind," the "halt," and the "invalids" Emerson enlists to define the liberal individual by opposition are, above all else, icons of bodily vulnerability. The "invalid" body is impotence made manifest. By barring the disabled figure from his definition of the universal "man," Emerson reveals the implicit assumption of an exclusionary physical norm incorporated in the ideal of an autonomous individual self. With the specter of physical vulnerability exiled into "a protected corner" along with the feminine, Emerson's naturalized "man" emerges as Murphy's "American Ideal,"unimpeded by the physical limitation that history and contingency impose upon actual lives.

Emerson's juxtaposition of an unrestricted cultural self with a muted other thwarted by physical limits exposes the problem of the body within the ideology of liberal individualism. The "American Ideal" posited by liberal individualism is structured by a four-part self-concept that is profoundly threatened by what Richard Selzer has called the "mortal lessons" that disability represents.[59] The four interrelated ideological principles that inform this normate self might be characterized as self-government, self-determination, autonomy, and progress. Such a self-image parallels the national ideal in an individualist egalitarian democracy that each citizen is a microcosm of the nation as a whole. A well-regulated self thus contributes to a well-regulated nation. However, these four principles depend upon a body that is a stable, neutral instrument of the individual will. It is this fantasy that the disabled figure troubles. For my purposes here, it is useful to disentangle these national and individual principles of self to examine how each relies on the disabled figure to absorb what it refuses.

Egalitarian democracy demands individual self-government to avoid anarchy. A system in which individuals make laws and choose leaders depends upon individuals governing their actions and their bodies just as they govern the social body. Consequently, the disabled figure is a unique and disturbing construct among the cultural others opposed to the ideal American self. It is perhaps easier to establish difference based on relatively stable, although highly policed, bodily markers like gender, ethnic, and racial characteristics than it is to distance disability. Disability's indisputably random and unpredictable character translates as appalling disorder and persistent menace in a social order predicated on self-government. Furthermore, physical instability is the bodily manifestation of political anarchy, of the antinomian impulse that is the threatening, but logical, extension of egalitarian democracy.[60] The disabled body stands for the self gone out of control, individualism run rampant: it mocks the notion of the body as compliant instrument of the limitless will and appears in the cultural imagination as ungovernable, recalcitrant, flaunting its difference as if to refute the fantasy of sameness implicit in the notion of equality. Even more troubling, disability suggests that the cultural other lies dormant within the cultural self, threatening abrupt or gradual transformations from "man" to "invalid." The disabled figure is the stranger in our midst, within the family and potentially within the self.

Just as the principle of self-government demands a regulated body, the principle of self-determination requires a compliant body to secure a place in the fiercely competitive and dynamic socioeconomic realm. The idea of self-determination places tremendous pressure on individuals to feel responsible for their own social stations, economic situations, and relations with others. Among the emerging middle classes of the nineteenth century, from whom traditional group affiliations had been shorn, the desire for identity produced conformity that was expressed in an intolerance of differences—precisely those distinctions that freedom encouraged. Because democracy precluded former class alliances and generational continuities, people had only one another after which to model themselves. By 1835 Tocqueville noted this tendency to conform, observing that "all of the minds of the Americans were formed upon one model, so accurately do they follow the same route."[61] Furthermore, the developing mass culture mandated by equality further encourages a uniformity that stabilizes threats of anarchy, enforcing conformity and punishing difference. Thus, democracy's paradox is that the principle of equality implies sameness of condition, while the promise of freedom suggests the potential for uniqueness. That potential amounted for many Americans to a mandate for distinctiveness—the kind of nonconformity that Emerson and Thoreau so vehemently extol in their efforts to formulate an individual self free from all restraint.

What often goes unstated is the body's crucial role in this paradoxical ideology of self-determination. For instance, nineteenth-century concern with health, especially the obsession with bodily functions such as elimination, cleanliness, and what G. J. Barker-Benfield calls "spermatic retentiveness" can be seen as a physical expression of pressures to control the corporeal self. Moreover, the rhetoric of nonconformity and anti-authority coexisted with the development of mass-produced goods and the standardization of appearance through reproducible images, encouraging the uniformity of lifestyle that serves modern consumer and mechanized culture.[62] The disabled figure speaks to this tension between uniqueness and uniformity. On the one hand, the disabled figure is a sign for the body that refuses to be governed and cannot carry out the will to self-determination. On the other hand, the extraordinary body is nonconformity incarnate. In a sense then, the disabled figure has the potential to inspire with its irreverent individuality and to threaten with its violation of equality. Indeed, I argue in the next chapter that a part of the fascination the freak show held for nineteenth-century Americans was this doubleness inherent in the extraordinary body.

Just as the dominant culture's ideal self requires the ideological figures of the woman to confirm its masculinity and of the black to assure its whiteness, so Emerson's atomized self demands an oppositional twin to secure its able-bodiedness. The freak, the cripple, the invalid, the disabled—like the quadroon and the homosexual—are representational, taxonomical products that naturalize a norm comprised of accepted bodily traits and behaviors registering social power and status. Thus translated, physical difference yields a cultural icon signifying violated wholeness, unbounded incompleteness, unregulated particularity, dependent subjugation, disordered intractability, and susceptibility to external forces. With the body's threat of betrayal thus compartmentalized, the mythical American self can unfold, unobstructed and unrestrained, according to its own manifest destiny.

Melville's Ahab: The Whale-Made Man

This paradoxical, simultaneous demand for individuality and equality is perhaps what renders *Moby Dick*'s Captain Ahab—perhaps the quintessential disabled figure in American literature—so compelling a character. Although certainly not Emerson's impotent invalid, Herman Melville's Ahab nevertheless suggests the problem of the body in America's grand experiment of liberal individualism.[63] Both self-government and self-determination require individual autonomy, the hypothetical state of independence Emerson calls self-reliance. The disabled figure profoundly threatens this fantasy of autonomy, not so much because it is seen as helpless, but rather because it is imagined as having been altered by forces outside the self. After all, even though Ahab uses the crew to carry out his revenge, his indignation is personal: the whale impinged upon his body. Autonomy assumes immunity to external forces along with the capacity to maintain a stable, static state of being, like the "possessive individualism" described by C. P. MacPherson. According to such logic, physical alterations caused by time or the environment—the changes we call disability—are hostile incursions from the outside, the effects of cruel contingencies that an individual does not adequately resist.[64] Seen as a victim of alien forces, the disabled figure appears not as transformed, supple, or unique but as violated. In contrast, the autonomous individual is imagined as having inviolate boundaries that enable unfettered self-determination, creating a myth of wholeness.[65] Within such an ideological framework, the figure whose body is a neutral instrument of the self-governing will becomes a free agent in contractual relations. Conversely, the disabled figure represents the incomplete, unbounded, compromised, and subjected body susceptible to external forces: property badly managed, a fortress inadequately defended, a self helplessly violated. Ahab's outrage compensates for his vulnerability, rendering him both a sublime and a threatening version of the disabled figure.

Ahab is, perhaps above all else, different from other men. At once compelling and repelling, he represents both the prospective freedom of nonconformity and the terrible threat of antinomianism. The outer mark of his difference is his ivory leg, and the inner manifestation is his monomaniacal fury. Neither loss of function nor pain motivates Ahab's vengeful quest as much as his profound sense of violation by the whale, a force from outside.[66] Cast as an intractable external will, the whale has breached Ahab's individual boundaries, altered his very being, and determined his future. The whale's incursion and its power over Ahab's destiny mock the ideas of self-determination and autonomy. Ahab is not a self-made man, but a whale-made man; his disabled body testifies to the self's physical vulnerability, the ominous knowledge that the ideology of individualism suppresses. For such apostasy, Ahab's body is violently and definitively separated from the rest of the community on the *Pequod* as the whale pulls Ahab from the ship with the harpoon rope, controlling him in death just as in life.[67] Ahab's nobility, like his menace, arises from his physical difference, the symbol of bodily limitation and vulnerability that threatens the notion of the autonomous, inviolable self. Ahab, along with other disabled figures, poses the troubling question of whether any person is independent of physical limitations, immune to external forces, and without need of assistance and care from others.[68] The disabled body exposes the illusion of autonomy, self-government, and self-determination that underpins the fantasy of absolute able-bodiedness.

The life of a well-governed, self-determined man is imagined as a narrative of progress on which Protestant perfectionism, the doctrine of success, and the concept of self-improvement all depend. Democratic nations, Tocqueville notes, are particularly invested in the notion of human perfectibility and likely "to expand it beyond reason."[69] But the disabled figure flies in the face of this ideal, renouncing with its very existence the fiction of self-improvement and at the same time presenting the ultimate challenge to perfection and progress. Such diverse phenomena as faith healing, cosmetic surgery, medical separation of conjoined twins, and Jerry Lewis's Telethons testify not only to the cultural demand for body normalization, but to our intolerance of the disabled figure's reminder that perfection is a chimera. As a cultural emblem for the restricted self, the disabled body stubbornly resists the willed improvement so fundamental to the American notion of the self. Indeed, lurking behind the able-bodied figure is the denied, and perhaps intolerable, knowledge that life will eventually transform us into "disabled" selves. In the end, the body and history dominate the will, imposing limits on the myth of a physically stable self progressing unfettered toward some higher material state.[70]

The Disabled Figure and the Problem of Work

The Proper Pauper

As I have suggested, disabled people are often imagined as unable to be productive, direct their own lives, participate in the community, or establish meaningful personal relations—regardless of their actual capabilities or achievements. In fact, the limitations disabled people experience result more often from interaction with a social and physical environment designed to accommodate the normate body. In other words, people deemed disabled are barred from full citizenship because their bodies do not conform with architectural, attitudinal, educational, occupational, and legal conventions based on assumptions that bodies appear and perform in certain ways.

Nowhere is the disabled figure more troubling to American ideology and history than in relation to the concept of work: the system of production and distribution of economic resources in which the abstract principles of self-government, self-determination, autonomy, and progress are manifest most completely. Labor, the definitive creed of Puritan through contemporary

America, transforms necessity into virtue and equates productive work with moral worth, idleness with depravity. The figure of the self-made American man has always held much cultural authority, especially in the nineteenth century, although poverty was widespread and industrialization was rapidly converting work into unrecognizable forms. The concepts of autonomy and independence essential to the work ethic became contorted as wage labor supplanted self-employment, the fragile economy surged up and down, and machines began to damage workers on a new scale. As modernization proceeded, the disabled figure shouldered in new ways society's anxiety about its inability to retain the status and old meanings of labor in the face of industrialization and increasing economic and social chaos.

American individualism is most clearly manifest in the conviction that economic autonomy results from hard work and virtue, while poverty stems from indolence and moral inferiority.[71] Paupers had to be held culpable for their socioeconomic situations in order to support the cherished belief that in a democratic society each individual was a self-determining free agent in a progress narrative of economic manifest destiny. However, a moral dilemma and contradiction emerge when this creed is applied to the "disabled," people whose bodies are different or transformed by life. What happens to the link between virtue and work when a person's body, through no one's volition, suddenly or gradually no longer fits the work environment? How, in short, can a culture founded upon and committed to the values of liberal individualism deal with physical disability?

In a world increasingly seen as free from divine determinism and subject to individual control, the disabled figure calls into question such concepts as will, ability, progress, responsibility, and free agency, notions around which people in a liberal society organize their identities. Moreover, secular thinking and a more accurate scientific understanding of physiology and disease prevented nineteenth-century Americans from interpreting disability as the divine punishment it had been labeled in earlier epochs. The problem of how to formulate disability as a social category arises from a conflict between the need to preserve a social hierarchy linked to individual economic condition and the need to recognize the freedom from divine intervention that makes individual achievement tenable. The disabled figure's existence mandates that society consider under what circumstances a person should be held responsible for "earning a living" and, conversely, when one should be released from that expectation because of circumstances beyond one's control. The social category "disabled" is a grudging admission of human vulnerability in a world no longer seen as divinely determined, a world where self-government and individual progress purportedly prevail. Such a classification elicits much ambivalence from a national consciousness committed to equating virtue with independent industry, especially during periods in which public policy toward those outside the labor force is being formulated.[72] That ambivalence expresses itself as social stigmatization and as rigorous, sometimes exclusionary supervision of people obliged to join the ranks of the "disabled."

The dawning industrial transformation of antebellum America forced the U.S. legal system to address the issue of physical disability as contingency rather than divine punishment, as industrial accidents began to increase and stable communities and older forms of production began to dissolve. For example, as power was being transferred from male parents to male judges during the first half of the nineteenth century, a defining decision written by Lemuel Shaw in 1842 legally framed the disabled social category according to the precepts of contractarian economic individualism. Shaw reversed the common-law precedent that made masters liable for their servants' actions by formulating the fellow-servant rule that defined negligence in favor of employers, thus serving business interests at the expense of disabled workers by making it very difficult for injured workers to sue for compensation.[73] This ruling interpreted both employer and employee as autonomous agents entering freely into a contract in which the market wage compensated for the risk of injury. That this legal formulation did not follow the precedent, established early on, of compensating wounded soldiers may have represented an effort to free economic development, seemingly separating issues of private justice from state justice. Nevertheless, newly disabled workers had little recourse but charity or poor relief. As long as economic resources from the public sphere were not equitably available for injured workers, they not only lost their jobs but also dropped out of sight into a private sphere of charity where the marketplace and the state were no longer accountable for their economic situations. That a man might be a virtuous worker one day and an indolent pauper the next doubtless raised uneasy questions about an individual's capacity for unlimited self-determinism.[74]

Even though the legal and socioeconomic category of disabled admits to contingency, this classification must, nevertheless, be assiduously delineated and monitored, so great is its threat to Americans' belief in the link between "hard work" and economic and social success. If the myth of autonomy and self-determination is to remain intact, those whose situations question it must be split off into a discrete social category governed by different assumptions. Indeed, at least since the inception of English Poor Laws in 1388, the state and other institutions concerned with the common welfare have molded the political and cultural definition of what we now know as "physical disability" in an effort to distinguish between genuine "cripples" and malingerers, those deemed unable to work and those deemed unwilling to work.[75] Although "ability" and "will" are certainly complicated and questionable concepts in the social relation called "earning a living," it is clear that in distributing resources the state and the populace insist upon trying to draw a firm boundary between these two groups of people.[76]

From Compensation to Accommodation

While the social history of disabled people has generally remained consistently one of stigmatization and low status, the state's response to "disability" in America has widened and shifted from early and continuing reimbursement such as veterans' pensions for public service, to workmen's compensation for civilian workers in industrial America, to the mandate in the Americans with Disabilities Act of 1990 that accommodation rather than restitution is the appropriate response to disability. The notion of compensation that characterized disability policy before 1990 implies a norm, the departure from or loss of which requires restitution. Seen this way, disability is a loss to be compensated for, rather than difference to be accommodated. Disability then becomes a personal flaw, and disabled people are the "able-bodied" gone wrong. Difference thus translates into deviance. Moreover, the focus on war wounds and industrial accidents as definitive disabilities supports a narrow physical norm by limiting economic benefits to those who once qualified as "able-bodied workers," barring people with congenital disabilities and disabled women from economic "compensation" because they could not lose a hypothetical advantage they never had. According to the logic of compensation, then, "disabled" connotes not physiological variation, but the violation of a primary state of putative wholeness. The logic of accommodation, on the other hand, suggests that disability is simply one of many differences among people and that society should recognize this by adjusting its environment accordingly.

The twin myths of bodily wholeness and bodily lack that underpin a compensation model of disability structure the history of public policy toward the extraordinary body. The concept of able-bodiedness and its theoretical opposite, disability, were continually reshaped as the state attempted to qualitatively distinguish between people whose physical or mental conditions legitimately prevented them from obtaining wage labor and people who simply refused to work. As disability became increasingly medicalized with the rise of science and technology, methods for distinguishing between the "sick poor" who deserved aid and the "frauds" who merited punishment and discouragement became the state's guiding principles. Yet even as ideology demanded the separation of the "able-bodied" from the "disabled" to preserve the myths of autonomy and self-governance as keys to economic success, the conflicting impulses to comfort and castigate paupers often merged in public policy and social attitudes so that neither was accomplished effectively. The history of public and private distribution of resources to people termed the "disabled" has been tinged with the punitive and the paternalistic as well as the compassionate and the just.

Science and medicine promised mid-nineteenth- and twentieth-century America the means for cordoning off the group of people it needed to class as unable to work so that supposed slackers could be rehabilitated. Medical technology such as the stethoscope and the X-ray finally provided what society believed was an objective and quantitative measure of a person's physical capability for work. In addition, a new understanding of specific disease-causing agents attributed disabling illnesses and impairments less to lack of personal responsibility and more to fate. Medical validation of physical incapacity solved the problem of malingering by circumventing the testimony of the individual. Under this confirmation scheme, the doctor sought direct communication with the body regarding its condition, eliminating the patient's ability for self-disclosure and, ultimately, for self-determination.[77] Rather than closing the gap between the work environment and the exceptional body, legal compensation further alienated disabled workers by separating their bodies from their conscious experiences of them. As a result, "disabled" became, in the twentieth-century welfare state, a medicalized category by which the state could administer economic relief in a seemingly objective and equitable manner.[78] Moreover, in constructing that legal social group, quite distinct conditions merge into a single administrative and social identity. Thus, a disabled figure whose bodily configuration was earlier read as divine retribution for some nameless sin was exonerated. Yet the new, clinically disabled category defined the person with a disability as a figure excluded from economic opportunities and therefore without free agency, self-determinism, and self-possession, the ennobling attributes of the liberal American individual.

To socially and legally construct a category of "proper paupers" whose extraordinary bodies exclude them from the burdens and privileges of work is to partially relieve anxieties about physical vulnerability by displacing them onto an identifiable group of corporeal others. Furthermore, granting exemption from work due to a "physical disability" is in one sense viewed as a proper act of mercy, if not moral generosity—the simultaneous recognition of human limitation and human obligation. Although the very young and the very old are released from official labor by similar logic, the disabled social category is harder to escape and far more stigmatizing than youth or age, which are seen more as stages in the lives of productive people than as immutable identities. On the other hand, to be officially or sympathetically relieved of the obligation of productive labor—cast out of the public economic realm into the private sphere of charity—is also to be excluded from the privilege of laboring in a society that affirms work as what Daniel Rodgers calls "the core of moral life."[79] Thus, the moral generosity that seeks to compensate for physical differences makes cultural outcasts of its recipients by assuming that individual bodies must conform to institutional standards, rather than restructuring the social environment to accommodate physical variety.

JULIA PASTRANA.
From a photo in the possession of the Anthropological Institute, London.

"Julia Pastrana," whose photograph we reproduce above, was born in Mexico, and died in the year 1860, after giving birth to a child, at Moscow. Both bodies were embalmed and preserved in that city, being at present in Prausher's Museum. Her upper eye-teeth and incisors are missing.

Billed as "The Ugliest Woman in the World," as well as "Bear Woman," "Ape Woman," and "Hybrid Indian," Julia Pastrana, a hirsute Mexican-Indian woman, sang and danced before audiences from 1854 until her death in 1860. This photograph of her embalmed corpse, which was exhibited in shows and circuses for over one hundred years after her death, illustrates that the freak's body is equally valuable whether alive or dead.

MISS JULIA PASTRANA
L'indescriptible (de Mexico)
La plus grande curiosité de monde
Elle parle anglais et espagnol, elle chante et danse

MISS JULIA PASTRANA
the nondescript, (from Mexico)
The greatest natural curiosity in the world
she speaks english and spanish sings and dances

MISS JULIA PASTRANA
Die Unbeschreibliche von Mexico)
Die grösste Natur-Seltenheit der Welt
Sie spricht englisch und spanisch, singt und tanzt

MISS JULIA PASTRANA
Die Unbeschreibliche (von Mexico)
Die grösste Natur-Seltenheit der Welt
Sie spricht englisch und spanisch, singt und tanzt

Miss Julia Pastrana, "The Nondescript," is advertised here in her various costumes.
A major convention of freak display was to exaggerate the freak's combination of the
ordinary, such as Pastrana's feminine figure, voice, and dress, with the extraordinary,
such as her beard and supposedly simian features.
Harvard Theater Collection, The Houghton Library

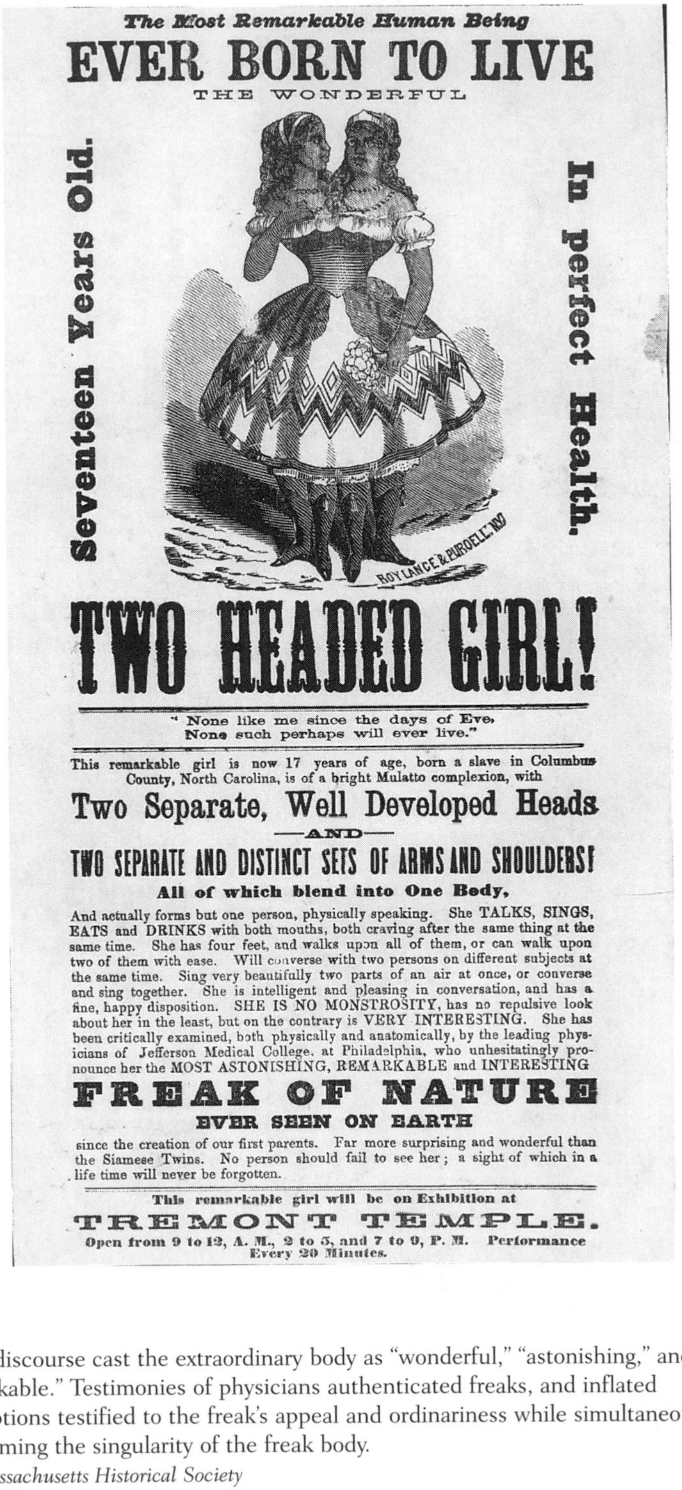

The Most Remarkable Human Being

EVER BORN TO LIVE

THE WONDERFUL

Seventeen Years Old.

In perfect Health.

TWO HEADED GIRL!

" None like me since the days of Eve,
None such perhaps will ever live."

This remarkable girl is now 17 years of age, born a slave in Columbus County, North Carolina, is of a bright Mulatto complexion, with

Two Separate, Well Developed Heads

—AND—

TWO SEPARATE AND DISTINCT SETS OF ARMS AND SHOULDERS!

All of which blend into One Body,

And actually forms but one person, physically speaking. She TALKS, SINGS, EATS and DRINKS with both mouths, both craving after the same thing at the same time. She has four feet, and walks upon all of them, or can walk upon two of them with ease. Will converse with two persons on different subjects at the same time. Sing very beautifully two parts of an air at once, or converse and sing together. She is intelligent and pleasing in conversation, and has a fine, happy disposition. SHE IS NO MONSTROSITY, has no repulsive look about her in the least, but on the contrary is VERY INTERESTING. She has been critically examined, both physically and anatomically, by the leading physicians of Jefferson Medical College. at Philadelphia, who unhesitatingly pronounce her the MOST ASTONISHING, REMARKABLE and INTERESTING

FREAK OF NATURE

EVER SEEN ON EARTH

since the creation of our first parents. Far more surprising and wonderful than the Siamese Twins. No person should fail to see her; a sight of which in a life time will never be forgotten.

This remarkable girl will be on Exhibition at

TREMONT TEMPLE.

Open from 9 to 12, A. M., 2 to 5, and 7 to 9, P. M. Performance Every 20 Minutes.

Freak discourse cast the extraordinary body as "wonderful," "astonishing," and "remarkable." Testimonies of physicians authenticated freaks, and inflated descriptions testified to the freak's appeal and ordinariness while simultaneously proclaiming the singularity of the freak body.

The Massachusetts Historical Society

The freak show exhibited exoticized racial others in order to define by staged
visual contrast the white, male subject of democracy as civilized, self-controlled,
and rational. *Harvard Theater Collection, The Houghton Library*

The contrast between this Ubangi woman and this Euro-American establishes the terms of beauty and ugliness in American culture. Lip discs, a pipe, and an androgynous costume render this African woman the grotesque opposite of the white woman, presented in standard, sexualized feminine garb, hair, and makeup.
Circus World Museum, Baraboo, Wisconsin

P. T. Barnum's "What Is It?," created from a microcephalic black man, challenged viewers to determine whether this "most marvelous creature living" was a "lower order of man" or a "higher order of monkey." Freaks were often staged as hybrids in order to provide their audiences with an opportunity to exercise their expertise at defining truth.

Shelburne Museum, Shelburne, Vermont. Photograph by Ken Burris

The first freak P. T. Barnum exhibited was Joice Heth, the supposed 161-year-old nursemaid to George Washington. Heth, a black, old, toothless, blind, crippled slave woman was a domesticated and trivialized version of what the ideal American self was not, thus assuring her audiences of their identities.
Somers Historical Society, Somers, New York

In circus sideshows, textual, spatial, and oral discourses made up of lurid banners, signs, showmen on stands, music, pitchmen, and stages framed the freak figures as extraordinary and exaggerated their strangeness.
Circus World Museum, Baraboo, Wisconsin

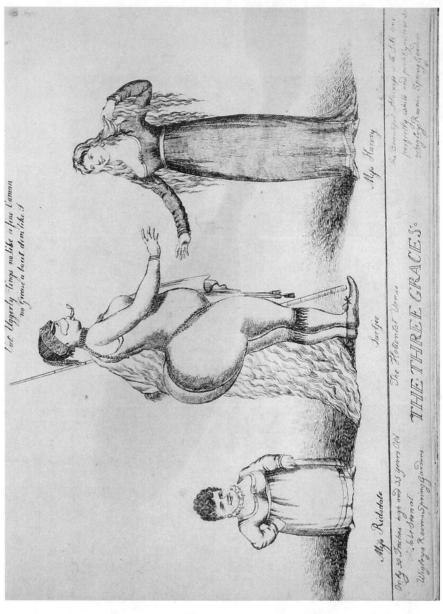

Sartjee, "The Hottentot Venus," is flanked here by a dwarf and an albino woman. Female freaks were created by publicly displaying women with extraordinary bodies to establish by contrast the contours of the ideal Euro-American woman, who remained in private.
Library of the College of Physicians of Philadelphia

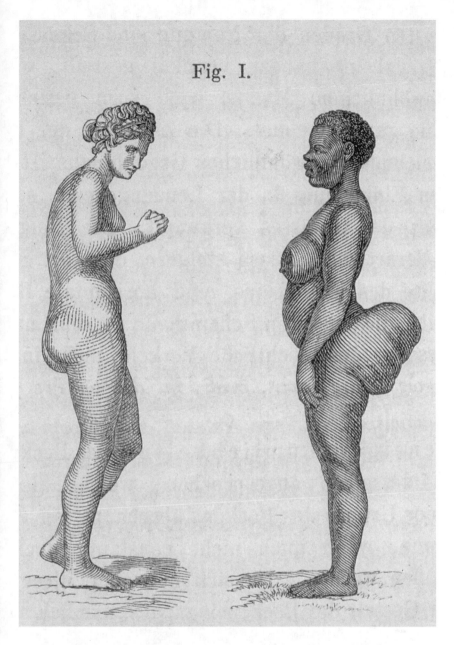

Fig. I.

Scientific illustrations such as this one of a female "Caucasian" and her mutually defining counterpart, a "Hottentot" woman, attempted to biologize cultural differences and establish an irrefutable hierarchy of embodiment, marking the poles of humanity for the nineteenth-century Western mind. Scientists recruited "Hottentots" like Sartje Baartman to embody an inferiority that affirmed European superiority.
British Library

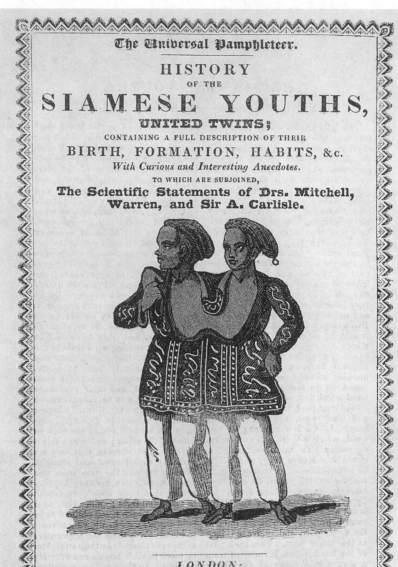

27,

Souvenir life narratives sold at shows fused medical with entertainment discourses. These pamphlets augmented visual displays by providing detailed descriptions and scientific authentications of the extraordinary body as well as exaggerated accounts of the freaks' lives.
Library of the College of Physicians of Philadelphia

The freak show stage brought together people whose bodies could signify the enormous, the excessive, the miniature, the exotic, the lacking, the profuse, the indeterminate, or the alien to produce a motley chorus line of physical difference that made the onlookers' bodies seem ordinary and banal by comparison.

Circus World Museum, Baraboo, Wisconsin

The interiors of dime museums and sideshows usually displayed a series of freaks, each surrounded by a hyperbolizing environment designed to produce the greatest illusion of difference and distance from the viewers.

*Circus World Museum,
Baraboo, Wisconsin*

Freaks made from people with congenital disabilities usually performed mundane tasks in alternative modes choreographed to amaze audiences. Here Charles Tripp, a famous Armless Wonder, whittles with his toes while surrounded with other props such as a teacup and writing and cutting implements, all of which he uses with his toes as a part of the exhibit.

Circus World Museum, Baraboo, Wisconsin

By juxtaposing the very large with the very small, freak exhibitions created wondrous giants and midgets, figures now vanished—"cured" by modern medical treatment.
Circus World Museum, Baraboo, Wisconsin

PART II

· · · · ·

*Constructing Disabled Figures:
Cultural and Literary Sites*

THREE

·····

The Cultural Work of American Freak Shows, 1835–1940

The Spectacle of the Extraordinary Body

In 1822 a native Brazilian woman called Tono Maria was exhibited in London's Bond Street as "the Venus of South America." Her body bore nearly one hundred scars, each ostensibly representing an act of adultery. According to her pitch man, her culture's social code allowed a maximum of 104 such scars but punished the one hundred-fifth sexual transgression with death. Her sexuality was thus purported to have reached the edge of even her own ostensibly savage society's standards. Complementing the display of this "Venus's" signifying scars was her performance, which consisted of eating to satiety despite the encumbrances of a large lip-stretching device and toothlessness. A contemporary journalist summed her up as "lazy" and "nasty," describing in detail "the emetic spectacle" of her sybaritic achievement. Regardless of his disgust, the observer gleaned from Tono Maria's show a useful lesson: having previously failed to fully appreciate English women, he would forever after "pay the homage due to the loveliest works of creation, enhanced in value by so wonderful a contrast."[1]

Stripped of her own cultural context and framed by the lurid interpretations of the Englishman and his society, Tono Maria's body became a malleable image upon which her audience projected cultural characteristics they themselves disavowed. Following conventions of displaying and interpreting the extraordinary body that go back to the beginning of human history, this ritual spectacle combined and exaggerated female characteristics in order to sharpen the distinction between the ideal Englishwoman and her physical and cultural opposite. Tono Maria's performance testified to an inherent female sexual deviance, indolence, carnality, and appetite tempered only by Western civilization. Personifying cultural and sexual aberration, Tono Maria not only confirmed the Englishman's sense of physical self-mastery, but also provided a cautionary tale of the natural female appetite, unmanaged by social sanctions.

In America, free enterprise and the rise of a democratized and fluid middle class fostered the proliferation of exhibitions like Tono Maria's in institutionalized shows that flourished and then faded between about 1840 and 1940.[2] An integral part of museums and circuses of the time, the American freak show—a phenomenon that today is almost synonymous with bad taste—descended from a tradition of reading the extraordinary body that can be traced back to the earliest human representation. Stone Age cave drawings record the births of the mysterious and marvelous bodies the Greeks and early scientists would later call "monsters," the culture of P. T. Barnum would call "freaks," and we now call "the congenitally physically disabled." Our unremitting fascination with the extraordinary, especially as manifest in our own bodies, is evident in explications that begin as early as the seventh century B.C. with cuneiform tablets at Nineveh describing sixty-two human congenital disabilities and their religious meanings, and culminates in scholarly treatises such as "Julia Pastrana, the Nondescript: An Example of Congenital, Generalized Hypertrichosis Terminalis with Gingival Hyperplasia," in the 1993 volume of *The American Journal of Medical Genetics*.

Scrupulously described, interpreted, and displayed, the bodies of the severely congenitally disabled have always functioned as icons upon which people discharge their anxieties, convictions, and fantasies. Indeed, the Latin word *monstra*, "monster," also means "sign" and forms the root of our word *demonstrate*, meaning "to show."[3] A fervent and persistent human impulse to account for corporeal exceptions surfaces in nearly every writer who casts his eye on the natural world, beginning with Cicero's linking of monstrous births to divination and culminating today with Oliver Sacks's wonderment at men who confuse their wives with their hats. Every historical era reinterprets the figure of the prodigious monster or nature's caprice, the freak. Pliny catalogues bodily anomaly as proof of nature's marvelous abundance, and Augustine delights in curious and inexplicable bodies as signs of his Christian god's benevolent purpose and constant intervention in the universe. In striking counterpoint to premodern narratives of awe and wonder inspired by bodies that defied the presumed "natural law," Aristotle initiates in the *Nicomachean Ethics* the devaluation recognizable today, claiming that a norm depending upon a mean represents virtue and superiority, while an excess of or departure from that standard constitutes vice.[4] John Block Friedman tells us that during the Middle Ages a monster was a prodigy, "a showing forth of divine will . . . a disruption of the natural order, boding ill [and in Christianity] they were a sign of God's power over nature and His use of it for didactic ends." By the thirteenth century *monstra* began to shift in meaning, from portent to wonder, designating what Friedman calls "part of the stock exoticism of the literature of entertainment."[5] Marvelous narratives of these extraordinary bodies were disseminated popularly in the sixteenth and seventeenth centuries via French canards, English chapbooks, wonder books, and the common broadside ballad that often accompanied displays of freaks on the street. Commerce—the precursor of capitalism—and curiosity—the precursor of science—brought the prodigious body into secular life, enriching the exclusively religious interpretations. By the eighteenth century the monster's power to inspire terror, awe, wonder, and divination was being eroded by science, which sought to classify and master rather than revere the extraordinary body. The scientist's and philosopher's cabinets of curiosities were transformed into the medical man's dissection table. The once marvelous body that was taken as a map of human fate now began to be seen as an aberrant body that marked the borders between the normal and the pathological.

Physically disabled bodies that qualified as prodigies—the conjoined twins, the spectacularly deformed, the hirsute, the horned, the gigantic, and the scaled—were always presented by priests, greedy or desperate parents, agents, philosophers, scientists, showmen, and doctors. Consequently, the concerns and careers of these mediators determined the narratives and the fates of these unique people. Indeed, extraordinary bodies have been so compelling—so valuable—*as bodies* throughout human history that whether they were alive or dead had little consequence. If live exhibition was enhanced by animation and performance, the display of a dead prodigy embalmed as a spectacle, pickled as a specimen, or textualized as an anatomical drawing derived from dissection was equally profitable, and often more readable and manipulable. Freaks and prodigies were solely bodies, without the humanity social structures confer upon more ordinary people. Not only were these bodies a source of profit, but the narratives of pathology derived from monstrous bodies built reputations at the Royal Society and the Académie des Sciences. For example, the embalmed body of Julia Pastrana, known as "The Ugliest Woman in the World," was displayed on the freak show circuit for well over 100 years after her death in 1860. Such practices moved Robert Wadlow, the world's tallest man, who resisted during his lifetime what David Hevey has called "enfreakment," to request at his death in 1940 that he be buried in a reinforced concrete slab to discourage grave robbers who might seek to display his skeleton.[6]

The century-long heyday of American freak shows represented a dramatic resurgence of the tradition of publicly displaying and reading extraordinary bodies. Fueled by the developing entrepreneurial spirit, dramatic social instability, and increasing mobility, these itinerant exhibitions institutionalized earlier forms and conventions in the service of present concerns from the Jacksonian Era through the Progressive Era. Even as the freak show burgeoned in America as a kind of democratic version of the eighteenth-century scientist's cabinet of curiosities, it was being discredited by the very institution of science that had shaped it since the Renaissance. Though still an oracle, the extraordinary body was transferred from the public gaze to the sequestered scrutiny of experts by the mid-twentieth century. Thus the wondrous monsters of antiquity, who became the fascinating freaks of the nineteenth century, transformed into the disabled people of the later twentieth century.[7] The extraordinary body moved from portent to pathology. Today the notion of a freak show that displays the bodies of disabled people for profit and public entertainment is both repugnant and anachronistic, rejected but nevertheless recent and compelling in memory.

P. T. Barnum, the apotheosis of American entrepreneurship, brought the freak show to its pinnacle in the nineteenth century by capitalizing on America's hunger for extravagance, knowledge, and mastery, along with its simultaneous quest for self-apprehension. As Neil Harris has pointed out, Barnum's freak shows were popular tests of knowledge that paralleled and intersected the halting emergence of scientific quantification as the elite, dominant method of subduing the material world by naming and measuring it. In addition to its penchant for information, especially numerical calculation, the nineteenth century was an era of display. "Truth" needed to be demonstrated and understood objectively: science measured and counted; what Thorstein Veblen called "conspicuous consumption" proved status; photography captured the "real"; and freak shows defined and exhibited the "abnormal."[8] By highlighting ostensible human anomaly of every sort and combination, Barnum's exhibits challenged audiences not only to classify and explain what they saw, but to relate the performance to themselves, to American individual and collective identity. With bearded ladies, for example, Barnum and his followers demanded that American audiences resolve this affront to the rigid categories of male and female that their culture imposed. With Eng and Chang, the famous "Siamese" twins, the freak show challenged the boundaries of the individual, asking whether this entity was one person or two. With dwarfs as well as armless and legless "wonders," the pitchmen charged their audiences to determine the precise parameters of human wholeness and the limits of free agency. The freak show thrived in an era of unbounded confidence in the human ability to perceive and act upon truth. These collective cultural rituals provided dilemmas of classification and definition upon which the throng of spectators could hone the skills needed to tame world and self in the ambitious project of American self-making. Furthermore, freak shows were to the masses what science was to the emerging elite: an opportunity to formulate the self in terms of what it was not.

The first freak Barnum displayed was Joice Heth, a black woman already on exhibit in Philadelphia in 1835 as George Washington's 161-year-old nursemaid and "The Greatest Natural and National Curiosity in the World." Barnum bought the right to show her for one thousand dollars, five hundred of which he borrowed, turning his new possession into the first act of a long and profitable career.[9] Dismissed by the public as a hoax and later renounced with a mixture of chagrin and pride by Barnum himself, Joice Heth is nevertheless the quintessential American freak. A black, old, toothless, blind, crippled slave woman, she fuses a combination of characteristics the ideal American self rejects. Joice Heth thus represents America's composite physical other, the domesticated and trivialized reversal of America's self-image. Droll and mundane as this old woman might seem, her body functions as the monster manifest in the ordinary rather than the extraordinary. She becomes a freak not by virtue of her body's uniqueness, but rather by displaying the stigmata of social devaluation. Indeed, Joice Heth is the direct antithesis of the able-bodied, white, male figure upon which the developing notion of the American normate was predicated. This black, disabled woman commodified as a freakish amusement testifies to America's need to ratify a dominant, normative identity by ritually displaying in public those perceived as the embodiment of what collective America took itself *not* to be.

As the inaugural exhibit of America's Golden Age of Freak Shows, Joice Heth exemplifies the cardinal principle of enfreakment: that the body envelops and obliterates the freak's potential humanity. When the body becomes pure text, a freak has been produced from a physically disabled human being. Such accumulation and exaggeration of bodily details distinguishes the freak from the unmarked and unremarked ordinary body that claims through its very obscurity to be universal and normative.[10] In *Struggles and Triumphs*, Barnum's autobiography, the showman's description of Heth exemplifies this accretion of bodily detail that generates the freak narrative:

> Joice Heth was certainly a remarkable curiosity, and she looked as if she might have been far older than her age as advertised. She was apparently in good health and spirits, but from age or disease, or both, was unable to change her position; she could move one arm at will, but her lower limbs could not be straightened; her left arm lay across her breast and she could not remove it; the fingers of her left hand were drawn down so as nearly to close it, and were fixed; the nails on that hand were almost four inches long and extended above her wrist; the nails on her large toes had grown to the thickness of a quarter of an inch; her head was covered with a thick bush of grey hair; but she was toothless and totally blind and her eyes had sunk so deeply in the sockets as to have disappeared altogether.[11]

Joice Heth's story illustrates in another way this process of being reduced to pure body through representation. Because medicine was eager to establish its authority, and because Barnum sought controversy as well as publicity, the showman promised David L. Rogers, the respected New York surgeon, that he could dissect Heth after her death. When she died in 1836, a much-publicized and -disputed postmortem was conducted before a large crowd of doctors, medical students, clergymen, and editors, each of whom paid fifty cents to observe. Although charging to watch autopsies was common, viewers were dismayed when Rogers announced that Heth was probably not yet eighty. Heth's handlers made seven hundred dollars from the autopsy and ten to twelve thousand dollars from the entire affair, all of which was actively discussed in the papers. As this account makes clear, freaks are created when certain bodies serve as raw material for the ideological and practical ends of both the mediators and the audiences.

Freak shows framed and choreographed bodily differences that we now call "race," "ethnicity," and "disability" in a ritual that enacted the social process of making cultural otherness from the raw materials of human physical variation.[12] The freak show is a spectacle, a cultural performance that gives primacy to visual apprehension in creating symbolic codes and institutionalizes the relationship between the spectacle and the spectators.[13] In freak shows, the exhibited body became a text written in boldface to be deciphered according to the needs and desires of the onlookers. The show's conventions of display situated the extraordinary body both spatially and narratively. For example, the elevated freak platform—sometimes, particularly in circuses, it was a pit instead—held the observer's gaze like a magnet, not only foregrounding the body on display, but exposing it in such a way that the physical traits presented as extraordinary dominated the entire person on exhibit.

On the freak show stage, a single, highlighted characteristic circumscribed and reduced the inherent human complexity of such figures as the Dwarf, the Giant, the Bearded Woman, the Armless or Legless Wonder, and the Fat Lady. Showmen barked embellishing adjectives like "wild" or "wondrous" and anachronistic, ironic pseudo-status titles like "King," "Queen," or "General" (as in the case of Charles Stratton, the famous "General Tom Thumb") that emphasized the extraordinary qualities of the body on display. Posters and broadsides extravagantly proclaimed the peculiarity of the freak's body, provoking the spectators' curiosity with taunts such as "What Is It?" that heightened the difference between the common observer and the marvelous body. If hyperbolic assertions such as "The Most Marvelous Creature Living" enhanced expectations, the crude illustrations on advertisements imaginatively distorted the freaks' bodies into grotesque caricatures. An illustrated, printed narrative pamphlet almost always accompanied the actual exhibit, authenticating the freak with a "true life" story and medical testimonies that served as both advertisement and souvenir, augmenting the pitchman's oral spiel. These souvenir narratives embellished the freak's exotic history, endorsed the exhibit's veracity, and described the freak's physical condition from a scientific or medical perspective, as titles like "History and Description of Abomah the African Amazon Giantess" and "Biography, Medical Description, and Songs of Miss Millie/Christine, the Two-Headed Nightingale" make clear. In addition to staging and costuming, narrative transfigured what, for example, would have been in a mundane context an ordinary "deformed darkey" into the "Beast of Borneo."[14] Together, the staging, the pitchman's mediating spiel, the scientific testimony, and the written narrative fixed the mute freak as a figure of otherness upon which the spectators could displace anxieties and uncertainties about their own identities. Embroidered by such elaborate conventions, the sideshow freak was made to exceed wildly the common, familiar expectations set by the spectator's own ordinary body.[15]

The new technology of photography helped transform extraordinary bodies into freak exhibits, its development intertwining with the show's evolution. Extremely popular during the Victorian era, photographic portraits of freaks represented the extraordinary body in a mode similar to Barnum's "lecture room" where freaks were displayed. Both conventions claimed proof of authenticity while producing meaning through visual images and studied contexts. In a description strikingly evocative of the freak show's mode of presentation, John Tagg characterizes the photographic images used in the nineteenth century to document and identify the "truth" of "cases" like prisoners, beggars, and the insane: "We have begun to see a repetitive pattern [in these photographs]: the body isolated; the narrow space; the subjugation to an unreturnable gaze; the scrutiny of gestures, faces and features; the clarity of illumination and sharpness of focus."[16] As dual cultural methods of producing the legible body witnessing its own deviance, both photography and freak shows—frequently merging in photographs of freaks—created an iconography of otherness set in a manipulated, yet naturalized, context of objective fact. For example, the conventional Victorian individual or family studio portrait, many of which were made by Matthew Brady and Charles Eisenmann in their Bowery studios, highlighted the incongruity of the freak's extraordinary body by juxtaposing it with formal social propriety and ordinary family life.[17] A particularly interesting conjunction between photography and freak shows occurred in the *cartes de visite*, extremely popular photographic portraits collected widely from the 1860s through the 1880s. Form and content clashed in a stunning irony as the popular *cartes* of celebrated freaks disseminated an iterated, mass-produced image of an icon that stood for precisely the reverse of the infinitely reproducible print: the singular, astonishing body of the freak.

The freak show consequently created a "freak," or "human curiosity," from an ordinary person who had a visible physical disability or an otherwise atypical body by exaggerating the ostensible difference and the perceived distance between the viewer and the showpiece on the platform. The spatial arrangement between audience and freak ritualized the relationship between self and cultural other. As in the social relations of domination and subordination based on race and gender, here too the differentiating stigmata literally took center stage, magnified and intensified, while the unmarked position of power, agency, and voice remained veiled. The freak simultaneously testified to the physical and ideological normalcy of the spectator and witnessed the implicit agreement assigning a coercive deviance to the spectacle. This determining relation between observer and observed was mutually defining and yet unreciprocal, as it imposed on the freak the silence, anonymity, and passivity characteristic of objectification. What the spectator assumed was a "freak of nature," was really, as Susan Stewart observes, a "freak of culture" whose body had been enlisted and paid at the expense of engulfment by his or her own stigmatization in order to confirm the spectator's status and identity.[18]

Perhaps the freak show's most remarkable effect was to eradicate distinctions among a wide variety of bodies, conflating them under the single sign of the freak-as-other. Freaks are above all products of perception: they are the consequence of a comparative relationship in which those who control the social discourse and the means of representation recruit the seeming truth of the body to claim the center for themselves and banish others to the margins. Nothing better illustrates this than the fact that the two main types of people presented as freaks were "normal" non-Westerners and "abnormal" Westerners. As in the ancient and medieval traditions of imagining foreign races as monstrous, all the bodily characteristics that seemed different or threatening to the dominant order merged into a kind of motley chorus line of physical difference on the freak show stage. Actually called "Nig shows" in circus lingo, freak shows traded indiscriminately in both cultural and corporeal otherness.[19] Hence, a nondisabled person of color billed as the "Fiji Cannibal" was equivalent to a physically disabled, Euro-American called the "Legless Wonder." Giants, dwarfs, visibly physically disabled people, tribal non-Westerners, contortionists, fat people, thin people, hermaphrodites, conjoined twins, the mentally disabled, and the very hirsute—all shared the platform equally as "human oddities," playing the assigned role of aberrant other to their audiences. Nevertheless, the most successful freaks melded both bodily and cultural difference. For example, foreign exoticism apparently intensified the physical exceptionality of "Chang, the Chinese Giant" or "Piramal and Sami," the conjoined twins billed as the "Hindoo Enigma." Chang and Eng, the original "Siamese Twins," were probably the most famous freaks, notorious for their merged extraordinary bodies and mysterious foreignness. Similarly, two microcephalic Central American natives were staged and costumed as "The Last of the Ancient Aztecs," their atypical physical appearance and non-European features combining to create the antithesis of the ideal American self-image and prompting debates about the comparative capacities of their brains and the relative states of their souls.[20] In an era of social transformation and economic reorganization, the nineteenth-century freak show was a cultural ritual that dramatized the era's physical and social hierarchy by spotlighting bodily stigmata that could be choreographed as an absolute contrast to "normal" American embodiment and authenticated as corporeal truth.

Constituting the Average Man

The constructed freak occupies the alarming and chaotic space at the borders that delimit the "average man," a concept formulated by the Belgian statistician Adolphe Quetelet in 1842. Enthusiastically adopted—although not uncontested—in America, the notion of *l'homme moyen physique* and the knottier issue of *l'homme moyen moral* mathematically formalized the egalitarian political idea of the Jacksonian common man and laid the theoretical groundwork for scientific norms that define our modern concept of deviance.[21] The cultural dilemma regarding the extent to which individual variations could be tolerated within a society based on freedom and equality was solved by installing the average man—a common version of Emerson's Representative Man—in the position previously held by the dethroned exceptional man, the aristocrat or the king. An abstract construct mandated by the idea of democracy, the multiply measured average man embodied humanity's regularity and stability, around which particularities ranged on a short leash. The freak show's prevalence after about 1840 can be seen, then, as serving to consolidate a version of American selfhood that was capable, rational, and normative, but that strove toward an ontological sameness upon which the notion of democratic equality is predicated. Extravagant in its repudiation of the typical, the displayed freak flattened the spectators' peculiarities and aligned them with the familiar.

The freak show thus quelled a range of anxieties accompanying the social disorder in the United States. America's great experiment in democracy posited a social system free from the stagnant stratification of the European patriarchy, but required a new basis of social organization consonant with egalitarian individualism and ostensibly limitless geographic and economic opportunities. This ideological leveling of class distinctions set the stage for a new social hierarchy based on ability—expressed, for instance, in the Jeffersonian idea of natural leadership—and produced a distinct aristocracy of the body. The American ideal self at the top of this hierarchy was an autonomous producer—self-governing and self-made—a generic individual capable of creating his own perfected self.

But recognizing that abstract ideological construct in oneself or one's neighbor was impossible without material markers. Since identifying and claiming status is perhaps the greatest anxiety in a theoretically egalitarian and volatile modern order, the boundaries of power must be clear. The body's material authority provides a seemingly irrefutable foundation upon which the prevailing power relations can thus be erected. The figure of the freak is consequently the necessary cultural complement to the acquisitive and capable American who claims the normate position of masculine, white, nondisabled, sexually unambiguous, and middle class. As I suggested in chapter 2, such an exclusive, idealized self develops within an expanding market economy as a self-controlled individual responsible for shaping his destiny and the social order by competently manipulating his acquiescent, standard body, along with personal skills and technological tools. Freak shows acted out a relationship in which exoticized disabled people and people of color functioned as physical opposites of the idealized American explicitly and implicitly delineated in such cultural representations as Emerson's intellectual man in "Self-Reliance," the independent Thoreau of *Walden*, and the folk hero Davy Crockett.

Safely domesticated and bounded by the show's forms and conventions, the freak soothes the onlookers' self-doubt by appearing as their antithesis. The American produces and acts, but the onstage freak is idle and passive. The American looks and names, but the freak is looked at and named. The American is mobile, entering and exiting the show at will and ranging around the social order, but the freak is fixed, confined by the material structures and the conventions of the staging and socially immobilized by a deviant body. The American is rational and controlled, but the freak is carnal and contingent. Within this fantasy, the American's self determines the condition of his body, just as the freak's body determines the condition of his self. This grammar of embodiment culturally normalizes the American and abnormalizes the freak. At the freak show, cultural self and cultural other hover silently for an historical instant, face to face in dim acknowledgment of their unspoken symbiosis.

The immense popularity of the shows between the Jacksonian and Progressive Eras suggests that the onlookers needed to constantly reaffirm the difference between "them" and "us" at a time when immigration, emancipation of the slaves, and female suffrage confounded previously reliable physical indices of status and privilege such as maleness and Western European features. The more heterogeneous the bodily traits of the enfranchised became, the less clearly marked power was in the egalitarian social order. Those whose social rank was most tenuous—immigrants, the urban working class, and less prosperous rural people—frequented the shows, which were always on the fringe of respectability and often were vehemently condemned by such icons of the status quo as Henry Ward Beecher in his *Lectures to Young Men*.[22] The extravagant and indisputable otherness of the freak's physiognomy reassured those whose bodies and costuming did not match the fully enfranchised and indubitably American ideal.

One might speculate further that the freak show's popularity at this time was also a response to several specific historical situations. Both the Civil War and escalating industrial accidents from machinery produced many disabled persons among the working classes. Perhaps the heightened anxiety of actual or possible disablement among that group drove them either toward an encounter with the physical other as distanced and domesticated or toward sympathetic identification with the stigmatized body. In addition, expansionist acts like Indian removal and the Mexican War, as well as slavery, required propagation of a white supremacist ideology that the freak show enacted in its display of cultural others. The white working classes who were competing with immigrants and people of color for scarce resources during this period also benefited from the self-image of able-bodiedness and racial normalcy that the freak show provided its spectators.[23]

Freak shows affirmed their newly democratized audiences in other ways as well. Freaks embodied the threat of individuation running rampant into chaos—the fear of antinomian logic that lurked under the optimistic surface of ardent American egalitarian democracy. The freak's body mocked the boundaries and similarities that a well-ordered democratic society required to avoid anarchy and create national unity. By exoticizing and trivializing bodies that were physically nonconformist, the freak show symbolically contained the potential threat that difference among the polity might erupt as anarchy. Heightened by the modes of exhibition, the freak's extraordinariness invoked the tensions between uniqueness and uniformity, particularity and generality, randomness and predictability, exception and rule, by extending the former so far as to disrupt the latter. The spectator was at once shaken by the limitless possibilities unleashed by the freak's anarchic body and mollified by having his own seeming ordinariness verified and the peril of difference restrained. Hence, domesticating the freak for entertainment and profit became one way to efface suspicions that the world might indeed be intractable, chaotic, and opaque.[24] As the subdued token for all that is inexplicable and unpredictable, the colonized freak makes democracy safe for the world by signifying the anarchic potential of individuality contained and mastered.

Identification and the Longing for Distinction

Although American ideology encouraged the citizen to become *l'homme moyen*, the freak as *l'homme extraordinaire* clearly held much attraction for those who enthusiastically flocked to see the shows and buy the photographs. Freaks were celebrities as well as spectacles, their popularity suggesting that audiences simultaneously identified with and were repulsed by the performers.[25] Becoming ordinary erased the markers that emblematized power and prestige in the repudiated European aristocracy, so as icons of the extraordinary, freaks were anachronisms in a nineteenth-century democracy. As we saw in chapter 2, a cultural reversal in the significance of individuality occurred around the Enlightenment as Western society shifted from a feudal to a modern order.[26] In the premodern era, the marks of individuation both enhanced and identified personal power. Ceremonial costumes, genealogies, even the stigmata of Christian saints testified to exceptional status; for example, aristocrats were highly marked by ritual and decoration—crowns, wigs, and similar differentiating tokens.Criminals, heretics, and witches routinely were forced to appear in public in a penitential, ordinary shirt that symbolically stripped them of all markers of individual personhood and status.[27] In the gradual move from a highly stratified, stable form of social organization to the modern order characterized by isolated individuals and fluid social relations, uniqueness came to be read as deviance, while the common became the basis of normalcy. The nineteenth-century Western cultural preoccupation with measuring and quantifying human differences illustrates some of the anxiety provoked by this cultural reversal. This validation of the common is consonant as well with the rise of masculinist egalitarian democracy and the demise of political and religious hierarchical patriarchy. Taking itself as the apotheosis of the modern egalitarian impulse, Jacksonian America, for example, deeply opposed the ceremonies, insignia, and lineage that had separated the corrupt European aristocracy from the undifferentiated masses it hoped to empower.[28]

Along with that distrust of the exceptional, however, came an apparently insatiable fascination with the extraordinary that made men like Barnum rich. For instance, Victorian America's obsession with the curious, the grotesque, and the anomalous is well documented.[29] Playing to that obsession, freak shows were vestiges of pre-Enlightenment European culture fashioned into entrepreneurial and communal rituals that both verified and questioned the order of things. The extraordinary body's display formalized the relatively recent reversal of prestige and power markers in relations between ordinary and unusual citizens. The freak show offered those who identified themselves as the American common man a trivialized parody of the old order as well as a nostalgic respite from modern pressures toward standardization. The freak's indelible physical markings mocked the insignia and conventions the sacred stigmata, so to speak—that distinguished the extraordinary man from the ordinary one in the fixed social hierarchy that America imagined resisting. Pseudonymous titles such as "King," "Queen," "Prince," and "Princess," as well as aristocratic-sounding stage names and the pretense of elite pursuits like writing poetry and speaking many languages were intended to suggest that freaks were luminaries or perverse aristocrats.[30] As an ironic celebrity, the freak seemed at once to burlesque, vitiate, reproduce, and bow down to an aristocracy that America rhetorically denigrated during its cultural oedipal phase. Freak shows thus conflated kings and fools in a tawdry, satiric extravaganza that inverted the old ceremonial spectacle of royal pomp and power by ritually displaying a person stigmatized by bodily particularity, silenced by the pitchman's imposed narrative, and managed by the showman.

This cultural ritual thus served more complex and compelling purposes than simply dispelling its patrons' self-doubts. Like the disabled figure discussed in chapter 2, the freak provided a site where a fundamental paradox at the heart of egalitarian democracy could be probed. While the ideology of freedom recommends cultivating individual differences, the ideology of equality encourages sameness of condition and expression among democratic citizens. So even as Emerson's representative voice defined the individual as independent and exhorted his fellow countrymen to resist conforming, Tocqueville observed that a remarkable conformity was the American way. Despite the rhetoric of individualism so basic to our national self-image, the individual, as John W. Meyer has observed, "achieves freedom and power only under the condition that he become isomorphic, or similar in form, to all the other individuals in the society."[31] Snagged by the contradiction between freedom and equality, Americans were apparently at liberty to become stiflingly alike; shorn of traditions and contemptuous of authority, they had only one another as examples. So while achieving a national identity required Americans to imagine themselves as independent, self-determining individuals, the culture itself increasingly standardized individuals through a range of institutions: universal education, mass production, interchangeable parts, mechanical reproduction of images, advertising, and mass print culture. Evidently, democracy in practice does not tolerate dissimilarity.

So although the anarchic body of the domesticated freak reassured audiences of their commonality, at the same time the extraordinary body symbolized a potential for individual freedom denied by cultural pressures toward standardization. One explanation for the nineteenth-century freak show's immense popularity could be that it provided a safe, ritualized opportunity for banal democrats to voyeuristically identify with nonconformity. Many spectators who were disabled by war or accident or excluded by ethnicity were no doubt drawn to these displays by an identification with the freak's extraordinariness. Sympathy and affiliation surely flowed along with smugness and differentiation, as some onlookers probably used the shows to explore the limits of human variation. If the nineteenth century was a time of identity crisis for Americans, it was partly because the intensifying capitalist imperative to distinguish oneself economically and to mark that distinction clashed with the egalitarian, antiaristocratic social imperative to emulate the idealized common man or yeoman farmer.[32] Yet, as the persistent rhetoric of nonconformity from Thoreau and others suggests, achieving some meaningful differentiation may have been difficult, in spite of their anxious efforts to distinguish themselves economically from their neighbors. The repudiation of authority, the refusal to follow traditions, and the disavowal of lineage suggested by the freak's extravagantly different body may have fascinated the onlooker whose egalitarian ordinariness seemed to betray the promise of distinction inherent in the concept of individual freedom. So the spectator enthusiastically invested his dime in the freak show not only to confirm his own superiority, but also to safely focus an identificatory longing upon these creatures who embodied freedom's elusive and threatening promise of not being like everybody else.

Not only was the image of the independent common man in whom Jefferson, Crèvecoeur, and Whitman placed so much faith being threatened by the standardization wrought by mass culture and mechanical reproduction, but his putative autonomy was undermined by the division of labor that ceded authority to the specialists and experts of the new middle class. The freakish body functioned as a kind of egalitarian shrine where the underclass and the immigrants could for a dime or a quarter exercise their authority as readers of this extraordinary phenomenon. America's fixation on the extraordinary body revisited the notion of the prodigy, the ambiguous body in which people had for centuries found the meanings and explanations that verified their perspectives.[33] The freak platform both mapped the boundaries of human physical and cultural otherness and generated a liminal space where ontological categories mingled. The freak's body confounded the classification systems that organize collective cultural perceptions, yielding hybrid exhibits like "The Frog Man" and "The Camel Girl."[34] A little boy with abnormal pigmentation became "The Leopard Child," while a hirsute Russian was "Jo-Jo, the Dog-Faced Boy." Such stage names illustrate how an interpretive grid placed them in reference to anxiously fixed social categories such as human and animal. Hermaphrodites such as Bobby Kirk, the "Half and-Half," compelled because they violated the rigid cultural boundaries between male and female. Several physically and mentally disabled black men were displayed under the title "What Is It?," a name that expressed the freak's ambiguous humanity and challenged spectators to resolve the disparity between this body and their expectations. Barnum's advertising poster challenged onlookers to make the distinction: "Is it a lower order of MAN? Or is it a higher order of MONKEY? None can tell! Perhaps it is a combination of both." Billed as "missing links," the "What Is It?" figures complemented after midcentury a growing interest in Darwinian distinctions between humans and gorillas. For instance, in 1860 Barnum introduced William Henry Johnson, a black microcephalic man, as a "What Is It?," depicting him as "a most singular animal" who was neither human nor beast, but "a mixture of both—the connecting link between humanity and brute creation."[35] Human exhibits like these, whose freakdom was founded on ambiguity, provided audiences with a rich icon of directed meaning. Perhaps even more provocative were conjoined twins. While Eng and Chang were two complete bodies joined at the chest, more transgressive instances of what the medical world now calls "major terata" upset the boundaries of the ordinary human body. The Tocci Brothers, for example, were from the waist up two boys and from the waist down only one, while Mrs. "B" was from the waist down two bodies and from the waist up only one. The famous East Indian "Laloo," as well as several other monsters recorded from medieval times forward, had parasitic miniature twins growing from their abdomens.

Such beings inadvertently flaunt the erratic and spurn the stable, becoming emblems of physical and cultural anarchy and magnets for the anxieties and ambitions of their times. Invested with the liminality that Victor Turner suggests threatens both to transform and to disrupt the social order, extraordinary bodies carry a range of attributed cultural meanings projected upon them by astonished onlookers.[36] After 1840, freak shows may have been one of the last sites where the ordinary citizen could exercise the authority to interpret the natural world, a right bestowed by the Reformation that was being incrementally revoked by the class division of labor—what Barbara Ehrenreich and Deirdre English have called "the rise of the experts."[37] The instability of traditional life undercut the layman's belief in the authority of his own senses, making ordinary people more receptive to the professional control of scientists and doctors. In fact, the consolidation of medical authority occurred during the freak show era.[38] Existing as definitive examples of the Emersonian "not me" rendered freaks malleable to spectators' speculations. The shows were the final opportunity for epistemological speculation available in a lay context. By 1940 the prodigious body had been completely absorbed into the discourse of medicine, and the freak shows were all but gone.

From Freak to Specimen:
"The Hottentot Venus" and "The Ugliest Woman in the World"

To trace the development of freak shows through the nineteenth century to their virtual extinction by the mid-twentieth century, we can focus on two freaks whose disturbing cultural images and personal histories exemplify and clarify the process of enfreakment. The construction as freaks of both the now relatively well-known Sartje Baartman and the much more obscure Julia Pastrana was inextricably linked to cultural productions of gender and race. Cast in opposition to the ideal American self—who is, among other things, male by definition—the freak is represented much like the woman: both are owned, managed, silenced, and mediated by men; both are socially defined as deviations from the ideal masculine body; both are marginalized in the realm of economic production; both are appropriated for display as spectacles; both are seen as subjugated by the body. The exhibitions of Sartje Baartman, billed as "The Hottentot Venus," and Julia Pastrana, billed as "The Ugliest Woman in the World," functioned as inverted, parodic beauty pageants. Exhibition framed these women's bodies as grotesque icons of deviant womanhood that confirmed the West's version of femininity. Displaying "The Ugliest Woman in the World" suggested to her viewers what the prettiest woman in the world should look like, while parading "The Hottentot Venus" instructed her audience how appropriate female sexuality should appear. Sanctioned femininity was at once veiled and elaborated by way of its oppositional spectacle.

These women's titles testify to the essential role that the sexualized physical standard we call "beauty" plays in defining the female. In both titles, one term perverts the other: "Hottentot," which signified to the Western mind savagery and irredeemable physiological inferiority, is paired with "Venus," the West's apotheosis of femininity; "Ugliest" cancels out beauty, the defining essence of the subject "Woman." The presentations of Baartman and Pastrana as grotesque versions of received womanhood amplified this paradox, destabilizing the very category of woman even while validating the standard notion of womanhood. The exhibits forced their enraptured audiences to explain how these creatures could gesture at once to familiar womanhood and its unsettling, threatening opposite. Posing this question gave the onlookers who flocked to such displays the authority to provide speculative answers.

The public lives and deaths, indeed the public *bodies*, of Sartje Baartman and Julia Pastrana expose how gender, sexuality, colonization, race, and pathology interrelate in the process of constructing cultural icons. Baartman was a native African indentured servant brought from South Africa in 1810 to be exhibited for profit in London and later in Paris until her death from smallpox, complicated by alcoholism, in 1815.[40] Although a member of a San tribe, she was billed a Hottentot, the exotic label that stood for everything the Englishman considered himself not to be. Emerging scientific discourse identified the Hottentots as the most primitive species of humans, the "missing link" in the chain of being that science was reforging and later manifested in Darwinian thought. Science's obsession with measurement and classification served white supremacism and legitimated colonial exploitation, its powerful evaluative lens locating the Hottentots on the very edge of humanity, equally human and bestial.[41] In the European view, then, Baartman was not only a Hottentot—a humanlike ape or an apelike human—she was also a female body deviant by definition, and doubly so in her particular female configuration, pathologized as a condition called "steatopygia." Sartje's definitive feature, the mark of freakdom, was her buttocks, which were quite differently shaped and considerably larger than the average European woman's. Like other freaks, Baartman was recruited and managed by a series of white men who profited from her performances. One acted as her "keeper" during presentations in which she was "produced like a wild beast, and ordered to move backwards and forwards, and come and go into her cage, more like a bear on a chain than a human being," according to a contemporary report.[42] The keeper, like the freak show pitchman, mediated between the silent spectacle and the paying viewers, collecting an additional fee for them to touch her as well. Although Baartman's buttocks were prominently displayed by a tight-fitting, flesh-colored garment, suggesting nudity, her genital area, widely rumored to be her secret and most dramatic anomaly, was hidden, withholding gratification from the voyeuristic spectators. In the tradition of Aristotle's view of women as mutilated males, female genitalia—for the Western culture that later produced Freud—were the stigmata marking the putative absence that defined female lack. By contrast, Baartman's notorious buttocks and genitalia became an icon for dangerously excessive and grotesque female sexuality, simultaneously embodying the opposite of supposedly domesticated, European female sexuality and warning of what that sexuality might become if not rigorously managed. Her cage dramatized both the urgency and the reality of female containment.

Caging Baartman for public inspection of her "overdeveloped" genitals ritually enacted one of our culture's most egregious forms of ethnocentrism. The freak show's modes of representation reveal that an icon of cultural otherness was interchangeable with one of physical otherness. In these exhibitions, absolutely no distinction existed between this African woman, whose body shape was typical of her group, and the conjoined twins, congenital amputees, or dwarfs who also fell outside the narrow, culturally constructed borders that distinguish the normal from the abnormal. Baartman's display as a freak forces us to recognize the relativity of all physical standards and to acknowledge that seemingly self-evident categories such as "abnormal" or "physically disabled" arise from a historically shifting sociopolitical context that interprets human variations for its own ends.

Baartman's American counterpart, Julia Pastrana, also simultaneously represented to her Western audiences cultural, physical, and sexual otherness. A member of a Mexican Indian tribe characterized in her exhibition pamphlet as "semi-human" with features having a "close resemblance to those of a Bear and Orange Outang," Pastrana was first displayed in New York in 1854 when she was about twenty years old.[43] Like Baartman, she had a brief, lurid career as a freak, dying in childbirth while on tour in Russia in 1860. Clearly, both Pastrana's and Baartman's non-Western ethnicity was essential to their enfreakment, suggesting that the medieval practice of figuring alien ethnic groups as monstrous persisted well into the nineteenth century. Whereas Baartman's body was read as a sign for grotesque and hyperbolic sexuality, Pastrana's body became freakish somewhat differently: it violated the male/female and the human/animal dichotomies, two of our most sacred cultural constructs. Her distinctive physical features were extreme hirsuteness and the shape of her nose and mouth, from which a simian appearance could apparently be construed. A description by Dr. J. Z. Laurence in an 1857 issue of the British medical journal *Lancet* describes her with the same attention to bodily detail used by Barnum in his account of Joice Heth and suggests the disturbing liminality projected upon her body:

> [Her] main peculiarity consists in her possessing hairs nearly all over the body, and more especially on those parts which are ordinarily clothed with hairs in the male sex. . . . She is four feet six inches in height, thick-set, and exceedingly well-proportioned in the trunk and limbs, the chief peculiarities residing in the face. She has a large tuft of hair depending from the chin—*a beard*, continuous with smaller growths of hair on the upper lip and cheeks—moustache and whiskers. Her eyebrows are thick and bushy; the hair upon her head remarkably copious. . . . The rest of the face is covered with similar short hairs. Indeed, the whole of the body, excepting the palms of the hands and the soles of the feet, is more or less clothed with hairs. In this respect she agrees, in an exaggerated degree, with what is not very uncommonly observed in the male sex. . . . In other respects she agrees with the female. Her breasts are remarkably full and well-developed. She menstruates regularly.[44]

In this first part of his description, Laurence reveals that Pastrana's deviance is in her body's combination of male and female markers, in the troubling coincidence of "a beard" and "moustache and whiskers" with "remarkably full" breasts and menstruation. This interpretation of in-betweenness was encouraged by exhibition titles both animal and human, such as "Bear Woman," "Apewoman," "Nondescript," "Baboon Woman," and "Hybrid Indian," all apparently intended to inflame the imagination and challenge the perceptions of onlookers.

The discourse's anthropological as well as medical style textualizes the body that was fixed under Laurence's gaze:

Her face is peculiar: the alae of the nose are remarkably flattened and expanded, and so soft as to seem to be destitute of cartilages; the mouth is large, and the lips everted [sic]—above by an extraordinary thickening of the alveolar border of the upper jaw in front—below, by a warty, hard growth arising from the gum. The lower set of teeth is perfect; but in the upper set the front teeth are all but deficient, the molars alone being properly developed. Her ears are unusually long. The physiognomy is not that of the negro: the facial angle is rather small. Her skin is of a yellowish-brown colour. The voice is that of a female, as is especially brought out in her higher notes when she sings.[45]

Strewn with words such as "extraordinary," "perfect," "deficient," and "unusually," this very detailed account of Pastrana's body is actually more a comparison than a description; it is haunted by the implied figure of the normative European woman, the neo-Platonic, ideologically inflected standard relative to whom Pastrana seems both hideous and less human. Yet for all her physical alienness in the European gaze, her "remarkably full" breasts and her lovely singing voice—upon which her chroniclers remark repeatedly—are a remnant of the expected, ideal figure. Thus Pastrana's role as freak and her fascination for audiences depends not upon her absolute otherness, but rather upon the conflicting presence of radical differences and familiar traits.

Indeed, Pastrana's handlers amplified this coincidence of the recognizable and the unidentifiable, as did all freak displays. Just as Baartman moved back and forth in her cage and wore clothes that set off her extraordinary body, so Pastrana gave an elaborate show in which she sang Spanish and English songs and danced flings and Pepitas. She wore elaborately embroidered dresses styled to accentuate her ordinary feminine body and emphasize by contrast her extraordinary face, described by the naturalist Francis Buckland in 1888 as "simply hideous." Yet Buckland went on, in the same vein as Laurence, to marvel at the juxtaposition of that face with her "sweet voice" and her "figure [which] was exceedingly good and graceful, and her tiny foot and well-turned ankle, *bien chausse*, perfection itself."[46] As the exhibitions of Pastrana and Baartman illustrate, the compelling power of freaks lay in their apparent straddling of the categories that underpin Western rationality. As so many slaps in reason's face, freaks were dangerous and alluring figures that had to be contained. The discourse of wonder had accommodated a pre-Enlightenment world view that placed God's inscrutable will at the center, but that reading of the extraordinary body could not articulate the mastery of the natural world that modern man saw as his destiny. Thus, as the nineteenth century progressed, the ever-worrisome freak was cast less in the language of the marvelous and explained more and more in the ascending scientific discourse of pathology.[47]

Although circus and entertainment narratives defined the freak in nine-teenth-century Western society, this popular and transient medium was no match for the emerging, authoritative, enduring scientific discourse that framed these people according to a medical model. By the 1940s, American shows were gone in part because scientists had transformed the freak into a medical specimen. The conventions of the freak show derived from earlier cultural practices that fixed individual deviance through ritualized spectacle, such as public executions and other communal displays of social debasement like the scaffold scene and stigmatic mark around which Hawthorne created *The Scarlet Letter*. The ancient mind translated the extraordinary body's hy-bridity and excess into the supernatural, often sacred, pantheon of cyclopses, satyrs, centaurs, minotaurs, and hydras. But the modern mind officially re-translated those qualities into science in 1822, when Isidore Geoffroy Saint-Hilaire coined the term "teratology" to mean the study of monsters. Rather than responding with fear or wonder, as in the past, the modern medical man competed with God, experimentally producing monstrous fish and mammals to discover the etiology of what came to be known in the twentieth-century as "birth defects." Gradually changing awe and superstition into rational expla-nation, science intently set upon such projects as classifying human variation and creating cleft palates in pigs.[48]

The discourse of the extraordinary body as medical specimen finally eclipsed the traditional freak show spectacle by the mid-twentieth century. Al-though scientific and sideshow discourses had been entangled during the freak show era, they diverged toward opposite ends of a spectrum of prestige and authority as time went on. Freak shows were always part of popular or low culture, while medical science has become increasingly elite and powerful in modern times. Nineteenth-century churches in America, for example, tar-geted freak shows for reform legislation and censure because they were con-sidered immoral and encouraged riff-raff, not because they exploited freaks.[49] By the mid-twentieth century, physicians and scientists, rather than the pub-lic and the entrepreneur, governed the production of freaks. In the transition period, scientists raided freak shows for observations and specimens and ref-ereed sideshow debates, while the freak show exploited scientific rationaliza-tion to authenticate its exhibits. For example, the narrative pamphlet that announces Julia Pastrana's exhibition at Boston's Horticultural Hall in 1855 by hawking her as "The Misnomered Bear Woman," also contains official-sound-ing medical accounts drawn from physical examinations of Pastrana's body. Dr. Alex Mott proclaims that she is a "hybrid" while Professor Brainerd, who has examined "the hair of the specimen," declares that there is "NO TRACE

OF NEGRO BLOOD," and the anatomist Samuel Kneeland—no less—from the Boston Society of Natural History testifies that she is indeed human.[50] While the medical man's elite discourse was inflected by the positivist ideology of scientific progress and humanitarian concern, the showman's popular discourse appealed to the notion of egalitarian entrepreneurship and the empowerment of the common man. Yet both the medical man and the showman vied for control of the extraordinary body upon which their careers and fortunes depended.

As we saw earlier in the case of Joice Heth's profitable public dissection, the freak was equally valuable in life and in death. Such extreme textualization of the human body demonstrates how representation attempts to convert people into things.[51] Variations on a theme, yet each with its own bizarre twist, the remarkable fates of Sartje Baartman and Julia Pastrana capture the competition between showman and scientist for control of the extraordinary body, as well as that body's transformation from awesome spectacle to medical specimen.

When Baartman died in 1815, the eminent French zoologist Georges Cuvier dissected her body, thus assuring her continuing freakdom by literally and discursively making her a medical specimen. Cuvier authorized a plaster casting and a painting of Baartman's nude body before dissecting it; he then presented the scientific community with both a written report and her actual, excised genitals, "suitably prepared" in a jar that remains to this day on a shelf in the *Musee de l'Homme* in Paris.[52] Both her preserved skeleton and the cast of her corpse are still among the museum's collections as well. But the idea of a Hottentot Venus shaped the cultural consciousness long after Baartman's body had been made to act out that script.[53] Sander Gilman notes that Baartman's history influenced scientific descriptions of Hottentot women throughout the nineteenth century, focusing descriptions on their genitals in an effort to establish biological differentiation of a separate race that was closer to animals than to Europeans. By 1877 Hottentot genitals were being described in gynecological handbooks as a "congenital error" involving a "malformation" of the clitoris associated with excessive sexuality that led to lesbianism.[54] Thus, from 1810 to 1877, Sartje Baartman's physical interpretation shifted from freakishly fascinating to clinically abnormal, inextricably fusing the culturally extraordinary and the physically extraordinary in a modern narrative of pathology.

Like the bodies of Baartman and Joice Heth, Julia Pastrana's body was also transmogrified into text and capital. Pastrana was managed by a man who married her after she became extremely profitable, perhaps to assure his control over her exhibition. When Pastrana died on tour in 1860 several days after giving birth before a curious crowd to a stillborn infant boy who closely resembled her, her manager/husband sold her body, along with their dead child's, to Professor J. Sokolov of the Anatomical Institute of Moscow University so that Sokolov could use his new method to embalm the bodies. So successful was Sokolov's embalming procedure that Pastrana's husband/manager repurchased her corpse for three hundred pounds more than he had been paid. He continued to exhibit Pastrana's body and their son's and to rent them to museums until he died in 1884. The bodies have traveled across Europe, changing hands, disappearing from and reappearing into public view, being stolen and retrieved. They toured the United States with a circus as recently as 1972. Now Pastrana's time-ravaged body, an embarrassment to the Norwegian government that owns it, is stored in the basement of Oslo's Institute of Forensic Medicine. Although the entrepreneurial purposes of the showman may seem to have prevailed in the textualization of Pastrana's body, the discourse of pathology has in fact had the last word. An academic debate now persists that requires radiographic examination of Pastrana's skull and microphotographs of her hair samples to determine whether her "condition" is "congenital, generalized hypertrichosis terminalis" or "congenital, generalized hypertrichosis languinosa," along with the question of whether her dentition is "normal" or "abnormal." All of this is documented in the 1993 volume of the *American Journal of Medical Genetics*. As was the case with Baartman, the social process of enfreakment made Pastrana's body into an icon of pathology, with only a trace of the human remaining.

Pathologizing cultural and corporeal others began with the Enlightenment faith in rationality as a means of predicting and regulating an intractable universe. The success of such positivism depends upon establishing absolute categories and routing the troubling paradoxes of contingency, indeterminacy, ambiguity, and impurity. If science justifies dominant power relations, as many have argued, it also legitimates the dominant body, which is both the marker of cultural power and the ticket of admission into that power.[55] Nineteenth-century scientists obsessively established hierarchical physical taxonomies, eventually reforging God's great chain of being into Darwin's and creating the idea of the norm, what Foucault calls "the new law of modern society."[56] Stephen Jay Gould points out that the more a body defied the classification system, the more it threatened the scientific enterprise, causing scientists to focus on the most paradoxical bodies. Hence, the most wondrous freaks— such as conjoined twins (one person or two?) or mentally disabled Africans (human or ape?) or hermaphrodites (men or women?)—presented the knottiest scientific dilemmas.[57] By the end of the century, medicalization rather than freakdom legitimated such notions as white supremacy and such political practices as colonialism, eugenic legislation, and compulsory institutionalization or sterilization. The extraordinary body shifted from its earlier visible, public position as strange, awful, and lurid spectacle to its later, private position as sick, hidden, and shameful, producing finally the fully medicalized freak who after 1940 was removed from the stage platform to the teaching hospital amphitheater, the medical text, and the special institution. This is the role that today's disability activists are attempting to cast off.[58]

The life-to-death trajectories of Sartje Baartman's and Julia Pastrana's bodies show how the consolidating authority of Western science and medicine transmuted sideshow freaks into pathological cases during the nineteenth century. Sartje in her cage and Julia on her stage have transmuted into diagrams and microphotographs in scientific texts, and challenges for reconstructive or cosmetic surgery, suggesting the totalizing discourse that now medicalizes all extraordinary bodies. Not only did Cuvier's presentation of Baartman's genitals and Solokov's embalming of Pastrana's body create what Sander Gilman calls a "pathological summary" of these women, but these literal synecdoches fuse the racial, gendered, and classed axes of cultural otherness.[59] This full-breasted and hirsute body, circulating for over 130 years beneath the curious gaze, and this bit of flesh in a jar on the museum shelf invoke an entire, complex cultural, historical, and political system.

The End of the Prodigious Body

The freak show era, then, charts a shift from prodigious to pathological in the cultural construction of the extraordinary body. Rapid social changes after 1830 allowed the ancient practice of reading monstrous bodies to thrive in the invigorated form of the American freak show. A cluster of cultural conditions dovetailed to produce the climate in which the freak show flourished: immigration, class repositioning, and increased social stratification pressed an insecure polity to invent a corporeal other whose difference relieved their apprehensions about status. Industrial accidents, war wounds, and increased concern about appearance may have heightened an anxious identification with the extraordinary body, while standardization, mass production, and mass culture produced the notion of an unmarked, normative body as the dominant subject of democracy. Railroads, mass education, photography, popular publishing, and a restless mobility made freaks highly visible and created a taste for novelty. Science as an ideological concept encouraged explanation and stimulated curiosity. Wage labor and the investing of professionals with authority threatened the common citizen's sense of mastery and autonomy. The emerging entrepreneur capitalized on all of this. Yet those very conditions eventually drove the showman from the stage and swept his freaks into the institutions, hospitals, and medical textbooks. By 1940, freaks had become inappropriate for the public eye, cast as private "cases," surrounded and defined by a professional apparatus of doctors, counselors, and rehabilitation specialists.

Both the narrative of the spectacle and the narrative of the specimen objectified the extraordinary body, ultimately serving the interests of the mediators. The social and economic success of the showman and the scientist depended equally on how freakish the bodies of their cultural/physical others could be. Nevertheless, each brought some benefit to the specimen/freak: the showman offered economic independence at the expense of cultural normalcy; the medical man offered normalizing procedures that often required submission to bodily intrusion and painful reconstruction. In order to reap the showman's benefits, the person with an extraordinary body had to agree to total immersion in the freak role. But the doctor's normalization requires denying aspects of one's individual body as well as negotiating the risks and psychic compromises of "passing."

The medical model that governs today's interpretation of disability assumes that any somatic trait that falls short of the idealized norm must be corrected or eliminated. Indeed, one of our strongest cultural taboos forbids the extraordinary body, as the generally uncontested advocacy and practice of reconstructive surgery, abortion of "defective" fetuses, and other normalization procedures attest. Extraordinary bodies are seen as deviations to be standardized, rather than as unique, even enriching aspects of individuals that might be accepted.[60] Ironically, the medical model's technology actually facilitates the survival of many disabled people at the same time that it pathologizes them. Whole groups who would have died even thirty years ago—like people with spina bifida or paraplegia—exist now, often only to await being "fixed."[61] Yet while more disabled people survive and are normalized through medical technology, developing procedures to detect disabled fetuses for probable elimination is a high medical priority.[62] Thus, the fundamental change in cultural perceptions has been neither clearly progress nor regression, but merely a conversion of wondrous, ominous pre-Enlightenment monsters to fascinating freaks on circus stages and, finally, to medical cases that fade into hospitals, physicians' texts, and specimen shelves.

In nineteenth and early twentieth-century America, freak shows produced a generalized icon of corporeal and cultural otherness that verified the sociopolitical status quo and the figure of the unmarked normate, the ideal subject of democracy. The freak show gave the American citizen a ceremonial cultural forum in which to examine apprehensions about the grand democratic experiment and the citizen's relationship to it. Admission fees were good investments for those who could walk away from the freak show with their self-image affirmed, although a vague identification with the freaks and a desire to witness again their anachronistic, extravagant individuation might linger. The extraordinary human icon in this sociopolitical drama, however, was denied the cultural validation such a ritual provided the unexceptional spectator. Instead, cultural necessity transformed the freak's extraordinary body into an enveloping and onerous mantle that appeared both prodigious and pathological to captivated onlookers.

FOUR

• • • • •

Benevolent Maternalism and the Disabled Women in Stowe, Davis, and Phelps

The Maternal Benefactress and Her Disabled Sisters

Whereas the freak shows discussed in chapter 3 display extraordinary bodies as entertainment and wonder, sentimentalism uses disabled figures in a parallel spectacle to generate sympathy. Although sentimental fiction seems to validate disabled figures while the freak show sensationalizes them, in fact both modes of representation appropriate disabled figures in the service of individualist ideology. Both conventions construct the disabled figure as burdened by the limitations and uncertainties of individual embodiment, displacing these burdens from the liberal individual onto that distant other marked by visible bodily difference. In other words, freak shows, sentimentalism, and Emerson's oppositional figures of the "blind," the "halt," and the "invalid" discussed in chapter 2 were all elements of a larger nineteenth-century project that made an abstract, disembodied self the cultural ideal.

Indeed, we can find the disabled figure entangled with liberal ideology in a surprising collection of texts whose announced purpose is advocacy for the very figures that Emerson excludes from liberal selfhood. Three novels—Harriet Beecher Stowe's *Uncle Tom's Cabin* (1852), Rebecca Harding Davis's *Life in the Iron Mills* (1861), and Elizabeth Stuart Phelps's *The Silent Partner* (1871)—employ disabled female figures in the sentimental tradition as essential rhetorical elements in their arguments for humanitarian social reform.[1] I will explore here the complex interconnections in these works between liberal individualism and a program, which I call "benevolent maternalism," that both revises and replicates liberalism. Further, by tracing the shift in the way these novels present disabled figures, I will suggest that benevolent maternalism not only restates the terms of liberal individualism, but also, by moving from sympathetic identification with the disabled figures to a distancing repudiation of them, ultimately dramatizes individualism's most vexing internal contradictions.

Uncle Tom's Cabin, Life in the Iron Mills, and *The Silent Partner* all turn upon relationships between idealized white maternal benefactresses and marginalized female figures who require spiritual and material redemption through their efforts. Differentiating each of these subordinate but mutually defining figures is what we would today call a visible physical disability. This mark operates as a badge of innocence, suffering, displacement, and powerlessness, rendering the disabled woman a sympathetic and alarming figure of vulnerability who cries out from the narrative for rescue. As Stowe deplores slavery's inhumane separation of families, as Davis reveals the iron mill's callous victimization of workers, and as Phelps censures the textile industry's abuse of mill girls, each writer highlights nondisabled heroines or narrators who prevail or even triumph. Their disabled sisters, however, stay on the narrative margins, degraded by oppressive institutions and ultimately sacrificed to the social problems the novels assail. Of Stowe's slave mothers, only the helpless Prue and Hagar, who are "crippled" by abusive slave practices, are beaten to death or sold away; Davis's Deb Wolfe, whose "hunchback" symbolizes her miserable fate as an exploited mill worker, retires and is cared for by others; and Phelps's blind, deaf, and feral Catty Garth is swept away in an apocalyptic conclusion. While the various maternal benefactresses radiate a transcendent virtue, agency, and power, the disabled women become increasingly subjugated, despairing, and impotent.

Crushed by capitalism's laissez-faire morality, Prue, Hagar, Deb, and Catty are icons of vulnerability who help generate a rhetoric of sympathy and scandal meant to propel readers from complacency to conviction. Despite their secondary or even minor parts in the actual narratives, these disabled women fulfill major rhetorical roles by arousing the sympathetic indignation that activates benevolent maternalism. This impulse was the springboard from which white, middle-class women could launch themselves into a prestigious, more influential public role that captured some of the elements of liberal selfhood. Each novel exposes and sharply castigates the exploitative institutions that favor the marketplace at the expense of social justice and human connections, extending to the disabled women a bridge of sympathy, acceptance, and identification across social and racial boundaries. At the same time, however, these novels diminish the very figures for whom they plead by casting them outside the exclusive program of feminine liberal selfhood the narratives map. As embodiments of the egregious injustices the novels condemn, these disabled figures constitute an escalating call—subtle in Stowe, plaintive in Davis, and strident in Phelps—for the narratives' moral, social, and spiritual program of feminine empowerment through humanitarian reform.[2] The characters function as what Paul Longmore calls "charismatic deviants," whose very presence evokes complex issues and potent sentiments.[3]

Yet as these complex, ambivalent relationships between the maternal benefactress and the disabled recipient of her bountiful endeavors develop from Stowe to Davis to Phelps, this program of feminine empowerment increasingly disavows the objects of its benevolence as it more anxiously idealizes its humanitarian figures. Over more than twenty years and two generations, the depiction of the disabled women registers growing tension about white, middle-class women's place in a changing social order. From novel to novel, the disabled women become increasingly prominent and repugnant, changing from minor sympathetic victims to pathetic, repudiated outcasts. In this progression, Stowe initiates a splitting off of the disabled woman from her idealized maternal benefactress, while Davis's Deb, and especially Phelps's Catty, increase this bifurcation. This division can be read as an attempt to resolve apprehensions about the place of the female body in an evolving socioeconomic sphere, the rise of oppressive scientific constructions of women, and concerns about the effectiveness of the discourse of domesticity—which was increasingly unable to provide a tenable framework for either individual feminine identity or social reforms. As a result, the novels incrementally and paradoxically revoke the insistent focus on the problems of female embodiment that they initiate. This progression culminates as Phelps severs the benevolent, ideal feminine self from the perilously corporeal female other in order to celebrate the benevolent woman as indomitable and triumphant, safe in her disembodied, transcendent beauty.

So although Emerson dismisses his invalids while Stowe, Davis, and Phelps sympathize with theirs, each employs the body marked as different—as "disabled"—as an emblem of definitive otherness. Whereas Emerson uses his blind, halt, and invalid figures to establish the boundaries of the liberal individual, Stowe, Davis, and Phelps paradoxically stigmatize some of the characters they seek to aid in their discourse of protest and empowerment.

Because readers must simultaneously feel sympathy for the victims and horror at their callous exploitation, this narrative strategy tends to conflate unethical practices with their effects, projecting the fear of becoming disabled onto the disabled person and confusing the victim with the crime. The characters' bodies thus become semiotic manifestations of social ills, evoking a tangle of empathy and disgust.[4] Such narrative slippage between body and situation derives from and plays on the largely unquestioned belief of many nondisabled people that disability is life's ultimate misfortune and a perpetual source of suffering. The fictional disability becomes, then, a concise trope for a wide range of human misery and corruption.[5] Detached from character, disability is a free-floating signifier for evil and woe that envelops and diminishes the figures so that they tend to become gestures of human wretchedness rather than characters with whom readers might identify.

The Disabled Figure as a Call for Justice:
Harriet Beecher Stowe's *Uncle Tom's Cabin*

To fully investigate the complex relationship between benevolent maternalism and disabled figures, we must examine the critique of liberal individualism that Stowe, Davis, and Phelps launch. The novels call for a more just society in which human needs and connections, rather than economic productivity and physical prowess, determine social worth. To accomplish this, exclusions and injustices surface in bold relief in scenes of suffering and victimization centering on figures who display visible signs of the body's violations and limitations.[6] Prue's scars, Hagar's crippledness, Deb's hunchback, and Catty's muteness and blindness symbolize physical incompetence and irrefutable difference, producing characters that are sympathetically human but incapable of successfully enacting that humanity. Such figures challenge the primacy of productivity and accumulation of wealth as measures of human worth. Distinguished by their disabilities, these women are icons of vulnerability who summon a clash between rights and responsibilities—between work-based and need-based systems of economic distribution—by exposing liberal individualism's denial of the body's needs and liabilities.[7]

The novels cast the disabled figures into the gap between liberalism's conflicting creeds of laissez faire individualism and democratic equality. The women's predicaments reveal the material and ideological disjunction between a value system—portrayed as feminine—that would allocate resources and assign privilege equitably according to human needs, and a market system—associated in the novels with masculinity—that would grant benefits based on individual advantages and effort. The disabled women are right-eously marshaled to exemplify those whose needs for care and support surpass their ability to perform socially valued tasks. Stowe, Davis, and Phelps intend to expose the moral bankruptcy of liberal individualism's model of an autonomous, self-interested, able-bodied individual, free from bodily limitation and the need for care from others. Pointing to liberalism's paradox, the novels assail the institutions that oppress the disabled women at the same time that they proclaim, and call feminine, liberalism's assertion of the equal worth of all individuals, regardless of physical configurations or capabilities.

A scene from *Uncle Tom's Cabin* exemplifies how the novels use disabled female characters to censure liberal individualism's view of the body. Two of Stowe's villains, the slave traders Haley and Marks, exchange stories ostensibly proving the illogical and intractable nature of female slaves. Marks offers the example of "a tight, likely wench" he bought once who was "considerable smart" as well but whose "young un" was "mis'able sickly; it had a crooked back." To his amazement the woman suffered miserably when he gave the child away to someone who would take it off his hands (*UTC* 124). Marks' surprise that the mother valued the child "more 'cause 't *was* sickly and cross" indicates his inability to comprehend the maternal devotion that, for Stowe, humanizes the slave. Haley follows with a similar tale about a slave mother whose "stone blind" child he "nicely swapped off for a keg o' whiskey." To Haley's astonishment, the mother defended the child "jest like a tiger," finally "pitch[ing] head first, young un and all, into the river" (*UTC* 125).

With these two children, Stowe initiates the critical strategy Davis and Phelps follow: using disabled figures to portray the clash between egalitarian concern with the equal value of all people and entrepreneurial laissez-faire individualism. The logic of slavery's unimpeded economic freedom equates human value with potential productivity, judging the disabled children useless and defective, their bodies liabilities rather than assets in a labor-intensive economy. According to the liberal ideal—represented and exaggerated by Marks and Haley—of autonomous, self-interested individuals competing freely in the marketplace, these physically disabled children are not fully human. Such an assumption violates the belief in inherent human equality that underpins Stowe's novel of social reform.

These disabled children—like their more fully developed counterparts, the disabled women—introduce the dilemma of corporeal difference into the novels. They plead the case of those whose bodies prevent them from acting out the role of the self-made man who freely pursues wealth, status, and power. Indeed, Stowe, Davis, and Phelps persistently invoke the physically disabled body to signify subjection to external forces to which embodiment in fact sentences all persons. Impersonal institutions or others' self-determination constrain the fate and control the body of each disabled woman. Slavery separates Prue and Hagar from their children; the economic hegemony of the mill bosses mocks Deb's feeble attempt to seize a chance at wealth for Hugh; Catty's life and death are dictated by the inhuman, mechanized working conditions in the textile mills. Moreover, the disinterested legal system enforces each unjust situation. The institutions these novels castigate literally shape these women's bodies, causing Prue's debility from her master's beatings and Catty's blindness from exposure to cotton residue. As emblems of imposed and innate inferiority, these women's bodies are not only the products of their oppression, but are the vehicles of their wretched fates as well. Their subjugated bodies demand acknowledgment that the liberal ideal of autonomy and self-determination denies physical differences and limitations to create a myth of the body as an acquiescent instrument of the individual will.

If Stowe's scene between the slave traders and the slave mothers is the prototypical rendering of liberalism's troubling contradiction, *Uncle Tom's Cabin* also offers a resolution: maternal devotion as a means of personal empowerment. Stowe's slave mothers refuse to depreciate their flawed and helpless children, underscoring the principle of universal, unconditional acceptance of all human beings that supports the novel's condemnation of slavery. Like Jesus, the mother regards her children as equally worthy regardless of their material and physical circumstances. Respecting no worldly social hierarchies, maternal affection distributes its resources according to need, not merit. As types for the undervalued and helpless, these disabled children's need for acceptance and love far exceeds their ability to inspire it; in Stowe's scenes, mother-love compensates for society's practice of rating people according to notions of physical adequacy rather than inherent worth. A feminized realm of ideal equality thus emerges—if only momentarily and in principle—in opposition to the dominant, masculine marketplace morality. Dismissed by liberal individualism's ethos of autonomy and productivity, these disabled children and their devoted mothers occupy the highest rung on the ladder of regard these novels offer as an alternative vision of human value. The disabled body, then, is a badge of unworthiness in the market economy and one of ultimate worth in the moral one.[8] Stowe's nameless infants and their other disabled counterparts serve as exclamation points in ambitious arguments for a more equitable socioeconomic order, a more human-centered value system, and a fuller acknowledgment of physical needs.

Such maternal agency is the narrative vehicle for what Philip Fisher calls "the romance of the object," which extends full humanity to figures from which it has previously been withheld.[9] With this "romance," Stowe adds to her rhetoric of protest the suggestion that maternal devotion on behalf of the vulnerable and devalued other produces a feminine self reminiscent of the liberal individual whose excesses Stowe so ardently condemns. Haley's misguided attempt to "swap off" the disabled infant elicits a vigorously offensive response from the slave mother, who "ups on a cotton-bale, like a cat, ketches a knife from one of the deck hands, and . . . [makes] all fly for a minit" before she recognizes the futility of resistance and drowns herself and the child, depriving Haley of his investment in her (*UTC* 125). In this narrative "minit," the presumably docile slave asserts her will, assaults her oppressor, arms herself, and boldly determines her own fate—just like Eliza does by crossing the Ohio, rescuing Harry, and eluding her captors, and as Cassy does by escaping from Legree after Emmeline's arrival. The mother transforms from the slave trader's passive pawn into an assertive figure charged with an independent will, defying external forces for at least a moment in an attempt to shape her own destiny. The maternal empowerment Stowe hints at here creates a figure resembling the idealized liberal self we associate with Emerson—self-reliant, willful, unimpeded by physical limitation. But this feminine selfhood differs from individualistic selfhood in that it does not claim detachment or self-interest, but instead admits the necessity of a dependent object for its fulfillment.[10] Indeed, Stowe's extension to slaves of this humane, feminized version of liberal selfhood reinforces her abolitionist argument: because slaves are capable of such feeling, they are in fact fully human and worthy of emancipation.

If Stowe's abolitionist project accords full dignity and agency to her black mothers, it simultaneously writes a comparable script for white women. As maternal benefactresses, they are to the undervalued and victimized women what the slave mothers are to their threatened children. Stowe reiterates this pattern in varying levels of complexity throughout her novel: Mrs. Shelby defends Tom and Harry; Mrs. Bird protects the pursued Eliza; Rachel Halliday mothers Eliza. Yet the principle white, female figures who gain personal authority this way are the angelic Eva and Stowe's ardent narrative voice, whose compelling and controlling presence suffuses the novel. Whereas the slave women display the valued qualities of liberal individualism through their humanizing roles as mothers, the white women accrue dignity, agency, and self-determination by acting maternally toward members of a devalued group. Although both Eva and Stowe's narrator act on behalf of a wide range of imperiled characters, I focus here on the relation between Eva and Prue and the one between Stowe's narrator and Hagar, for here Stowe presents the model for the relation between an empowered maternal benefactress and her disabled counterpart that Davis and Phelps take up later. It is important, however, to examine first how the figure of the maternal benefactress operates in these novels.

Empowering the Maternal Benefactress

Behind the explicit social reform these novels call for is the implicit task of framing a semi-public, socially and morally empowered role for heroines, narrators, and readers. This white, benevolent, maternal reformer was a new social position for middle-class women who, as the private and public realms in nineteenth-century America became increasingly separate, were shut out of economic production and status.[11] Excluded by gender from the status of the liberal individual, middle-class women cultivated this role partly to launch themselves into public life as their program negotiated tensions emerging from imposing domesticity on a world that increasingly marginalized the domestic sphere.[12] Arising from women's traditional caretaking and affective duties and appropriating Christian ethics, benevolent maternalism gained virtue and legitimacy by focusing on the needs and suffering of others and publicly advocating on their behalf. The narrators bespeak, and the white, middle-class heroines enact, a feminine liberal identity that blends traditional noblesse oblige, maternal affection, sororal affiliation, millennial optimism, evangelical fervor, resistance to patriarchy, and personal salvation. Alienated from the economic and political spheres, these domestic writers consolidate and disseminate what Nancy Cott calls "the rhetorical magnification of women's domestic occupation."[13] As they attempted to reshape the public world and their own image within it, middle-class women sought to extend their influence from the home to the worldly realm of humanitarian work.

The role of maternal benefactress, separated from its recipient by race and class, could generate for nineteenth-century middle-class women a feminine self that possessed many qualities of the liberal individual while still conforming to the main tenets of domestic ideology. Maternal benevolence fulfills domesticity's mandate that feminine identity be founded upon self-denial. Precluded from seeking status or power on their own behalf, middle-class women could only assert a form of liberal selfhood by identifying with, nurturing, and acting on behalf of others. If maternal benevolence conforms to domesticity's demand for feminine self-renunciation, it also depends upon a notion of self that approximates the self-determining, self-advancing figure of the entrepreneur.[14] Such a strategy enables the maternal benefactress to envision herself responsible for the troubles of strangers and capable of alleviating them, using an individual imagination and will that could range far into time and space, sculpting and subduing the world. Yet where capitalism posits a market economy based on contractual relations among individuals regarding labor and material resources, benevolence posits a moral economy of contractual obligations based on the pledge of human sympathy inherent in Christianity. Maternal benevolence, then, amounts to a social contract enacted by a woman who views herself, her covenants with God and her fellow humans, and her capacities for innovative action extending far beyond the realm of daily needs and kinship circles. Thus the benevolent matron secures a feminine liberal selfhood that maintains emotional connections and the appearance of self-sacrifice so essential to the ideal of true womanhood.

The disabled women not only activate their rescuers, but they also authorize the benevolent woman's passage from the confining home to the public realm. If true womanhood granted women the potential to be moral exemplars who emanated salvific Christian love, it also ensconced them in cottages that sheltered them from the very corruption for which they held the cure. The novels position each disabled woman, not at home—where disabled people were usually found in nineteenth-century society—but at risk inside the masculine institutions the novels criticize.[15] Stowe places Hagar on the auction block and Prue under the whip of a cruel master; Davis situates poor, naive, motherless Deb alone at the iron mill; Phelps allows motherless Catty to wander the streets of the mill town. Casting these characters as endangered children and grandmothers demands intercession in the public realm and invites women readers to respond as either mothers or grown daughters to the imperiled disabled women. The disabled figures thus legitimated the middle-class woman's move out of the sequestered home while remaining within the maternal role.

If the moral-social contract of maternal benevolence demands a recipient who is dependent upon her supporter, the disabled figure seen as unfit for both labor and society exactly fits this script. These characters call forth the reader's compassion and invite her to fight "jest like a tiger" on behalf of the suffering, vulnerable other, working for social change and securing liberal selfhood within the domestic role. Replicating the uneven power relationship between mother and child, the connections between disabled women and their maternal benefactresses are cemented by shared gender but unbalanced by race and class differences. Benevolent, white, maternal figures such as Stowe's Eva, Davis's Quaker woman, and Phelps's Perley achieve freedom, independence, and self-determination through a relationship with an other whose dependence is secured by disability, blackness, and/or lower-class status: Eva has Prue; Perley has Catty; the Quaker woman has Deb; the narrators have Hagar, Prue, and Deb. And the readers have them all.[16]

This feminine liberal self gains strength in part because the disenfranchised, vulnerable disabled figures are forced to occupy the position women traditionally hold in relation to men. The difference, of course, is that the feminine liberal self admits dependence on the other, naming it sympathy and identification, while the masculine liberal self claims autonomy, denying reliance on female support and the defining boundaries that it provides masculinity. Nevertheless, the presence of the sympathetic, marginalized disabled figures creates a triangle among the masculine liberal self, the white maternal benefactress, and the black or lower-class disabled woman. As a third term in the gender opposition so fundamental to these novels, the disabled figure partially disengages the maternal benefactress from her status as subordinate to white men, providing another social relation around which she might organize a more empowered and prestigious selfhood.[17] This discursive relationship thus secures for the white female a way to gain some of the liberal individual's status, which patriarchal ideology and industrial capitalism denied women. Legitimated, like Emerson's ideal man, by the defining presence of an inferior, the benefactress acquires agency, status, and invincibility, all secured by the disabled women's passivity, marginalization, and vulnerability.

Benevolent Maternalism's Flight from the Body: Harriet Beecher Stowe's *Uncle Tom's Cabin*

The female body, whether degraded or ideal, becomes the setting for this drama of empowerment and agency. The virtue Stowe's white maternal benefactresses derive from their relations with the disabled women manifests itself in an idealized, ethereal beauty and transcendent authority that is never so fully achieved by the slave mothers. Although the seeming self-sacrifice of motherly devotion makes all of Stowe's maternal heroines beautiful in their righteousness, no benevolent figure is more resplendent than Eva.[18] As "the perfection of childish beauty," Eva's dying body is cast as strangely incorporeal—in fact, as an angel. A model "little lady," she has a "cloud-like tread," "a buoyant figure," and "a visionary golden head," that make "beautiful Eva" into "the picture of some bright angel stooping to reclaim a sinner" (*UTC* 230–32, 263, 410). Not only is Eva "always dressed in white," but her association with the privileged, beautiful, white purity of benevolence grows stronger as her influence over others expands, culminating with her death and transformation into an angelic, idealized figure. Eva out-mothers everyone, becoming the apotheosis of maternal devotion, literally sacrificing herself to relieve Prue's and Tom's physical suffering and Topsy's heathenism, and becoming exalted and freed from the body in the process. Whereas Tom and Topsy inspire salvific love in Eva, Prue's gruesome tale of physical misery and vulnerability makes Eva "pale, and a deep, earnest shadow passe[s] over her eyes," accentuating her beatific whiteness, which is complete in her dramatic, white-draped *tableau mourant* "beneath an angel figure" (*UTC* 325, 429).

In direct opposition to Eva's progressively idealized, ethereal beauty is Prue's inescapable physical awfulness. A "low creature" whose "grunting," "scowling," and "sour surly" ways confirm her own conviction that "I's ugly,— I's wicked," Prue is "a poor, old, cut-up critter," an often-abused, suicidal alcoholic touchingly grieving for her lost child (*UTC* 319–23). Prue's body is a liability from which she cannot escape. It is the medium of her victimization, producing the child that she cannot defend, becoming the instrument of her drunkenness, compromising her labor, and finally provoking her master to beat her to death. Even though the nondisabled slave mothers—such as Eliza, Cassy, and Haley's and Marks's unnamed slaves—are humanized and gain self-determination through motherhood, Prue's and Hagar's dreadful fates acknowledge just how potentially vulnerable maternity makes women under the patriarchal slave system.

Stowe's disembodied narrative voice of benevolent maternalism offers Hagar to the readers as the tragic epitome of female impotence in the face of masculine subjugation. Hagar is "partially blind, and somewhat crippled with rheumatism" so that she responds with "shaking hands," "intense trepidation," and "sobbing" when confronted by the wills of others (*UTC* 194–95, 197). On the auction block where she is torn from her grown son because she can no longer work, Hagar is a "poor victim," a "despairing old mother, whose agony [is] pitiful to see," and whose disability summarizes her incapacity and defeat (*UTC* 197). Both Prue and Hagar fall prey to their own bodily conditions, their discomforting warning uneasily retracted by Stowe a few pages after the characters' introductions.

These disabled slave mothers' brief but rhetorically vital appearances comprise a counternarrative in *Uncle Tom's Cabin* that undercuts Stowe's proclamation that home and motherhood can redeem a world corrupted by secular and economic pursuits. Motherhood does not free Prue and Hagar, but instead it holds them hostage to its attachments and emotions, even while it humanizes them. These characters' disabilities signify exactly what the maternal heroines manage to escape: a physical vulnerability that undermines the will behind self-determination. While Eliza miraculously crosses the Ohio on the ice, Hagar's trembling, crying, and begging change nothing; and Prue's drinking, though it is excused, only destroys her. If Stowe leaves her readers momentarily heartbroken and wary at Hagar's and Prue's fates, she briskly moves beyond their helplessness to Eliza's and Cassy's heartening heroism. While the indomitable white maternal benefactresses and nondisabled slave mothers here become mistresses of their fates, the disabled figures lack the agency and self-determination that regulate and neutralize the body's vulnerability. Enveloped by forces they cannot control, Hagar and Prue lack the will to resist and the ability to anticipate the present's consequences on the future— both traits of the liberal selfhood essential to maternal benevolence. The disabled women's incapable, impotent bodies operate not as neutral instruments of sovereign wills, but as impediments subject to inexorable fate or irresistible forces, both cast as masculine. Were Prue and Hagar—or later, Deb and Catty—to act in their own behalf, the narrative frame of a power struggle between invincible maternal benevolence and masculine marketplace practices would collapse. Their vulnerability—marked by a disability that simultaneously justifies and enforces their material and psychological destitution —rhetorically activates the benevolent maternalism the novel seeks to inspire in readers.

The Female Body as Liability

As the sharp contrast between Eva and Prue suggests, the female body elicits much anxiety in these novels. The shift in representation from Stowe's sympathetic but promptly erased disabled slave mothers, to the repulsive but touching Deb and the bestial and pathetic Catty, suggests a growing uneasiness about the female body and the script of benevolent maternalism. While the female body had always been in some sense cast as a liability, this became especially so for middle-class women, who were by the mid-nineteenth century pressed into new roles and culturally restricted by the institutions that created what Gerda Lerner terms the middle-class "cult of the lady."[19] The rise of industrial capitalism, the emergence of the middle class, the notion of separate private and public spheres, the professionalization of work, the increasing hegemony of the scientific-medical perspective, and the escalation of consumerism interacted to produce an ideology of womanhood that required the white, middle-class female body to be idle, frail, and beautiful.[20] Each of these cultural developments found an ideological site in the newly configured middle-class female body. For example, as the factory, the sweatshop, and the putting-out system for piecework replaced the independent home as the principle site of production, middle-class women, now excluded from the transformed market economy, became ornaments and consumers, markers of the status their husbands and fathers were toiling to achieve. Banishment from the workplace, a mandate to consume, and a focus on appearance thus created the standard of the frail and idle beauty. That standard was policed by an authoritative scientific-medical discourse that not only pathologized femaleness itself, but enforced the restrictions of middle-class domesticity by declaring education, work, and creativity other than reproduction as physically dangerous and destructive of womanliness. As such socioeconomic demands and power relations were literally inscribed on the bodies of middle-class women, the women must have struggled with a heightened sense of their own vulnerability as the ideal female body shifted from a hearty mother and worker to a delicate, expensive, indolent ornament barely fit for reproduction.[21]

Many women rebelled, of course. Locating the issue squarely in the female body, Stowe responded by drawing a sharp contrast between an idealized but lost figure of domestic productivity and the current, denigrated successor who was unfit for useful physical work. Lamenting in an 1864 essay the "fragile, easily fatigued, languid girls of a modern age," she nostalgically recalls the "strong, hardy, cheerful girls . . . of old times" who could "wash, iron, brew, bake, harness a horse and drive him," as well as "braid straw, embroider, draw, paint, and read innumerable books."[22] For Stowe and her colleagues who championed a domesticity based in female work, the banishment of middle-class women from productive activity created an often defensive and despairing vision of female embodiment. Anxiety over economic changes rendering the middle-class female body essentially a decorative ornament rather than a productive implement may have contributed to the periodic breakdowns, nervous disorders, and chronic bouts of ill health that these authors and many of their contemporaries experienced.[23] The example of Phelps illustrates the schizoid response that ambition could produce in women acculturated for a limited, domestic role. Phelps asserts in an 1886 *Harper's* essay that "the notion that women are made to be taken care of, to depend upon somebody, to be toiled for, to play among the roses of life while their husbands and fathers are on its battle-fields, is degrading to the last degree." Yet after writing *The Silent Partner*, she endured a five-year illness that was probably a reaction to her father's disapproval and anti-feminism.[24]

To be excluded from earning a living in a society that equates virtue with work is profoundly diminishing. Yet the image of the "fragile" woman in the "degrading" position of needing "to be taken care of" because she is outside meaningful production is precisely that of both the disabled figures in these novels and middle-class women. So while the novels extend a narrative hand of sympathy across a chasm of difference to the disabled figures, the actual distinctions between "dependent" and "degraded" Hagar, Prue, Deb, and Catty and their middle-class sisters may not have seemed so clear to the authors or their readers. Redundant and displaced in the transforming marketplace, cast as dependent and frail, seen as victims of their uteruses, vulnerable to institutional subjugation, and possessed of bodies that were increasingly deemed useless, middle-class women were in a position parallel to that of people with physical disabilities.[25]

This cultural effigy of womanhood was exactly what articulate, ardent, and ambitious women like Stowe, Davis, and Phelps were trying to overthrow. Being in a parallel position to her disabled counterpart produces both a compelling compassion and a potent threat that generate an escalating, uneasy ambivalence culminating in a representational breach between the maternal benefactress and her disabled beneficiary. Increasingly divergent in their figuration, the two groups personify the poles in a narrative of feminine embodiment in which the disabled women offer a tale of admonition while the nondisabled women stand as apotheoses of womanly physicality. Beginning with Stowe, and more fully with Davis and Phelps, these novels offer two possible scripts for women, one disabled and one enabled, to instruct readers about the perils and potential of being a woman in mid-nineteenth century America. While the maternal benefactresses are empowered with voice, self-determination, and agency, the vulnerable figures languish on the narrative margins, ensnared by the limitations of their own bodies. The novels simultaneously embrace in compassion and resist in dread these reminders of bodily impotence and victimization. The disabled women become discursive lightning rods for a growing sense of feminine vulnerability that the authors dare not fully concede. Their shadowy, terrible fates constitute a muted counternarrative of female subjugation and bodily liability that the maternal benefactresses flee.

Two Opposing Scripts of Female Embodiment:
Rebecca Harding Davis's *Life in the Iron Mills*

As this reform narrative develops, the disabled figures become progressively more prominent and more degraded, while the maternal benefactresses become more idealized and disembodied. As Davis and Phelps expand and complicate Stowe's rhetorical use of disabled figures to mobilize benevolent maternalism, they intensify the cautionary tale of female vulnerability in the stories of Deb Wolfe and Catty Garth. Deb's and Catty's marked bodies function first as debased instruments of ineffectual wills and second as liabilities that condemn them to desperate situations. The disabled women represent precisely the possibility that liberal individualism refuses to concede: that the body might impede rather than implement the development of selfhood. In stark contrast, the maternal benefactresses—Davis's seemingly guilt-ridden narrator and her ethereal Quaker woman as well as Phelps's idealized, beautiful Perley Kelso—are free from the vulnerability that endangers the disabled figures.

By centering its representation of womanhood on the vulnerable body of the sympathetic but miserable and inept "hunchback" Deb Wolfe, *Life in the Iron Mills* reverses Stowe's focus on the heroines in order to highlight the victims. Davis converts Stowe's Southern racial hierarchy to a more Northern concern with class differentiation, her less sanguine narrative voice of benevolent maternalism exposing the failure of domesticity to impose moral order.[26] Whereas the home endures as a site of salvation in Stowe's world, Davis points explicitly to how industrial capitalism splits whites into a class hierarchy that decimates working-class families, squelches individual fulfillment, and renders home life inconsequential. A barren remnant of Stowe's idealized family, the Wolfes subsist in a hovel of impotent misery and wretchedness. The motherless Deb is one of Stowe's disabled and devalued children, grown up and cast out like Hagar and Prue, defenseless before her oppressors. Although she serves as a caretaker, Deb is denied motherhood, that conduit to dignity, identification, and sympathy for Stowe's slaves. Stronger on cultural critique than domestic solution, *Life in the Iron Mills* focuses on the mill and prison, effacing both the middle-class home and the Quaker community from which the maternal benefactresses spring.

Whereas Stowe focuses on an idealized Eva, Davis obscures her benefactresses, although she grants them the story's only positive power. Both the narrator and the Quaker woman are strikingly insubstantial, compared to the wretched mill workers whose bodily suffering floods us with vivid detail. Like Stowe's narrative voice before her, Davis's narrator is not unequivocally a woman; yet the tone of both voices is so strongly aligned with female benevolence as to seem feminine. While the narrator shapes readers' responses with provocative descriptions and goading judgments, she reveals almost nothing about herself, particularly the details of her own body. We learn only that she has known the community since childhood even though she seems to be quite apart from it, narrating from a window above the workers' "massed, vile, slimy lives" (*LIM* 13). Only at the end is the presence that has guided us through "the poor Welsh puddler['s]" dreadful story revealed as that of a writer whose library now houses Hugh's korl statue of the woman, guiltily "hid behind a curtain" (*LIM* 64). A vast rhetorical disparity looms between the middle-class, presumably white, writer, whose entire characterization consists of acts of will such as "I open," "I can detect," "I look," "I want," "I choose," "I dare," and— most important—"I write," and the mill workers, whose miserable material lives and degraded bodies, down in the "fog, and mud, and foul effluvia," she so frankly depicts (*LIM* 11–14).

The unnamed benevolent Quaker woman who appears at the end of Deb's prison term is as effectual as, and more embodied than, the narrator. In total command of herself and the tragic situation, this "homely body coarsely dressed in gray and white," with a "strong arm" and a "strong heart," appears to rescue Deb and to transport Hugh's corpse to a proper burial among the hills and trees (*LIM* 62–63). In this idealized Quaker woman—so similar to Stowe's Rachel Halliday—no dissonance exists between body and will; her body functions efficiently and capably so that she arrives, cleans, leads, buries, and begins "her work" of redeeming Deb without the slightest hindrance (*LIM* 64). Perpetually in the service of others, yet mistress of herself, her body, and the consequences of her actions, she is Deb's opposite, the liberal feminine self free from the liabilities of female embodiment.

Deb is, by contrast, tethered to a body that frustrates—even perverts—volition as well as obstructing the achievement of her desires. "[A] type of her class," she is the wretched mill life made flesh (*LIM* 21). A degraded version of Hugh, whose artistic commitment redeems his bodily restrictions, Deb emblematizes the unredeemed, subjugated body that impedes her will. While Hugh's "finer nature" remains unsullied because of his "groping passion for whatever was beautiful and pure," Deb, reduced to a body spoiled by fate and society's disfavor, is "[m]iserable . . . like a limp, dirty rag—yet not an unfitting figure to crown the scene of hopeless discomfort" (*LIM* 21–23). Whereas cruel masters thwart Prue and Hagar, Deb's body itself is her primary oppressor, her defining feature, summing up for Hugh and the narrator everything ugly, revolting, and confining about mill workers' lives. Descriptions like "watchdog" and faithful "spaniel" relegate Deb to the status of an animal at the mercy of dominating masters, her own crude instincts, and a hostile environment (*LIM* 61, 23).

Although Deb's sole motivation throughout the story is to love and be loved by Hugh, he is "sickened with disgust at her deformity," and she is pathetic to everyone else (*LIM* 23). Rejected and pitied in her efforts to gain Hugh's love, she represents the ultimate threat to nineteenth-century female selfhood: a body that prevents her from attachment to a man, women's conduit to power and status. Repulsive to the male gaze, Deb's beleaguered body witnesses the domestic self's precarious dependence upon a body that must be approved and fulfilled by male selection. Even more alarming, Deb's only moment of bold agency, the self-sacrificing, quintessentially feminine act of stealing Mitchell's money for Hugh, ironically neither saves nor pleases him but leads instead to his death. Thus, Deb warns of the female body's worst possible betrayal: that it prevents all desires and needs from being realized. A figure for all the vulnerability, aberration, rejection, and impotence attributed to females, Deb, victimized by and because of her "thwarted woman's form," is at once sympathetic and monstrous, finally contained in, rather than empowered by, the Quaker haven (*LIM* 21). With Deb, then, this novella continues Stowe's process of sealing off the disabled figure who signifies female vulnerability into a narrative space of insurmountable bodily difference, freeing the maternal benefactress from a growing wariness of the female body's limitations on agency and will.[27]

Davis and Phelps intensify beauty and ugliness as opposing signifiers of feminine virtue. In Stowe the dichotomy follows racial lines, but in Davis and Phelps differences in physical appearance reflect class discrepancies. While Stowe uses maternal experience to flatten out physiological differences between Prue and Hagar and Eliza and Rachel, Davis and Phelps expunge motherhood and differentiate their sets of women by aligning beauty with social status. In the generation that separates Davis and Phelps from Stowe, class distinctions among women continued to solidify, and female beauty as an industry and ideology intensified.[28] By mid-century the life patterns of middle-class and lower-class women were very dissimilar, except that they were equally marginalized and disenfranchised.[29] That disparity is represented here by beauty, a commodity that was much more available to middle-class women than to their working-class sisters. For example, even though Davis's maternal benefactresses are too physically vague to be thought of as beautiful, the novel doggedly underscores the mill workers' ugliness: "deformed" Deb is the apotheosis of working-class grotesqueness, "even more ghastly, her lips bluer, her eyes more watery," than the repellent drunk, Old Wolfe (*LIM* 16–17). So while Hagar has only "shaking hands" and is merely "pitiful to see," Deb is a "weak, flaccid wretch," whose ugliness clearly is a mark and product not only of physical inferiority, but also of class distinction (*UTC* 197, *LIM* 17).

Davis's Janey also figures in this economy that equates physical beauty with female value, virtue, and power.[30] Although subdued by the mill life that has made Deb so ugly, Janey's beauty shows through enough in her "dark blue eyes and lithe figure" that Hugh loves her instead of the repugnant Deb (*LIM* 23). Deb's recognition that Hugh loves Janey's fragile and fading beauty produces in Deb a "jealousy" that the narrator uses to encourage the reader to identify with Deb despite class boundaries. "Are pain and jealousy less savage realities down here in this place I am taking you to," the benevolent narrator charges, "than in your own house or your own heart[?] . . . The note is the same, I fancy, be the octave high or low" (*LIM*, 23). This allusion to all women's dependence on male approval for fulfillment and status suggests that the threat of the "ugly" female body cannot be safely sequestered behind the wall Davis constructs between mill girls and middle-class women. So with the introduction of physical beauty and its links to class differences as a value system imposed on female bodies, the feminine liberal self asserted by benevolent maternalism becomes still more vulnerable, and must be bolstered repeatedly by the anxious opposition between the disabled figure and her benefactress.

The Triumph of the Beautiful, Disembodied Heroine: Elizabeth Stuart Phelps's *The Silent Partner*

Appearing in 1871, nearly twenty years after *Uncle Tom's Cabin, The Silent Partner* seems to accept as its premise *Godey's Lady's Book's* 1852 assertion that "It is a woman's *business* to be beautiful," and to amplify that assertion with both the domestic proposition that beauty equals virtue and the feminist proposition that women can live independently from men and marriage.[31] A kind of hybrid of Stowe's Eva and Davis's Quaker woman, Phelps's Perley Kelso is a full-blown figure of transcendental benevolent maternalism whose flawless beauty and unmitigated capability is contrasted with the ugliness and ineptness of the wretched Catty Garth. As with Davis, class distinctions manifest as beauty and ugliness separate Phelps's ultimate heroine, Perley, and ultimate victim, Catty. A self-made woman in the feminine economy of benevolence, the indomitable Perley repudiates marriage, instead using her inheritance to establish an all-female home centered on sororal affection, supposedly uncompromised by either patriarchy or class divisions.[32] Open to the mill workers, Perley's home serves as a stage upon which a class-based hierarchy equating beauty and virtue is repeatedly displayed. Capable of shaping her own destiny, Perley is "a superior woman," devoted to the less capable and less appealing, a "swift, strong, helpful figure" with a "womanly, wonderful face," whose virtue and physical faultlessness increase in proportion to her generosity toward the mill workers (*SP* 163, 217, 302). She is a grown-up, strengthened version of Eva whose beauty and goodness make her invulnerable and useful, an earthly rather than a heavenly angel. Several *tableaux vivants* juxtapose Perley's idealized, capable body with Catty's debased, inept one: "They were a startling pair to be standing side by side. . . . Perley's fine, finished smile seemed to blot out this miserable figure," who is habitually characterized as "an ugly girl" with a "repulsive" face (*SP* 86–88, 190). Echoing Eva, Perley—as her name suggests—is associated repeatedly with white: "Miss Kelso's elegant white[dress], without flaw, or pucker of trimming presented a broad and shining background to the poor creature's puzzled figure" (*SP* 230).

Phelps complicates this contrast, however, by creating a triangle composed of Perley, the humanitarian heiress; Sip Garth, Catty's older sister and a nondisabled mill girl; and Catty, the disabled woman whose helplessness elicits their devotion and emphasizes their power. Sip is aligned with Catty by low social class and its attendant lack of beauty, and with Perley by the self-determination with which she overcomes the liabilities of the body to which Catty succumbs. As if to suggest both the limits and the possibilities for upward social mobility, Sip stands midway between Perley's capability—embodied as beauty—and Catty's ineptitude—embodied as disability. Despite this suggestion of class permeability, class distinctions appear mainly as biological differences akin to racial categories: Sip is "just a little rough, brown girl" with a "pinched face," while the precious Perley has a radiantly white, "fine, rare face" (*SP* 294, 85, 302). Nevertheless, Sip's willfulness and self-control allow her to become Perley's understudy in their self-created, ambitious world of Christian benevolence independent of male influence. In contrast, Catty is blinded and deafened by mill work and finally swept away by an apocalyptic flood of logs, the mill's final destructive effect on her body. With this triangulation, then, Phelps shapes Stowe's model of relations between the disabled figure and the maternal benefactress into a class-based hierarchy that correlates with the behavioral value system of liberal individualism and is linked to physical characteristics.

Perley's beauty is not only the visible manifestation of her virtue; it functions as well as a synonym for the self-control that Catty lacks. Just as Perley's body is the "finished" and "flaw[less]" product of feminine moral usefulness, Catty's body is "ill-controlled" and "uncontrollable" (*SP* 85). Perley's asceticism contrasts with Catty's vices: the deaf and mute girl drinks, runs wild in the streets, and "worse"—is probably sexually promiscuous (*SP* 84). Entirely physical, with no restraining will, she constantly risks exploitation and sexual appropriation. Like Davis's Deb, Catty is "a miserable creature," a "[t]ype of the world from which she sprang" (*SP* 277–78). As her name implies, Catty is also bestial, cowering and "whining . . . like a hurt brute" and "snarl[ing] like an annoyed animal" (*SP* 188, 150). Suggesting a social Darwinist view of class and disability, Catty's face appears simian: not having managed "that difficult evolution of brain from beast," she is "a girl with a low forehead, with wandering eyes, with a dull stoop to the head, . . . [and] a thick drooping under lip" (*SP* 86).[33]

Catty is the body incarnate that frustrates and obliterates the liberal individual's narrative of progress toward physical mastery. Rather than functioning as, for example, the compliant implement that frees Thoreau from a restrictive social order, Catty's body is a liability, imperiling her and provoking the feral behavior implied by her name. Her wandering and appetites suggest prototypical male behavior that is self-destructive for a woman without male entitlement. Catty is the woman Perley must save, but also must never become. By depicting Perley as the sovereign will in the compliant body while Catty is the sovereign body that obviates the autonomous individual will, Phelps fastens all physical restrictions and perils to Catty's body, leaving Perley as pure soul and voice attached to a transcendent, tractable implement of feminine self-determination.[34]

The Silent Partner, however, does not focus on these negative aspects of Catty's portrayal. The repeated litany of emotion-encrusted sympathy for the "poor" disabled woman blurs Catty's implicit menace, obscuring the physical dangers she represents. The defensive, almost manic, quality of Perley's uplifting portrait also further mutes, even trivializes, the nevertheless insistent threat that Catty's vulnerable body poses to Phelps's benevolent feminine self. The narrative strategy of splitting the female characters into carnal and incorporeal figures becomes clear only if the spotlight is shifted from the narrative of class solidarity between Perley and Sip to the juxtaposition of Catty's awfulness with Perley's idealization, both of which are veiled by constant claims of "love." Indeed, their obsession with Catty's vulnerability secures the bond between Sip and Perley, her apocalyptic death freeing and inspiring them—as well as the readers—for unencumbered benevolent work and its concomitant female self-making.

With this shift in figuration of the disabled women and their maternal benefactresses, Davis and Phelps bear witness to an escalating anxiety, first expressed by Stowe, about the place of the female body in a society undergoing changes in work, gender arrangements, class relations, consumption, and enfranchisement. While America's progress narrative may have increased middle-class young women's expectations, the developing role of the white, frail, idle beauty enclosed in the middle-class home and severed from her working sisters represented a paradoxical threat registered by these women writers. The same frustrations and sense of restrictions among middle-class women that ignited their women's rights movement, officially launched in 1848, insinuate themselves into the portrayals we have examined here.[35] Uncle Tom's Cabin's idealization of maternity as physically empowering certainly liberates some of the slave mothers, but it also creates in benevolent maternalism a pattern in which the terms of celebration tend to undermine the project itself. The maternal benefactress transforms through *Life in the Iron Mills* and *The Silent Partner* into a defensive biologizing of beauty as the physical location of female power and prestige and of ugliness as its absence. Despite the desire to construct a rhetorical model of socially valued feminine selfhood, these novels could only modify the available, dominant script of the masculine liberal self, bending it toward the other-directedness and self-denial mandated by the female domestic role. In spite of their laudatory aims, these works reflect the limitations of liberal individualism's denial of bodily limitation and dependency. In ambitiously remaking the world and themselves, these writers reveal a suspicion that middle-class female embodiment was an increasing impediment. Yet that suspicion inadvertently sets in motion a narrative that betrays the very sisters it intends to support. The novels banish onto the disabled figures such troubling issues as female sexual exploitation, the failure of domesticity, the pathologizing of women, female economic dependence, and the equation of femininity with childhood. By projecting the liabilities of femaleness onto the disabled women, the novels open a narrative safe space where the maternal benefactress can create a moral society and a feminine liberal self unconstrained by the limits of embodiment.

Renunciation triumphs over identification in these novels because the disabled body signifies a physical vulnerability so troubling that it seems to undermine the writers' ambitions for middle-class white women. By declining to be re-formed, by stubbornly resisting rehabilitation, the disabled bodies defy notions such as self-improvement, self-reliance, self-determination, even progress itself—all valued, if illusory, tenets of liberal individualism. Eventually too great a threat to the project of benevolent maternalism, the disabled women are sympathetically but definitively cast out of the empowering scheme the novels promote for women. If presenting a vision of social justice that recognizes physical limitations is these novels' achievement, their disappointment is that the critique falters in applying this vision to the figure of feminine selfhood they advance. To confront the problems of the body that are embedded in benevolent maternalism and raised by the disabled women would require confronting the disparity between the ideal and the actual that these novels eschew. Though she is embraced, the disabled figure is above all what the maternal benefactress refuses to become. These novels at once claim and repudiate the identification between the two groups of women, offering compassion as an ambivalent compromise.

FIVE

• • • • •

Disabled Women as Powerful Women in Petry, Morrison, and Lorde

Revising Black Female Subjectivity

As we saw in chapter 4, sentimentalism's discourse of sympathy necessarily frames disability as a lack that middle-class female benevolence redresses. While benevolent maternalism's focus on race, gender, beauty, and disability seems to insist on the body as the ground of identity, the novels of Stowe, Davis, and Phelps ultimately flee from their own emphasis on the body to construct a feminine persona that conforms to the abstract notions of the liberal individual and the constraints of true womanhood. If the cultural work of nineteenth-century benevolent maternalism is introducing the body into politicized literary discourse, that work is continued by several twentieth-century African-American women writers who also use disabled figures in strategies of empowerment that recast benevolent maternalism's positive version of womanhood.

Perhaps the fundamental aim of African-American women's writing is to construct a black female subject that displaces the negative cultural images generated by America's aggregate history of racism and sexism. Such a collective project of cultural revision challenges the African-American woman writer to produce a narrative of self that authenticates black women's oppressive history yet offers a model for transcending that history's limitations.

In other words, the writer must recast the dominant representations of black womanhood without betraying the historical experience of being a black woman in America. Her task is thus to render oppression without reinscribing it: to build a figure of black female selfhood on the narrow space between victimization and assimilation, so that she neither repudiates her history nor embraces the conventional scripts of womanhood that have excluded her.

In Audre Lorde's explicitly revisionist narrative of self, *Zami: A New Spelling of My Name*, the narrator Audre/Zami at once poses this problem and implies a solution:

> My mother was a very powerful woman. This was so in a time when that word-combination of *woman* and *powerful* was almost unexpressible in the white american [sic] common tongue, except or unless it was accompanied by some aberrant explaining adjective like blind, or hunchback, or crazy, or Black. Therefore when I was growing up, *powerful woman* equaled something else quite different from ordinary woman, from simply "woman." It certainly did not, on the other hand equal "man." What then? What was the third designation?

Acknowledging that the dominant definition of "woman" excludes personal power, Lorde searches here for language to express her experience of the oxymoronic "powerful woman."[1] Rejecting both "woman" and "man," she imagines this iconoclastic black female as occupying a "third designation" distinct from the only two available normative options. This woman thus falls outside standard categories and necessarily into the realm of the "aberrant," intelligible only if inflected by "explaining adjective[s]" invoking that which is outside what counts as normal. For Lorde, the designations "blind," "hunchback," "crazy," and "Black" become the only available semantic vehicles into the ontological safe space of the extraordinary, where alternative ways of being can be articulated and validated. Using these adjectives, Lorde equates the body's form with subjective identity. Indeed, Lorde uses the devalued bodily characteristics associated with race and disability to represent any state or feeling that differs from the privileged norm. The material experience of always being extraordinary, of never coinciding with the normative requirements of womanhood or manhood is the fact of existence that shapes the identity Lorde creates in her "biomythography." The body is the source of both the freedom and the condemnation from which Lorde's mythic self, her own "third designation," emerges.

What is clear in this passage and throughout Lorde's "biomythography" is that difference, not sameness, is her principle of identity. Being outside the ordinary is both essential and emancipatory in her self-definition: she is a lesbian as well as "fat, Black, nearly blind, and ambidextrous," a cluster of attributions at once excluding and affirming for her (*Zami* 240). By claiming her extra ordinary body as the ground of identity, she repudiates the norms of "woman" and "man." Assimilation to the norm would be for her an act of self-effacement that would make her a deviant pretender. Instead, Lorde figures herself as inassimilable, so unique in body, birth, history, and behavior that distinction becomes the principle of her identity and her power.

Lorde's "third designation" is one manifestation of a figure sprinkled through African-American women's writings, a figure whose body bears the marks we think of as "disabilities." This figure's extraordinary body disqualifies her from the restrictions and benefits of conventional womanhood, freeing her to create an identity that incorporates a body distinguished by the markings—some painfully inflicted, some congenital—of her individual and cultural history. These disabled figures present a version of black female subjectivity that insists upon and celebrates physical difference. By flaunting rather than obscuring these figures' physical differences, the authors establish the extraordinary body as a site of historical inscription rather than physical deviance, and they simultaneously repudiate such cultural master narratives as normalcy, wholeness, and the feminine ideal.

I trace here a genealogy of this disabled figure—who might be more precisely called extraordinary—from its inception as Mrs. Hedges in Ann Petry's 1946 novel *The Street*; through more fully developed manifestations in Toni Morrison's first five novels, *The Bluest Eye* (1970), *Sula* (1973), *Song of Solomon* (1977), *Tar Baby* (1981), and *Beloved* (1987);[2] and finally to Audre/Zami in Audre Lorde's 1982 "biomythography," *Zami: A New Spelling of My Name*. Together, these disabled female figures gesture toward an antiassimilationist, politicized rhetoric of difference born of the civil rights and the Black Arts movements of the 1960s. Characters such as Morrison's Eva Peace, Baby Suggs, and Pilate Dead, and Lorde's Zami offer an African-American female self grounded in the singular body that bears the etchings of history and whose validation, power, and identity derive from physical difference and resistance to cultural norms. These women enable their authors to represent a particularized self who both embodies and transcends cultural subjugation, claiming physical difference as exceptional rather than inferior. Beginning with Petry's Mrs. Hedges, an ambiguous precursor in the modernist grotesque tradition, I examine here eleven figures and their rhetorical roles. Following Mrs. Hedges are Morrison's disabled women, Eva Peace, Marie Thérèse Foucault, Baby Suggs, Nan, and Pauline Breedlove; the physically marked figures of Pilate

Dead, Sula, Sethe, and her mother; and, finally, the multiply distinctive central figure of Audre in Lorde's *Zami*. In varying degrees, these figures each occupy the radical subject position Lorde terms the "third designation." In these revisionist narratives of black womanhood, the body as a site of history and identity is at once burden and means of redemption.[3]

Physically disabled characters appear with some frequency, but usually peripherally, in African-American literature. I focus here on the figures created by Petry, Morrison, and Lorde to reveal the shift in African-American literary representation from a modernist to a postmodernist mode, a change that parallels the ideological move of minority groups from assimilation to affirmation of cultural and ethnic differences.[4] Petry's novel, *The Street*, offers a modernist representation of disability that serves as a transition between the nineteenth-century sentimental novels I examine in the previous chapter and the postmodern, post-civil rights representation of disabled figures in Morrison and Lorde. While the sentimental fiction deploys a rhetoric of sympathy, the modernist mode invokes a rhetoric of despair, and the postmodern fiction enlists a rhetoric of celebration in representing disability.[5] All three are nevertheless rhetorics of protest in the shared political missions of exposing oppression, arguing for social justice, and supporting groups to whom it has been denied.

The earlier and more traditional uses of the disabled figure—Emerson's invalid, Melville's Ahab, the recipients of benevolent maternalism—exploit physical difference as a disqualifying trait, signifying vulnerability and subjection to external forces. As I suggest in chapter 2, disability is characterized as lack, loss, or exclusionary difference for which compensation is needed to achieve the equality justice promises. Within this framework, equality demands a sameness that casts disability not as variation but as deviance; compensation therefore requires advocacy by those who have normate status for those who do not. The sympathetic exchange that produces maternal benevolence can only exist, then, if disability is read as a condition that must be compensated for.

In contrast, the representation of disability I find in Morrison and Lorde—and to a degree in Petry—reflects a shift in the meaning attached to bodily difference that is consonant with the positive identity politics characteristic of the post-civil rights era, in which racial and gender variations are reinterpreted as differences to be accommodated or celebrated rather than erased or compensated for. This change in perspective on bodily difference can be traced historically from early legislation that compensated for disability in the workplace and the military, to the later legislation exemplified by the 1990 Americans with Disabilities Act requiring that disabilities be accommodated.[6] With their disabled figures, Petry begins and Morrison and Lorde develop a postmodern perspective of particularity in which physical differences—racial, gender, cultural, or sexual—are seen as politicized marks of variation that must be recognized and accommodated within a democratic society. The rhetorical framing of bodily difference thus moves from a politics of sympathetic advocacy to a politics of affirmative identity.

The Extraordinary Woman as Powerful Woman: Ann Petry's *The Street*

The conventions of naturalism structure *The Street*'s primary narrative, creating a modernist rendering of alienation and desperation.[7] Petry's "street" is a neutral—even hostile—world, bereft of transcendental signifieds, without the traditional ideologies of unity and meaning that could provide adequate tools for living. Rooted in racism and sexism, the novel's rhetoric of despair renders all characters except the heroine, Lutie, as modernist grotesques, of which Mrs. Hedges is the paradigm. Focusing on Lutie's unswerving journey toward disaster, *The Street* traces the failure of the dominant versions of True or New Womanhood to come to terms with modern, institutionalized racism and sexism.[8]

A subdued counternarrative can be extracted from this novel, however, by imaginatively reading Petry's physically disabled antiheroine, Mrs. Hedges. This character anticipates the positive identity politics that African-American women's writing articulates after the 1960s and tentatively begins forging a new, specifically black, figure of womanhood. The model of black female subjectivity that Mrs. Hedges inaugurates refuses the derivative cultural script of the patriarchal woman and instead acknowledges the violations and exclusions of the oppressed body. Defining herself apart from the conventional model of white femininity from which she has forever been excluded, Mrs. Hedges and her heiresses extravagantly claim the authority of their bodies as well as their individual and collective histories as the basis of their identities. This version of black womanhood is fully developed in the physically disabled figures created forty years later by Morrison and Lorde. As their prototype, Mrs. Hedges embodies not the rule, but the exception, testifying to the dialectical relationship between the subjugation and the realization of the black female self in modern American culture.

Mrs. Hedges functions as a foreboding and forbidding element of the deterministic environment that defeats Petry's spunky and earnest protagonist, Lutie Johnson. A "very black" woman of "enormous bulk," Mrs. Hedges is "so huge that the people [in her home town] never really got used to the sight of her" (*Street* 5, 242). A frightening precursor to Lorde's "powerful woman," she is "a mountain of a woman" with "powerful hands," whose strength and size violate the diminutive and delicate stereotype of womanhood and defy categorization. Mrs. Hedges is an inexplicable monster who seems to Lutie like "a creature that had strayed from another planet" (*Street* 237, 236). If Mrs. Hedges's hugeness precludes the femininity of which Lutie is the black type, it is her physical disability that definitely renders Mrs. Hedges Lutie's grotesque opposite. The reader knows from the outset that Mrs. Hedges has some mysterious, awful bodily condition that she hides by wearing a bandanna and staying at home, sitting at her window above the rest of humanity in the street. She operates as an ominous quasi-monster who evokes the Gothic and embodies the grotesque, conventions that create the sense of impending, menacing, impersonal fate characteristic of both naturalist and modernist narrative.

Not until halfway through the novel does Petry humanize Mrs. Hedges by revealing the story of her disability, the "mass of scars—terrible scars" covering most of her body after she escaped from a tenement fire by squeezing herself through a tiny basement window (*Street* 237). When Petry briefly shifts the omniscient narration typical of naturalism to Mrs. Hedges's perspective to explain her disability, the novel allows the reader some empathy and understanding, but refuses Mrs. Hedges any pity. Recounting the incident that has determined Mrs. Hedges's life and identity, the novel conceals her interior, just as Mrs. Hedges hides her scars from public view. We learn what she does to survive, but not how she feels about it. She appears chiefly through a normative perspective:

> When she walked into [employment agencies], there was an uncontrollable revulsion in the faces of the white people who looked at her. They stared in amazement at her enormous size, at the blackness of her skin. They glanced at each other, tried in vain to control their faces or didn't bother to try at all, simply let her see what a monstrosity they thought she was (*Street* 241).

Mrs. Hedges remains throughout the novel resolutely other, apparently unmoved, and finally inscrutable. As the grotesque, toughened embodiment of the brutal life dictated by the street, she inspires mainly "dismay" or "horror," leading Lutie to conclude that "[i]t would never be possible to develop any real liking for her" (*Street* 247, 239).

Nevertheless, a striking ambiguity in Mrs. Hedges's figuration suggests a possible oppositional subtext in which she is the literary foremother of the postmodern black heroines. Narrative comments such as "all those years [Lutie had] been heading straight as an arrow for that street," indicate that *The Street* is primarily intended as a narrative of social determinism in which the "walled enclosure" of racism and its institutions finally surrounds the heroine (*Street* 426, 430). Such generic constraints demand that Mrs. Hedges function as the disturbingly grotesque product of racism and poverty. Representing the unacceptable fate that the hapless heroine must endure if she is to thrive on the street, Mrs. Hedges—who offers Lutie the alternative of prostitution— is part of Lutie's oppressive social environment. As both the street's victim and its threat, Mrs. Hedges recalls Deb in Davis's sentimental prenaturalist work, *Life in the Iron Mills*, who also embodies the condition that novel criticizes.[9] However, unlike the ineffectual Deb, Mrs. Hedges not only remains unrescued and survives the street, she becomes its queen—precisely because she is the antithesis of the conventional Lutie.[10] Juxtaposing Lutie and Mrs. Hedges makes *The Street* not simply a fatalistic vision of racist, sexist society, but a feminist critique of conventional womanhood inflected by race issues. Moreover, viewed from this perspective, Mrs. Hedges allows us to explore her potential as a radically revised heroine.

Mrs. Hedges is precisely what Lutie is not: the perfect lady, a version of the nineteenth-century domestic heroine, cast out of the patriarchal home for which she was fashioned and abandoned in Harlem during World War II. Motherless and fortuneless, Lutie must make her way in the world, in the tradition of the heroines of nineteenth-century women's fiction.[11] Armed with beauty, morality, a spunky industriousness, self-reliance, faith in the American success narrative, and what Nancy Cott has called "passionlessness," Lutie is a granddaughter of the True Woman, the traditional feminine version of the self-made man.[12] Her only available cultural model for life is Ben Franklin, whom she undauntedly invokes in a paradoxical mantra of self-blame and self-encouragement.[13] Ready to sacrifice herself for the manhood of her son and her husband, Lutie is republican motherhood incarnate. In this sense, she is a modern version of Stowe's Eliza and kin to Phelps's exultant Perley Kelso. Writing in 1852 and 1871, an ardent Stowe and Phelps suggest that their model of womanhood will equip Eliza and Perley with the individual resources to triumph over all obstacles. Lutie, however, can never triumph in Petry's realm of implacable racism and sexism. Petry's vision nearly one hundred years later, in 1946, is much less sanguine, reflecting the universalized impotence and alienation so characteristic of the modernist aesthetic.

Each of Lutie's conventional feminine assets turns out to be a disastrous liability in the twentieth-century context of "the Street." Rather than evoking respect and admiration, Lutie's beauty compels the lust of every man she meets, inciting men to fight for ownership of her as if she were a piece of meat. Her idealized passionlessness makes their desire for and power over her a greater threat than necessary. For example, Boots, whom she bludgeons to death in a self-destructive moment of released rage, might have made a suitable lover if Lutie had been able to somehow accept his sexuality and avoid his coercion. Her Emersonian self-reliance and fear of moral contamination of herself and her son prevent her from bonding with women such as Mrs. Hedges's "girls" or anyone else who might help her negotiate life on the street. Lutie's adopted mode of femininity is so ineffective in a world shaped by racism and sexism that she literally and metaphorically cannot even read the signs in Petry's wind-whipped opening scene. Every act, every decision comes from the individualist sensibility that seems to Lutie the only coherent narrative of self, but that leads her inexorably toward ruin.

Whereas the street and its dangers are illegible to Lutie, Mrs. Hedges is almost omniscient. Instead of retreating because of her disability, she actively engages the world on her own terms from her window, refusing to "expose herself to the curious, prying eyes of the world" (*Street* 247). The opposite of sexually objectified Lutie, Mrs. Hedges has the gaze, a voice, and agency—the personally empowering elements that culture has persistently denied women. With her "rich" and "sweet, voice," she gently but authoritatively advises, manages, and connects with the folks on the street (*Street* 5, 8). Her "unwinking," "eager-eyed stare" clearly apprehends and comprehends both the street's squalor and its potential (*Street* 245, 68). Displaying no emotion but much generosity, she is the powerful "lady with the snake's eyes" that seem to penetrate people, reading their thoughts (*Street* 8). Both malevolent and benevolent, Mrs. Hedges uses her powerful body to rescue the defenseless Lutie from her predatory landlord and to regulate his sexual aggression thereafter.

Seeing without being seen, knowing without being known, staging without being staged, acting without being acted upon, the figure of Mrs. Hedges inverts the cultural choreography of gender so concisely described by John Berger: "men act and women appear."[14] In contrast, the guileless and exposed Lutie is ceaselessly the victim of both her inadvertent and deliberate attempts to capture the male gaze—for example, when she heads to Junto's bar for relaxation or auditions for singing jobs. Mrs. Hedges's body may be violated and shaped by her history of enduring racist and sexist institutions, but it is also the instrument with which she is able to define herself apart from the cultural script of womanhood that destroys Lutie. By juxtaposing these two women, *The Street* effectively dislodges the gender system's myth of the power and advantage of feminine beauty and the rewards of male devotion, suggesting alternative forms of female empowerment.

Anticipating Lorde's call for a "third designation," Mrs. Hedges repudiates the dominant script of femininity without falling into a masculinized mode. Instead, she establishes a woman-centered life and maintains a truce of sorts with the coercive male power that controls the street. In the brutal environment of racism, sexism, and poverty, Mrs. Hedges forges a community of women that figuratively and literally nourishes its members even while it is circumscribed by an inescapable power hierarchy that would grant her nothing but scorn. Outside of the sexual economy herself, Mrs. Hedges has set up a household of "girls" who manipulate the sexual exchange system to satisfy their own material needs. Above all, the figure of Mrs. Hedges insists upon the demands, restrictions, and obligations of the body. Because, as she notes wryly, "Mary and me don't live here on air," she begins to charge the young men who come around for sex (*Street* 250). Nevertheless, her relations to this prostitution and to Junto, the omnipotent white male who controls the street, are very ambiguous. Mrs. Hedges is in one sense utterly complicit with the dominant order that oppresses them all and is the ultimate threat to Lutie's freedom. Yet her actions are an adaptation to brutal adversity that allows her and the girls to make a life for themselves mostly on their own terms: choosing their customers, tending the sick, watching kids after school, and looking out for one another. Despite being—from Lutie's perspective—perversely compromising, threatening, and repellent, Mrs. Hedges nevertheless testifies with her indomitable corporeality to the grandeur and authority of "an absolutely incredible will to live" (*Street* 245). While Lutie's attempted inviolable self proves brittle and vulnerable, Mrs. Hedges refuses victimization, witnessing with her extraordinary body the abiding power of the violated self to endure injustice and yet prevail.

From the Grotesque to the Cyborg

Even though Petry's portrayal of Mrs. Hedges is one of qualified positive empowerment, *The Street*'s treatment of this character seems nevertheless to be dictated predominantly by the conventions of the modernist grotesque. Such a reading implies the grotesque might be worth exploring as a problematic yet potentially suggestive way of representing physical disability. The problem occurs when we employ an aesthetic category such as the grotesque in an inherently politicized critical project. When the interpretative framework of the grotesque's visual fantasies and extravagances is translated into the predominantly realistic conventions of literary representation and criticism, the grotesque becomes equated with physically disabled characters. Therefore, using the grotesque as an analytic strategy invites both critics and readers to view representations of disability through an aesthetic rather than a political framework. Aestheticizing disability as the grotesque tends to preclude analysis of how those representations support or challenge the sociopolitical relations that make disability a form of cultural otherness.

A full consideration of this representational dilemma requires examining the convention of the grotesque, an aesthetic category appearing as early as the fifteenth century and referring to ornamental designs modeled on Roman frescoes found in underground caves, or *grotte*. Opposing principles, such as human and beast, merge to produce supernatural forms that confuse categories and violate boundaries. Gothic manifestations of the grotesque are fantastic fusions such as gargoyles, chimeras, or mermaids. Hieronymus Bosch, of course, is the master of the demonic, marvelous grotesque. But the specific aesthetic category of the supernatural grotesque eventually became so generalized that Wolfgang Kayser characterized it in 1957 as anything capable of evoking human "estrangement," "radical alienness," or the world's "essential absurdity."[15] Migrating from architecture and the visual arts, the grotesque has been appropriated as a fundamental concept in modernist criticism and literature, where it is a fitting trope for the alienation and disorientation that define modernism. In fact, so taken was modernist criticism with the grotesque as a figure for the existential estrangement and rupture of meaning advanced relentlessly by its canon that William Van O'Connor argued in 1962 that it was the essence of American literature.[16] The restrictions of mimetic figuration thus transform the fantastic grotesque into the "abnormal" grotesque. The modernist gargoyle is the physically disabled figure, a metaphor for depravity, despair, and perversion. Depoliticized and aestheticized by the authoritative critical frame of the grotesque, the disabled body is perpetually read as a sign for a degenerate soul or a bankrupt universe.[17] The notion of the grotesque thus discourages literary critics and authors from a politically conscious perspective that might examine disabled characters in terms of minority culture issues.

The grotesque as a mode of liminality that blurs accepted categories is nevertheless suggestive for my purposes, as I indicated with the discussion of Mary Douglas's concept of anomaly in chapter 2. Geoffrey Galt Harpham defines the grotesque figure as "stand[ing] at the margin of consciousness between the known and the unknown, the perceived and the unperceived, calling into question the adequacy of our ways of organizing the world, of dividing the continuum of experience into knowable parts." Such a sense of the grotesque as "something illegitimately *in* something else" tends to neutralize alienation and repugnance and to highlight the potential for an iconoclastic liminality that can accommodate new forms of identity—precisely the project of the African-American women writers I consider here. Anthropologist Victor Turner contends that liminal figures occupy "a realm of pure possibility whence novel configurations of ideas and relations may arise."[18] Anthropologist Robert Murphy's ethnography of his own disability, *The Body Silent* explicitly recognizes the disabled category as a liminal social state. But while Murphy's social liminality robs him of status and tenable roles, Turner's notion of liminality as "pure possibility" can yield affirmative representational forms, such as Lorde's "powerful woman," that are unconstrained by conventional categories. Whereas Murphy's idea of liminality is restrictive, Harpham's and Turner's expansive liminality predicts figures such as the Bakhtinian disorderly body of the Carnivalesque tradition and the disabled women I discuss here.

By refusing with their very beings to conform to social rules and categories, the disabled women operate as embodied alternatives to the status quo. Their opposition to the dominant order is not intellectual; rather, it is an immutable ontological state. The perception of bodily lack, difference, and marginalization is recast here as a radical, affirmative state of alternative physical configuration particularized by history.[19] When a figure that might ordinarily appear merely as grotesque—like Mrs. Hedges—is thus reformulated through liminality, a sociopolitical perspective begins to emerge.

Mrs. Hedges's figuration as an ambiguous modernist grotesque opens the way for a postmodern representation of disabled figures that more fully exploits the potential of third designations and liminal identities. The most fundamental aspect of postmodern thought for the purposes of this analysis is its willingness—perhaps its demand—to relinquish the principles of unity and sameness in interpreting self and world. What I am calling postmodern here are alternative, affirmative narratives that do not depend on a faith in oneness or a range of valued concepts such as wholeness, purity, autonomy, and boundedness—characteristics of the ideology of unity that both sanction the normate self and generate its opposite, the corporeal other. The disabled figures in these novels explore narratives of the body in a post-normal world, similar to the "post-gender world" sometimes invoked by feminists, which upsets the traditional normal/abnormal dichotomy.[20]

The principle of unity undergirds the dominant discourse of normal/abnormal, expressed in ideas such as social Darwinism and the statistical conception of the norm, both of which arose in the nineteenth century. The notion of a human norm—Quetelet's *l'homme moyen*, discussed in chapter 3—that polices human physical variation both generates a unified community whose differences are effaced and defines an outside and inside. The concept of the norm that Foucault finds emerging in the eighteenth century thus characterizes bodies with the differences we call disabilities as deviant rather than distinctive. So while prodigious or "monstrous" bodies have always been a focus of human interest, the normal/abnormal dichotomy of the modern mind limits the explanation of differences to pathology. Although the idea of abnormality as an interpretive frame for physical disability displaced such rationales as divine punishment or moral corruption, the dichotomy of normal/abnormal nevertheless devalues disability rather than defining it on its own terms. Like "powerful woman," the term "disabled person" is oxymoronic because "disabled" nullifies the dominant version of personhood expressed in, for example, the Emersonian self-possessed individual.[21]

Donna Haraway's popular notion of the cyborg might serve as a theoretical prototype for constructing a self that can negotiate the incompatibility between "disabled" as physical fact and social identity and "person" as member of the human community. Similar to the grotesque-as-liminal but freed from its negative connotations, the cyborg is "a hybrid of machine and organism, a creature of social reality as well as a creature of fiction" that Haraway offers as a model for self in a postmodern world. As a hybrid, the cyborg breaks down a profusion of distinctions fundamental to the modern self, transgressing the boundaries between animal and machine, organic and mechanical, me and not-me. The cyborg makes it possible to imagine a coherent entity characterized by "permanent partiality," shifting multiple identities that Haraway calls "affinities," and the kind of "illegitimate fusions" suggested by Lorde's "powerful woman" or the self-canceling category "disabled person."[22]

Whereas the notion of a hybrid self might act as a guiding metaphor for those who consider themselves nondisabled, for people with disabilities such hybridization is often consonant with actual experience. The disabled person always fuses the physically typical with the physically atypical. The disabled body is also often merged with prosthetics such as wheelchairs, hearing aids, or white canes.[23] Disability is also sometimes experienced as a transformation, or a violation, of self, creating classification dilemmas, ambiguous status, or questioning assumptions about wholeness. All persons with physical disabilities thus embody the "illegitimate fusion" of the cultural categories "normal," which qualifies people for human status, and "abnormal," which disqualifies them. Within this liminal space the disabled person must constitute something akin to identity. According to the principle of unity, the disabled person becomes grotesque either in the sense of a gargoyle, breaching boundaries, or in the sense of a eunuch, one who is incomplete, not whole. But if unity is no longer the organizing principle of world and self—as the modernists lamented and the postmodernists celebrate—then the grotesque sheds its twisted, repugnant, and despair-laden implications and becomes a cyborg: the affirmed survivor of cultural otherness, ready to engage the postmodern world on its own terms. The paradoxes of body, self, and world that positivism sought to untangle with taxonomies and that modernism bemoaned with grotesques have become the stuff with which a postmodern sensibility explains itself and—paradoxically—constructs its meaning.

The Extraordinary Body as the Historicized Body: Toni Morrison's Disabled Women

Such hybrid figures repeatedly appear in Toni Morrison's first five novels, published between 1970 and 1987. Among other things, each novel elaborates alternative modes of self for the African-American woman. The successors of Petry's Mrs. Hedges, Morrison's disabled and marked women have changed, we might say, from grotesques to cyborgs. Each character discussed here functions as what Morrison has called "the pariah figure":

> There are several levels of the pariah figure working in my writing. The black community is a pariah community. Black people are pariahs. The civilization of black people that lives apart from but in juxtaposition to other civilizations is a pariah relationship. . . . But a community contains pariahs within it that are very useful for the conscience of that community.[24]

Marginalized by the exclusionary hierarchy of appearance commonly known as "beauty" or "normalcy," Eva Peace, Marie Thérèse Foucault, Baby Suggs, Nan, Pilate Dead, Sula Peace, Sethe, and her mother are all pariah figures whose place in "the conscience of th[e] community" is to probe the interrelations of identity, history, and the body. Each woman is excluded from the cultural center because of her deviant bodily marks or configurations, as well as by being black, poor, female, and—in some cases—old. While some of these women are central and others peripheral characters, all of them possess a narrative power, often associated with the supernatural, that far outstrips the marginal social status accorded them by the dominant order. Their "deformities," "disabilities," and "abnormalities" are the bodily imprints and the judgments of social stigmatization—rejection, isolation, lowered expectations, poverty, exploitation, enslavement, murder, rape. Excluded because of their bodies from all privileged categories, Morrison's pariah figures explore the potential for being and agency outside culturally sanctioned spaces.[25]

These characters enable Morrison's novels to represent a narrative of self that simultaneously embraces and transcends the individual and collective history of oppression. Although Morrison's novels certainly celebrate black American culture, they also insist that its very shape and spirit have been informed by the institutions, injustices, and resonating, devastating consequences of racism. Nevertheless, Morrison's characters are not victimized or demoralized, nor do they lead diminished lives. A scene from *Beloved* succinctly illustrates how Morrison represents the tension between the need both to incorporate the experience of oppression and to surmount it. The young heroine, Sethe, just escaped from slavery, is able to look with full horror at the young black men hanging dead in the sycamore trees and, at precisely the same moment, to recognize the arresting beauty of those trees. Refraining from reconciling those images, and thus attenuating the contradiction's force, Sethe embeds the disharmony in her memory for a lifetime. Sethe's refusal to allow either spectacle to cancel out the other, her sharpening of this paradox that potentially threatens all meaning and coherence, exemplifies the mode of being and knowing that Morrison represents as fundamental to the African-American self. This self affirms the human ability to survive pain, loss, and the denial of both self and culture without abridging experiences of passion, beauty, attachment, and joy. As physical witnesses to violations and oppression, the extraordinary bodies of these women act as a collective conscience by testifying to the power and dignity inherent in this specifically African-American narrative of self.

The prototype for all eight women is Eva Peace, the matriarchal grandmother who pervades Morrison's 1973 novel, *Sula*. Eva's leg has been amputated, perhaps on her own initiative so that she can collect insurance money that will feed her children. Like Mrs. Hedges's forcing her imposing body through the basement window to escape the fire, Eva's act of tough desperation both reshapes her body and guarantees her survival. All of Morrison's protagonists are in similar situations: they literally constitute themselves with a free-ranging agency whose terms are tragically circumscribed by an adversarial social order. Self-violation, however, is no concession for Eva or for Mrs. Hedges; rather, it is an act of self-production that at once resists domination and witnesses oppression's virulence. Eva differs from her fellow amputee, Melville's Captain Ahab, in that Ahab's amputation enslaves him in an obsessive pursuit of Moby Dick, while Eva's amputation frees her from poverty. Ahab's transformation is wrought by wholly uncontrollable external forces, while Eva's is enacted as a limited choice. Indeed, physical disability neither diminishes nor corrupts Morrison's extraordinary women; rather, it affirms the self in context. Eva's disability augments her power and dignity, inspiring awe and becoming a mark of superiority, a residue of ennobling history.

Morrison represents Eva as a goddess/queen/creatrix character, rich with mythic allusions and proportions, even though she is by dominant standards just an old, black, one-legged woman who runs a boardinghouse. Eva is a rewritten, black Eve, striding the realms of the ordinary and the extraordinary, a female version of the African-American trickster whose asymmetrical legs suggest presence in both the material and the supernatural worlds and signal empowerment rather than inadequacy. The trickster is ambivalence personi- fied, violating behavioral norms with outrageous antics and reversing cultural categories that make sense of the social order.[26] As a trickster figure, Eva transgresses the existing social order, opening up the possibility for a tenable narrative of the embodied self as unique rather than normate. Revising as well the Biblical myth of Eve's original sin, Eva creates a mythic narrative of the maternal grounded in physical existence—eating, defecating, dying, and the material, mundane demands of earthly survival. Her power encompasses birth and nurturing as well as death: she severs her leg to sustain her "beloved baby boy," Plum, whom she later immolates when his heroin addiction blunts the life she once gave him (*Sula* 34). Morrison rewrites Eve's apple as the meager three red beets that remain for Eva to feed her children after her hus- band abandons her to poverty. In short, Eva is a goddess, not of the Western spiritual order, but of the flesh—flesh made extraordinary not by idealization but by history. Her enduring body is both her identity and her ultimate re- source.

Eva's legacy to her world is sustenance. Not always benevolent and never sentimentalized, Eva provides food and shelter, the material needs of life. Eva is the "creator and sovereign" of a peculiar, rambling, incoherent boarding- house, filled with living, singing, addiction, and casual lovemaking (*Sula* 29). This "woolly house" is replete with trees bearing womblike pears in the yard and "a pot of something always cooking on the stove" (*Sula* 29–30). Directing her children, as well as a continuous stream of friends, boarders, and adopted strays, Eva reigns—much like Mrs. Hedges—over an unorthodox communal household from her incongruous throne, a wagon in her third-floor bedroom where she reads dreams and distributes "goobers from deep inside her pock- ets" to gaggles of children (*Sula* 29). Naming her own children and renaming others with a mystical and determining vision, Eva possesses, like Adam, the power denied Eve: to name, and thus to define. For example, she renames three very different abandoned boys she adopts "Dewey King," apparently recognizing that the bond of a shared name would enable them to emerge from rejection and isolation and to survive (*Sula* 39). Thus, in the liminal space of what Michelle Fine and Adrienne Asch have called the social "rolelessness" of disabled women, Morrison erects a rich narrative countermythology around the pariah figure Eva, investing her with the power and authority that the dominant order would withhold.[27]

The quasi-supernatural character Marie Thérèse Foucault, from Morrison's 1981 novel *Tar Baby*, resembles Eva Peace. Thérèse's narrative role is essential, although she occupies little space in the novel. Known on Dominique for her "magic breasts," the blind Thérèse is a former wet nurse for white babies and a washerwoman for the wealthy whites who control a nearby island (*TB* 92). Like Eva, Thérèse has mysterious powers; she is a caretaker, a trickster, and an Eve figure whom the narrator calls "a lying crone with a craving for apples" (*TB* 93). Like the blind seer Tiresias, Thérèse has the knowledge associated with the gaze, but without the sense of sight. With omniscience reminiscent of Mrs. Hedges's, Thérèse senses the stalking presence of Son, the novel's protagonist, weeks before any of the sighted characters become aware of him. Like both Eva and Mrs. Hedges, Thérèse unobtrusively manages the main characters from her position on the edge of society. She leaves Son food, enables him to pilfer the white people's provisions, and finally escorts him through the dark to his ambiguous destiny. A spiritual mentor as well, Thérèse coaxes both Son and her nephew to reconnect with their black culture, their "ancient properties," after they have been lured away by white culture (*TB* 263). Personifying the mythical, supernatural element in the novel, Thérèse is suspected of being "one of the blind race" who escaped slavery and currently roam the island freely on horseback, seeing with "the eye of the mind" (*TB* 130–31).

Thérèse vividly illustrates an essential aspect of all the mythical disabled women in these novels: her narrative prestige and power—both magical and material—are exactly the opposite of the position the real world accords such figures. Thérèse's extraordinary knowledge and authority within the mythic black culture contrast starkly with her powerless, inconsequential, and even invisible position within the dominant culture. To the whites, she is an intractable servant, poor, old, blind, uneducated, haughty, superstitious, ungrateful—and bad at English. Repeatedly fired, she is simply rehired by her employers, who do not even recognize her. However, being resolutely outside the dominant order gives Thérèse authority. She will not speak to the deferential black servants, or "acknowledge the presence of the white Americans in her world," or include them in her imaginative stories, or even simply look at them (*TB* 94). Such denials free her from the cultural perspective that would obliterate her. Blind and invisible to the privileged, Thérèse nevertheless senses the pulse and sets the stride for the black community that Morrison celebrates. By elevating the lowest figure on the dominant scale of human value to power and status, the novel inverts that hierarchy.

Beloved, the 1987 fictional exploration of the female self under slavery, features two disabled figures, limping Baby Suggs and one-armed Nan, whose bodies bear witness to racism's violations and to their own survival.[28] Baby Suggs and Nan—following Eva, Thérèse, and Mrs. Hedges—nurture, guide, and tend to the material needs of the black community from an effaced position of authority. After her son buys her out of slavery, "Baby Suggs, holy" establishes a kind of maternal ministry and community welfare center, similar to Eva's, in her intergenerational, female home, where "two pots simmered on the stove," "the lamp burned all night," and she "loved, cautioned, fed, chastised and soothed" every black man, woman, and child who passed through (*Beloved* 87). Until she is worn out by life, Baby Suggs is also a priestess of the flesh, leading the community in neo-pagan, outdoor ceremonies, rich with dancing, crying, and singing, in which she delivers potent, moving sermons imploring the people to deeply love their own flesh, their strong and worthy bodies that are broken, tormented, and despised by others. Afterward, she "dance[s] with her twisted hip the rest of what her heart ha[s] to say" (*Beloved* 89). Baby Suggs knows the significance of the body for black women: her flesh has been owned by someone else, her eight children have been stolen from her, and her disabled hip has quite literally reduced her value in the perverse economy of slavery.

Less developed than Baby Suggs, Nan, Sethe's early caretaker, also has the power to survive, nurture, and connect. Like Thérèse, Nan is a wet nurse; like Eva, she is an amputee. Nan is also a preserver of culture and history, telling the young girl Sethe—*Beloved*'s protagonist—in their vanishing African language the story of Sethe's birth, revealing that she was the sole child whom her enslaved mother valued, the only one not born of a rape and thrown overboard. Although Sethe never acknowledges it explicitly, part of her mother's legacy is the certainly ambiguous moral capacity to commit infanticide, a paradoxical power shared with Eva Peace.

Morrison creates another group of women whose bodies are extraordinary, not because of functional limitation but because of formal particularity, "disability's" other manifestation.[29] The first is Pilate Dead, born without a navel, who is a priestess and the maverick aunt of Milkman Dead, *Song of Solomon*'s protagonist. Like Mrs. Hedges, Eva, and Baby Suggs, Pilate is the matriarch of an unorthodox household, "a collection of lunatics," where mysterious arts of the flesh such as winemaking, potion-making, and lovemaking are practiced. In Pilate's house, three generations of women reign like the three graces or Eumenides, black goddesses who sought vengeance for crimes against family members (SS 20). Self-named, Pilate ceremoniously hangs through her ear-lobe her Biblical name ensconced in a tiny brass box. Just as Thérèse lures Son back to his black roots, Pilate and her housewomen entice Milkman with their Siren songs, but instead of destruction he finds a revitalizing connection with his history and ancestors.

Pilate's extraordinary body differentiates her from the other characters, marking her off in a liminal, often magical, space of possibility. Morrison de-scribes this effect in an interview:

> I was trying to draw the character of a sister to a man, a sister who was different, and part of my visualization of her included that she had no navel. Then it be-came an enormous thing for her. It also had to come at the beginning of the book so the reader would know to expect anything of her. It had to be a thing that was very powerful in its absence but of no consequence in its presence. It couldn't be anything grotesque, but something to set her apart, to make her literally in-vent herself.[30]

Morrison suggests here that a character's embodied difference enables her to "invent herself," to realize a distinctive identity apart from the canonical body that acts out conventional, white scripts. All these women literally em-body a principle of identity formation predicated on the extraordinary rather than the ordinary. Assuming much narrative significance, these women's bod-ies resist assimilation into a narrow category of humanness and challenge all exclusionary physical standards in racial and gender systems. By seeing all of-fers of either assimilation or tolerance as condescension, they insist that there is nothing into which they wish to assimilate, and there is nothing in them-selves that must be tolerated.

Similar to Pilate Dead, Eva Peace's granddaughter, Sula, is set apart by a dark facial birthmark that gives "her otherwise plain face a broken excitement and blue-blade threat" (*Sula* 52). Sula's physical marking is both the cause and the manifestation of her otherness. Suggesting her ambiguous position within the community, Sula's birthmark is interpreted by others as a snake, a tadpole, her mother's ashes, or a rose, depending on each character's position. As a rose, the birthmark alludes to the blossoms on the skin that early Christians interpreted as stigmatic marks of grace, and alludes to the African goddess of love, Erzulie, whose sign is a rose.[31] The serpent, of course, associates Sula with the biblical Eve and with her grandmother, the revised, black Eve. The way that Sula's birthmark becomes the anchor for someone else's narrative meaning captures the essence of how cultural otherness is produced. What the dominant order perceives as bodily differences act as depositories of meaning that serve the psychological and political perspectives of that group. Like the monstrous bodies of ancient and medieval times, Sula's body is a hyperlegible text from which her community reads its own preoccupations, fears, and hopes. The extraordinary aspect of her body makes her a spectacle among spectators, the point of reference for social boundaries. The body that violates the norm becomes a marked pariah and disrupter of the social order. In such a role, Sula enables "others [to] define themselves" by offering up her differences so that the group can clarify itself (*Sula* 95). Like the other extraordinary women, her body serves as "the conscience of th[e] community."[32]

Both Sethe and her unnamed, enslaved, rebellious, hanged mother have markings that map their histories upon their bodies, at once imposing identity and differentiating them from the unmarked. Sethe's mother's slave status is literally integrated into her flesh, branded on her as on a steer or a Greek slave. Her mouth has also been permanently fixed in a ghastly, ironic "smile," fashioned by the master's punitive bit rather than by her own feelings (*Beloved* 203).[33] With the dignified, tough pride of a survivor, Sethe's mother, in her only direct encounter with her daughter, brandishes her stigmata before Sethe as a means of identification, prompting the innocent child to plead, "Mark the mark on me too" as a bond with her mother (*Beloved* 61). Answered with a slap from her outraged mother, Sethe finds eventually that the legacy of enslavement provides her with her own inscription, a deep intricate scar on her back from the brutal beating that was the price of her freedom. Recalling Sula's differentiating birthmark, Sethe's scar is interpreted by others, alternately as a chokecherry tree and a wrought-iron maze. Sethe herself must decipher this memory-charged inscription, borne on her back and hidden from her own view, in order to fathom her history and quiet her ghosts. This ambiguous badge, at once a curse and a gift from her mother, represents their bond as well as Sethe's redemption from her mother's fate. As with each marked female character, Sethe's bodily reconfiguration is paradoxical, embodying simultaneously the terrible price demanded and the extraordinary character produced by her history and identity. The role of the extraordinary women is to preserve otherness and its meanings with the very shapes of their bodies and to sustain the communal body by nurturing and care. Their marked bodies witness the shared bond created by slavery and the differentiation each individual history has wrought. These women's bodies *re-member*: they recall and reconstitute history and community.

Morrison's extraordinary women emerge most clearly when contrasted with a final physically disabled female character who serves quite a different rhetorical function from the others. Pauline Breedlove, mother and wife of the brutalized and brutal Breedlove family in Morrison's first novel, *The Bluest Eye*, bears the label of bodily deviance and the markings of history, just like her successors. But Pauline does not display the authority, dignity, or quasi-supernatural powers of figures like Eva, Thérèse, or Pilate. Although Pauline is a washerwoman and caretaker of white children like Thérèse, has a disabled foot and a limp like Baby Suggs, and has survived poverty, abuse, deprivation, and animosity, she is never a priestess or mythical goddess figure. Instead of enabling other members of her community, she devastates them. Indeed, Morrison strips Pauline of precisely what she endows the other disabled women with. While they are empowered, Pauline is diminished, for she has desecrated herself by her complicity with oppression. By internalizing the judgment of inferiority handed down to her, Pauline betrays her own flesh and consequently that of her children, husband, and racial community. The stigmata of being black in a white culture, being a woman in a man's world, being poor in a rich society, or even limping through a world that idealizes physical ability do not diminish Pauline and destroy her daughter, Pecola. Rather, the convergence of circumstances, character, and choice that make Pauline embrace "ugly" and her role of "the ideal servant" with neither question nor defiance rob her of the dignity, grace, beauty, and love accorded the other extraordinary women (*BE* 34, 100).

Pauline is Morrison's sympathetic study of violations of the soul and perversions of potential perpetrated by racism and sexism. Her misplaced priorities estrange her from the sustaining community of other black women so that Pauline never hears sermons by the likes of Baby Suggs, eats in kitchens like Eva's, or even feels the validating solidarity of the whores who live upstairs. Bereft of such sustenance, she is tragically seduced into self-loathing, squandering her potential by finding her praise and satisfaction keeping a rich white family's house and loving their blue-eyed, blond-haired girl instead of her own daughter. With no sources of resistance, Pauline accedes to the destructive ideologies of female martyrdom, bourgeois respectability, Christian denial of the flesh, and romantic love. Such beliefs lead her to accept disability as imperfection, to idealize white physical beauty as equal to virtue, and to embrace the role of the ideal praise-lulled black servant in a luxurious white household. Much like Petry's Lutie, Pauline has embraced the cultural scripts all the other marked women have rejected. Her faith in these ideological sins against blackness, femaleness, and self functions in the novel as an apostasy that nullifies her daughter, Pecola. For this violation, Morrison denies Pauline one of her chief rhetorical emblems of empowerment: the inclusive, woman-centered, black home where she might have reigned as a priestess of the flesh.

Through resistance, Morrison's marked and disabled women deny the dominant standards that would invalidate their beings while they simultaneously create their own alternative psychological and physical order of self-authorization. These characters suggest a transformed social order, one that reconfigures value hierarchies, norms, and authority structures. This alternative domain emerges from a rhetorical juxtaposition of realism and myth. Susan Stewart maintains that realism depends on the rules of everyday experience and a shared interpretive framework; besides physical laws, it recognizes, and to a certain extent agrees with, the dominant social norms, expectations, and behaviors.[34] For example, the opening scene of *Song of Solomon*, in which Mr. Robert Smith attempts to fly, refers to and is interpreted by a shared cultural image of disturbed suicidal people perched on ledges above absorbed crowds. Such a presentation, along with Mr. Smith's splat on the pavement, confirms common everyday experience, the status quo. However, the realism of this scene is undercut by Pilate, bursting into song as she watches from below. Violating the social rules of the situation, Pilate disrupts the flow of the expected. Pilate is a figure of doubleness here: a bag-lady figure whose crazy action elicits the "realistic" snickers from the crowd, and the "powerful contralto" whose words are italicized and set off from the rest of the text, suggesting their authority and oracular status (SS 5).

Although realism dominates this scene, different social rules achieve a foothold. The novel offers an alternative reality peopled by the oddballs and throwaways of the dominant social order, those called Pilate and Guitar rather than everyday names like Robert Smith. Myth, according to Stewart's narrative theory, is a fictional strategy that is one step removed from realism in its referential relationship with everyday experience. However, it is close enough to realistic representation to sustain our identification with, and willing belief in, the fictional realm in a way that irony and metafiction, for example, do not.[35] Stigmatized within the prevailing social system to which realism refers, Pilate nevertheless reigns in the contrapuntal mythical order *Song of Solomon* proffers and validates. Indeed, the novel's protagonist is progressing toward this domain where, possessed of his black heritage, he defies the social and the physical order by learning to fly. The mythic context begun by Pilate's song renders Milkman's final gesture of flight a revision of Mr. Smith's splat and a release from the social rules that governed the opening scene and would erase black culture. The conventions of mythic representation in Morrison's novels distance readers just enough to recognize and question the ascendant social order as only one system for interpreting, defining, and ordering experience. Myth allows the novels to put aside the dominant perspective and to establish a space—like Eva's, Pilate's, or Baby Suggs's houses—where things are run differently. Morrison casts the disabled and marked women doubly, as the queens of the mythic realm that the novels privilege and as outsiders in the dominant order.[36] Like Eva as trickster, each woman is a mediating liminal figure with a foot in each domain, a spiritual and physical cyborg equipped to negotiate a fragmented world.

Inversions, Stewart asserts, convert into nonsense the common-sense, everyday world.[37] For example, several inverted names in Morrison's novels suggest a perceptual incoherence: in *Sula*, the hills where the black people live above the white-owned valley are called "the Bottom;" in *Beloved*, the farm where the central characters are slaves is called "Sweet Home;" in *Song of Solomon*, "Not Doctor Street" and "No Mercy Hospital" are nonsensical names that also parody the dominant license to name and thereby define (SS 1, 13, 4). Since the presumed everyday world of common sense is filled with the dominant, exclusionary perspectives, values, hierarchies, and norms, narrative inversions undermine the status quo by rendering it unintelligible. That this mythic counterdomain is ruled by poor, black, manless, disabled women is, of course, a fundamental inversion of the power structure based on normate privilege and status. Eva Peace perhaps best illustrates the rhetorical effect of such reversals. Eva's humble throne is a wheelchair fitted into a child's wagon, so low that adults actually must look down on her; nevertheless, the narrative reverses that perspective, giving her audiences "the impression that they were looking up at her, up into the open distances of her eyes, up into the soft black of her nostrils and up at the crest of her chin" (*Sula* 31). In this mythical realm, the reliable coordinates of up and down, high and low do not apply. Instead, the extraordinary is entitled and the ordinary is impotent.

This mythical domain inverts dominant hierarchies as well. For instance, these women's world affirms every aspect of the flesh, as if to undo Western culture's denial of the body and abstraction of a discrete soul. Baby Suggs's sermon on loving one's own flesh is the sacred discourse; caretakers of the body are powerful; sexuality is natural; nourishment is sanctified; and even the ghost in *Beloved* has a body. Moreover, slavery, poverty, and rape appear not as economic or even moral issues, but—above all—as violations of the body, never mitigated by ideologies of martyrdom, asceticism, or self-denial. This domain also overturns traditional ideas of the self as an autonomous individual. Personal power tends not to follow the master-slave model of ownership or control over others, but operates for the most part to enable, feed, shelter, nurture, and minister to members of the group. Cooperation, community, and connection replace the emphasis on individual achievement, competition, and possession. Finally, a matrifocal, intergenerational kinship system replaces the nuclear, patriarchal household structure.

But this alternative mythic domain is no utopia. Even while the novels authorize and validate this world, they surround the women's lives by a realist, adversarial social order that circumscribes both their actions and their relationships. Although few characters actually occupy the normate subject position, it is nevertheless pervasive, a ubiquitous force that relentlessly disrupts and limits the black characters. The slave owner, Schoolteacher, for example, appears only briefly in *Beloved*; yet the dreadful consequences of his acts reverberate throughout the novel, rupturing and distorting relationships everywhere within the black community. Even the arguably benevolent white men such as Valerian in *Tar Baby*, Mr. Garner in *Beloved*, and Pauline's appreciative employer in *The Bluest Eye* unwittingly inflict damage because their normate perspective and values are incompatible with the well-being of black people. The cruel paradox fundamental to Morrison's novels is that the destructive interlocking of racism, sexism, ableism, and classism govern her characters even while the characters have power to act within those systems. We see this delimitation of agency, for example, in *Sula* when Eva severs her leg to save Plum from hunger and later burns him to save him from spiritual starvation, and—even more strongly—in *Beloved* when Sethe turns back the slave master by slashing her baby's throat.

By insisting that the historicized body informs identity, Morrison recalls Leonard Kriegel's "Survivor Cripple," whose principle is that "self-creation is limited by the very accidents that give it shape" and that agency lies in "the will to manipulate that which has manipulated him [sic]." The women's disabilities and marks are either material traces of racism and sexism or the congenital variations upon which cultural otherness is built. These physical traces are a discourse inscribed by history upon the flesh of human beings, what Paule Marshall calls "life-sores."[38] The disabilities, then, are not metaphors for lives twisted by oppression, but the identifying, affirming, and valued manifestations of bodily uniqueness and personal history. The body is a text that the women insist upon interpreting themselves, even as they resist fantasies and fears others project on them. Recalling Mrs. Hedges, these women's individual and communal histories are emblazoned upon their flesh, evidence of dignified endurance and profound vitality.

The Extraordinary Subject: Audre Lorde's *Zami: A New Spelling of My Name*

Whereas Petry's and Morrison's disabled women tend to occupy the margins of their fiction, Audre Lorde's 1982 "biomythography," *Zami: A New Spelling of My Name*, places the marked woman and the claims of her body at its very center, making her the narrator. Describing *Zami* as "really fiction" that "has the elements of biography and the history of myth," Lorde consciously constructs a narrative self, purposefully evading the naive referentiality behind the idea of objectively chronicling a life.[39] Her hybrid genre, "biomythography," fuses the opposing discursive categories of "myth" and "biography" signaling *Zami*'s thematic project of creating an embodied identity that transgresses all boundaries. The Prologue describes the work's fundamental concern with bridging dichotomous, narrowly restricting classifications of self:

> I have always wanted to be both man and woman, to incorporate the strongest and richest parts of my mother and father within/into me—to share valleys and mountains upon my body the way the earth does in hills and peaks (*Zami* 7).

Zami thus begins with the premise that Audre's lived and felt experience is at odds with normative categories of identity. She speaks of herself as "grow[ing] up fat, Black, nearly blind, and ambidextrous in a West Indian household" (*Zami* 240). Although this description thwarts valued self-representations, Lorde defiantly claims it nevertheless. From the pages of *Ebony*, to the "wasting" expression of whites, to the favoring of light skin in her family, to the special classroom for children "with various serious deficiencies of sight," Audre learns from early on that her body is not only different but wrong (*Zami* 5, 24). *Zami*'s mission is to reconstruct the narrative of deviance carried by "fat," "blind," "lesbian," and "Black" to create a discursive self that incorporates the bodily traits and experiences upon which these terms are based, yet infuses the words with value, power, and fresh meaning.

For Lorde, rigid oppositional categories such as man/woman, self/other, normal/abnormal, and superior/inferior straitjacket her lived, physical experience. *Zami* vigorously resists such imposed definitions of the self, refusing to capitulate to self-erasure as Pecola Breedlove does in Morrison's *The Bluest Eye*. The autobiographical form eliminates the dynamics of sympathy and the potential for objectification that often emerge when a narrator mediates between the reader and a marginalized character like Audre. By establishing a subjective perspective centered on lesbian sexuality and cultivating outsiderness, *Zami* denaturalizes the normate viewpoint and protests its dominance.

Both invoking and retooling autobiographical form and content, *Zami* shapes a multifaceted cultural and corporeal otherness into a coherent subjectivity, grounding her narrative of self in the kind of "third designation" discussed at the beginning of this chapter (*Zami* 15). To do this, Lorde intensifies her subject's differences from the dominant norm, rather than muting them, and highlights those differences in the text. Hence, what we might term "the intensely other" becomes the self in Audre's narrative, challenging the cultural norms that would shunt her to the margins. Explicitly representing lesbian sexuality in a cultural context where heterosexuality is the norm becomes a method for contesting normalcy itself. *Zami* extends Petry's and Morrison's explorations of new forms of black female identity by even more intensely founding its definition of self on the extraordinary rather than the ordinary, on the exception rather than the rule. If her physical difference is the source of her social alienation, she also makes it the source of her poetic and erotic affirmation. Such self-authorization, Lorde insists, is a political and personal act of survival, a "transformation of silence into language and action" that achieves significant cultural work.[40] Thus *Zami* illustrates that identity for these extraordinary women follows the postmodern impulse of repudiating the normate master narratives, conjoining subjectivity with embodied differences.

Audre/Zami draws on the conventional forms of the *Bildungsroman*, *Kunstlerroman*, picaresque, and autobiography to build a positive self-representation as a black, lesbian poet. Her development progresses through a series of relationships with women, beginning with her foremothers and culminating with Afrekete, the black love-goddess figure with whom Audre affirms herself as a Carriacouan, woman-loving poet. By representing these relationships with women, including her mother, as both erotic and constitutive of herself as poet, Lorde connects word and body.[41] The biomythography is a surprisingly linear, teleological, picaresque, selected account of relationships with women that together form a response to the work's initial, structuring questions: "To whom do I owe the power behind my voice, what strength I have become . . . ?" and "To whom do I owe the symbols of my survival?" (*Zami* 3). *Zami*'s closing statement reveals that Audre's composite self includes aspects of herself recognized in other women. The biomythography fashions these encounters into a patchwork identity drawn from lived experience and open to alteration by subsequent relationships:[42]

> Every woman I have ever loved has left her print upon me, where I loved some
> invaluable piece of myself apart from me—so different that I had to stretch and

grow in order to recognize her. And in that growing, we came to separation, that place where work begins. Another meeting (*Zami* 255).

Lorde imagines this self-creation as a renaming—what Claudine Raynaud has aptly called a "fiercely active denomination."[43] She begins the transformation from Audrey to Zami with her insistence, at age four, on severing the *y* from her given name, Audrey, and completes it by invoking the biological fact that the body regenerates itself every seven years. This reformulation is cast as a somatic reshaping: letters are amputated and lovers leave imprints on Audre. The body that shifts from Audrey to Zami has supple boundaries; it transfigures and is transfigured by its history in a dialectic between body and experience that recalls Morrison's disabled women, whose bodies literally are their histories.

Moreover, Lorde's narrative departs from the master narrative of the self-determining, autonomous individual. Audre's self, produced by affiliation with a series of women, contrasts starkly with the cultural self articulated in Emerson's "Self-Reliance" or Thoreau's *Walden*, for example, which repudiates all forefathers and influences, seeking to develop identity through differentiation. Audre's profound physical departure from the dominant type perhaps makes this affiliation both necessary and safe in a way that it might not be for someone closer to the norm. In other words, sameness with the loved ones could become an affirmation rather than the threat of undifferentiating effacement. Perhaps the almost obsessive denial of conformity in Emerson and Thoreau is a fear of being obliterated by ordinariness.

Lorde employs a structuring scheme similar to Morrison's, interweaving a mythic narrative of self with a realistic narrative of selected life events. For example, the italicized voice of the poet speaks the text's mythic account in such lyrical passages as, "*Snail-sped an up-hill day, but evening comes; I dream of you. This shepherd is a leper learning to make lovely things while waiting out my time of despair.*" This poetry intertwines with prosaic chronicles of education, work, family tension, tortured adolescence, and sexual initiation, such as "I had sixty-three dollars in my pocket. I arrived in Stamford on the New Haven local on Thursday afternoon. I went to the Black Community Center whose address I had gotten from a previous visit the week before" (*Zami* 190, 122). Audre's last and most affirming sexual encounter consciously weaves the mythic and realistic perspectives, portraying her lover alternately as the poetic "Afrekete" and the prosaic "Kitty." Kitty, "still trim and fast-lined, but with an easier looseness about her smile and a lot less make-up"—is of the real world, while Afrekete comes "*out of a dream to me*" bearing "*live things from the bush, and from her farm set out in cocoyams and cassava,*" conjuring the goddess in each of the women (*Zami* 244, 249). So from the devalued girl, Audrey, emerges the mythical, "*Zami. A Carriacou name for women who work together as friends and lovers*" (*Zami* 255). Juxtaposing realism and myth blends robust social criticism with a utopian impulse, accomplishing in *Zami* precisely the same end as in Morrison's work: the mythic perspective dislodges the dominant viewpoint, opening a discursive space for imagining new ways of being.

Lorde's "biomythography" fully realizes Petry's tentative use of physical difference as a means to a positive-identity politics. While *The Street*'s Mrs. Hedges possesses both vision and voice, *Zami*'s viewpoint confers upon Audre a gaze and voice produced through the autobiographical form, not simply as an effect of content. Because Audre's consciousness determines the narrative perspective, *Zami* not only generates a discursive self, but also creates an entire world apprehended, spoken, and legitimated by that self. Whereas Mrs. Hedges must protect herself from the intrusive stares of others, including the reader, to whom her body seems deviant, Audre cannot become a spectacle of otherness because her voice and perspective constitute the text. Thus a narrating Audre can resist becoming a grotesque spectacle while still parading her difference as a mark of distinction, of identity: "I was fat and black and very fine. We were without peer or category and on that day I was conscious of being very proud of it" (*Zami* 223). In *Sister Outsider*, Lorde writes movingly about the problem of exposure, the risk of becoming a spectacle when one intensifies difference. Discussing self-revelation, she mentions fear of contempt or censure, but asserts that "we fear the visibility without which we cannot truly live;" the "visibility which makes us most vulnerable is that which also is the source of our greatest strength."[44] Caught between rage at being unseen and the self-protective impulse for concealment, Lorde uses the biomythography to discursively display the extraordinary body and to simultaneously disengage from the exploitative dynamics of spectacle. Thus, Audre/Zami's self-display exalts the extraordinary body and banishes all mediators, insisting upon a direct, intimate relation with her readers.

The Poetics of Particularity

Petry's Mrs. Hedges, Morrison's marked women pariahs, and *Zami*'s Audre explore a politicized model of embodied selfhood inflected by collective and individual history. This self defined by distinctiveness revises the model of the uniform self predicted by democracy's premise of equality. As I discussed in chapter 2, in a post-Enlightenment society the ideological power of the norm parades the marked body as deviant, subordinate, and particular and grants the unmarked body status, privilege, and universality. If the principle of equality encourages uniformity while the principle of freedom invites distinction, American selfhood is balanced on the tension between the desire for sameness and the longing for uniqueness. Consequently, in modern society the tyranny of the norm makes extraordinary bodies into freakish bodies, which both compel and repel the normate sensibility.

I want to suggest here that some writers influenced by the black civil rights movement and the women's movement found in the extraordinary body precisely the rhetorical strategy with which to express a notion of self that literally incorporated into the body the essential distinctions implied by racial and gender identity.[45] The problem of representation in a post-black power era was that if black was to be beautiful, it had to be distinguished from standardized whiteness. The figure of the marked woman offers a vehicle for representing the extraordinary body that contradicts, even insults the privileged normate body that claims neutrality yet enjoys higher status and constitutes the cultural center. Thus, post-1960s black women writers such as Morrison and Lorde use the extraordinary body in the discourse of positive difference so integral to their fictional perspective, while Petry's much more ambivalent portrayal of Mrs. Hedges, written in 1946, was created before a positive-identity politics was commonplace. For these writers, the extraordinary body is a physical testimony to individual and collective experience. At the same time, these figures are differentiated absolutely from characters whose undistinguished bodies grant them the cover of banal, often fraudulent, normate status. In political terms, these extraordinary bodies demand accommodation, resist assimilation, and challenge the dominant norms that would efface distinctions such as racial, gender, and sexual differences and the marks of experience.

These black women writers not only appropriate marked figures for nationalist cultural work; they also rescue the extraordinary body from its modern, deviant incarnation. The disabled women are not only the racialized bodies of positive-identity politics, but also nonconformity incarnate, the quality lauded in Emerson's and Thoreau's visions of an independent self. These figures regain the power subdued by equality's assumption of sameness in standardized, mass culture. In other words, Petry, Morrison, and Lorde recover the figure of the freak, which has fascinated Western culture in general and Americans in particular. But whereas the freak show colonized extraordinary bodies to establish the boundaries of the spectators' normalcy, these black women writers transform the marked women figures into prodigies, whose bodies hold the secrets of an empowering identity. As politicized prodigies, these figures are cast in the mold of the wondrous pre-Enlightenment monsters whose bodies were not seen as flawed but as distinguished and awe-inspiring.

It is not surprising that the cultural work undertaken by African-American women writers is reformulating the dominant model of self, particularly the female self. In her history of African-American women, Paula Giddings stresses black women's uneasy relationship with dominant versions of femininity, from the ideology of True Womanhood in the nineteenth century, the New Woman image at the century's turn, the fifties middle-class housewife, and the contemporary mainstream feminist. Black women have always, as a group, been excluded by ideology and economics from these roles, yet simultaneously judged according to them. As early as 1861, for example, Harriet Jacobs pointed to this double standard in her narrative of slave women's sexual exploitation: "the slave woman ought not to be judged by the same standards as others."[46] Similarly, the standards of feminine beauty, based on Caucasian characteristics, have made black women's assigned physical inferiority seem an inherent characteristic. Cast primarily as slaves, sexualized prey, and domestic workers, black women's bodies have traditionally been opposed to white women's, even while they are praised or condemned by the same standards. As if in recognition of this paradoxical snare, all three writers deploy the extraordinary women figures in response to the judgment of deviance that has been imposed on the black female body.

For example, Morrison's novels—the most extensive body of work examined here—both continue and significantly revise the tradition of social protest and advocacy to which the nineteenth-century fiction of Stowe, Davis, and Phelps belongs. Specifically, Morrison's novels revise Stowe's *Uncle Tom's Cabin*. Both writers' rhetorical aim is to grant socioeconomic and political equality, as well as status, to a group excluded by the dominant culture. Morrison both extends and amends this tradition, substituting subjectivity for advocacy, thus neutralizing the problem of benevolent maternalism that shapes Stowe's black characters in controversial ways.[47] Morrison's novels actually rewrite many of Stowe's black women figures, bringing them from the edges of the abolitionist narrative to the heart of the African-American-centered perspective at the political and aesthetic core of her fiction. Topsy, the unruly feral child accused in *Uncle Tom's Cabin* of "drollery" and "witchcraft," who claims to have a "wicked heart" and be "a bad girl" (*UTC* 20), becomes in *Sula*, the pariah protagonist who introduces evil not as an "alien force," but simply—as Morrison says—"a different force."[48] Stowe's disabled slave mother,

Hagar, who is sold off from her beloved son and disappears from the narrative, reappears as *Beloved*'s Baby Suggs, the disabled slave mother whose son purchases her freedom and who establishes a ministry and a woman-centered household. One of Stowe's black heroines, Cassy, who confesses to Tom that she gave her baby laudanum because she could "never again let a child live to grow up," (*UTC* 521) reappears as Sethe, whose act of infanticide is the incident around which Morrison constructs *Beloved*. Aunt Chloe, the devoted wife and servant whom Stowe celebrates as a figure of Christian domesticity, becomes Pauline Breedlove, who in *The Bluest Eye* reveals the consequences of the good servant role. Stowe's bad servant, the humanized but victimized Prue, appears mythically empowered as *Tar Baby*'s Thérèse. Finally, the harshest of Morrison's transfigurations recasts Stowe's central redemptive child-heroine, Eva, as *The Bluest Eye*'s interchangeable figures of "cu-ute Shirley Temple" and "Lovely Mary Jane," with the "Smiling white face. Blond hair in gentle disarray, blue eyes looking . . . out of a world of clean comfort" (*BE* 19, 43). Lovable Eva's destructive potential becomes clear when the Eva figure appears as well in *The Bluest Eye* as "the little pink-and-yellow girl" of the Fisher family, to whom Pauline Breedlove devotes herself while forsaking her own daughter, Pecola (*BE* 87). The idealized white girl child undermines and obsesses the docile Pecola Breedlove, who comes to identify with the seemingly innocent image that dooms her. Such transformations constitute a pointed cultural critique that emerges when subjectivity and centrality are shifted from white to black consciousness. Thus, Morrison at once continues and interrogates the cultural work of the nineteenth-century social reform novels.

Just as Morrison's characters allude to and radically recontextualize Stowe's, the extraordinary women invoke the image of the wondrous freak while fundamentally refashioning it. Both the freak and the marked women inspire awe with the profusion of difference their bodies flaunt. Both astonish ordinary and perhaps complacent onlookers, challenging their viewers' supposedly superior status by rendering it banal. But while the freak show stage decontextualizes the atypical body to intensify the spectacle of otherness, these literary representations accentuate the marked body's historical context, infusing the material body with social meaning rather than metaphorical significance, surrounding them with life rather than props. By connecting physical being with individual history and culture, the extraordinary women figures define the self in terms of its uniqueness rather than its conformity to the norm.

But even while the extraordinary women appropriate the marvelous difference of freakdom, they repudiate the visual objectification that makes the freak a grotesque spectacle. Petry's ambiguous rendering of Mrs. Hedges suggests that the spectacle is produced by perspective and context. By thematizing both Mrs. Hedges's refusal to be a spectacle as well as her insistence on spectatorship and agency, Petry begins to move the disabled body from object to subject. Morrison continues the process by using mythic representation charged with supernatural power and gender to show bodily differences as the traces of history and the marks of racial experience. Lorde's autobiographical form, however, most fully disengages the dynamics of the grotesque spectacle. Her "biomythography" is a kind of textual self-exhibition that emphasizes "the source of [her] greatest strength," the physical traits that the dominant culture most devalues: "fat," "blind," "lesbian," and "black."[49] Lorde appropriates the freak show's exaggeration of deviance to reframe it as distinction. Yet while the freak's distinction separates it from the rest of humanity, Audre's distinction operates as eminence encouraged by the identification inherent in the autobiographical form. We might say that Lorde invites the freak show viewer to leave the audience and stand beside the freak on the platform so that they can gaze together at the normates below with amused superiority and faint contempt. Petry, Morrison, and Lorde thus infuse the traditionally muted, static spectacle of otherness with voice, gaze, and power to act—all without normalizing the extraordinary body.

In *Sister Outsider*, her manifesto of feminist and poetic radicalism, Lorde claims that "the master's tools will never dismantle the master's house."[50] We have since found that ownership of power is much more complex than Lorde's statement suggests. I would offer that Petry, Morrison, and Lorde improvise, refashioning what is at hand for their own uses by alluding to the traditional monster, the prodigiously embodied figure that has been eclipsed and trivialized by the modern, standardized figure of *l'homme moyen*. Perhaps because racist discourse has so closely aligned black women's bodies with the monstrous and the freakish, such extraordinary figures are to these writers the found material from which to forge the politicized prodigies they empower. As prototypes for postmodern heroines, the extraordinary women they create are neither good girls nor ladies nor beauties, but cyborgian figures whose foremothers are the wondrous freaks, as yet undiminished by the containing discourses of modernity. Alluding to the unmitigated, essential physical difference of the freak, the figures of the marked women resist assimilation and compensation that would erase their historical specificity. Retaining the awe of difference but rejecting the objectification of staging, Petry rewrites the freak show's fierce "Amazon Giantess" as Mrs. Hedges turned upon the predators of Harlem. Morrison continues by refiguring "The Legless Wonder" as Eva Peace—regal, commanding, and fully sexualized on her wagon-throne.

Barnum's "Armless Wonder" becomes *Beloved*'s Nan, who imparts sacred stories and dispenses nourishment. Morrison also transforms "The Amazing Tattooed Woman" into Sethe and Sula, their flesh inscribed with mysterious, inscrutable signs of their uniqueness. And the exotic "Circassian Beauty" is in Morrison's novels the alluring Pilate Dead, guiding men to a nationalist destiny. Julia Pastrana, dancing Pepitas before her gawking audience in a grotesque parody of femininity, becomes Morrison's Baby Suggs, leading her renegade congregation in a sacred dance celebrating her extraordinary flesh. Finally, Lorde renders "The Hottentot Venus" as Audre/Zami: "fat," "black," "lesbian," and humanized by voice, subjectivity, community, agency, and sexuality—yet still fully corporeal and extraordinary in every sense.

Conclusion

· · · · ·

From Pathology to Identity

This book aspires to broaden and shift our current academic conversation about identity production and physical differences. While its primary aim has been to explore the ways culture represents and social practices construct disability, a related goal has been to highlight the role of the body in these representations and constructions. Introducing the idea of disability into discussions about constructions of the body demands confronting the relation between visible bodily particularity and identity. This requires neither ascribing categories of physical difference to a naive essentialism nor allowing constructionism to erase the materiality of the body. Instead, focusing on cultural representations of disability reveals a politics of appearance in which some traits, configurations, and functions become the stigmata of a vividly embodied inferiority or deviance, while others fade into a neutral, disembodied, universalized norm. Such readings of the body are the coordinates of a taxonomical system that distributes status, privilege, and material goods according to a hierarchy anchored by visible human physical variation.

Disability, of course, is not the sole somatic marker in this economy. Including disability in the discourses that constitute race, gender, ethnicity, sexuality, and class complicates the body's cultural construction and acknowledges that all physical existence is inflected by multiple narratives of identity, felt or attributed, denigrated or privileged. By focusing on the intersections of the various systems that order and demarcate visible physical differences, I do not wish to suggest that identities are interchangeable—that gender and disability are synonymous constructs, or that disability is a form of ethnicity. Rather, I propose that gender, ethnicity, sexuality, and disability are related products of the same social processes and practices that shape bodies according to ideological structures. What I have tried to uncover here are some of the complexities of these processes as they simultaneously make and interpret disability.

As I have suggested throughout this book, the disabled figure operates as a code for insufficiency, contingency, and abjection—for deviant particularity—thus establishing the contours of a canonical body that garners the prerogatives and privileges of a supposedly stable, universalized normalcy. The figure of the cultural self, then, in its refusal to be fleshed out, is the twin subject of this study. Moreover, within this cultural choreography the disabled body is a spectacle—sympathetic, grotesque, wondrous, or pathological—in a complex relation between seer and seen, between the opposing subject positions of the intensely embodied, reified, and silenced object and the abstract, unmarked, disembodied normate. I have attempted as well to historicize this dynamic between spectator and spectacle by examining the disabled figure in the context of American liberal individualism, the work ethic, and specific representational genre.

In analyzing three generic sites of disabled identity production—the freak show, sentimental fiction, and black women's liberatory novels—I hope to accomplish three things. First, I have tried to reveal how the interconnections among various forms of physical otherness operate in actual representations. My aim here is ultimately to demonstrate the fundamental complexity of social formations by historicizing and contextualizing those representations. In particular, I want to complicate any simple dichotomy of dominant and marginal social categories. For example, by considering the internal dynamics of otherness in texts that already claim a position outside dominant discourse, I hope to press our analyses beyond dualistic conceptions of identity and to discourage the current practice of balkanizing analytical categories in a kind of cultural and critical separatism in order to ensure legitimacy.

Second, the freak show, sentimental fiction, and black women's liberatory novels are genres in which the representation of disabled bodies is especially ambivalent and unstable. It is easy enough to chronicle the stereotypical uses of disability. Yet by focusing on the freak show's framing of the extraordinary body as at once wondrous and repellant, and on sentimentalism's combination of advocacy and repudiation, I intend to highlight further complexities in the relations between those who assume the normate subject position and those whose bodies are enlisted to define the borders of that identity. With this study, then, I not only expose the master narrative of physical disability as the mark of embodied otherness, but I also unravel a counternarrative of physical difference as the mark of distinctive individual or collective history that interrogates the very definition of the ideal American self.

Finally, my assertion that black women's liberatory novels revise both the freak show's and sentimental fiction's ambivalent representations of disabled figures suggests a bias that I wish to acknowledge. While I have historicized my analysis of Morrison's and Lorde's uses of disabled figures by recognizing the post-civil rights impulse toward positive-identity politics in their celebratory portrayals of difference, I must confess that my own politics parallel these black women's attempts to render physical difference as distinction, uncoupled from modernity's devaluation of the atypical. This book imagines seeing disabled bodies in fresh ways: as extraordinary rather than abnormal. The rhetorical thrust of this book, then, is to critique the politics of appearance that governs our interpretation of physical difference, to suggest that disability requires accommodation rather than compensation, and to shift our conception of disability from pathology to identity.

Notes

· · · · ·

1. Disability, Identity, and Representation: An Introduction

1. For example, two recent books that analyze "race" and "gender," respectively, as historical, ideological constructions legitimated by physical differences are Thomas Laqueur, *Making Sex: Body and Gender from the Greeks to Freud* (Cambridge: Harvard University Press, 1990), and Kwame Anthony Appiah, *In My Father's House* (New York: Oxford University Press, 1992), an exploration of "the idea of the Negro, the idea of an African race" (p. x). Disability has been acknowledged in American studies by Douglas C. Baynton's study of the metaphorical construction of deafness in the nineteenth century, "A Silent Exile on This Earth: The Metaphorical Construction of Deafness in the Nineteenth Century" in *American Quarterly* 44 (2): 216–43; by David A. Gerber, "Heroes and Misfits: The Troubled Social Reintegration of Disabled Veterans in *The Best Years of Our Lives*" in *American Quarterly* 46 (1994): 545–74; and by Martin Norden in *The Cinema of Isolation: A History of Physical Disability in the Movies* (New Brunswick, N.J.: Rutgers University Press, 1994). Disability studies is a recognized and articulated subfield of sociology that tends to emphasize medical anthropology, social policy, and rehabilitative medicine, although the voices of cultural critics are emerging here as well. Several important studies of the social, political, and legal history of disabled people treat disability as a social construction; for example, see Deborah Stone, *The Disabled State* (Philadelphia: Temple University Press, 1984); Richard Scotch, *From Good Will to Civil Rights: Transforming Federal Disability Policy* (Philadelphia: Temple University Press, 1984); Nora Groce, *Everyone Here Spoke Sign Language: Hereditary Deafness on Martha's Vineyard* (Cambridge: Harvard University Press, 1985); Stephen Ainlay et al., eds., *The Dilemma of Difference: A Multidisciplinary View of Stigma* (New York: Plenum Press, 1986); Robert Bogdan, *Freak Show: Presenting Human Oddities for Amusement and Profit* (Chicago: University of Chicago Press, 1988); David Hevey, *The Creatures That Time Forgot: Photography and Disability Imagery* (New York: Routledge, 1992); Claire Liachowitz, *Disability as a Social Construct: Legislative Roots* (Philadelphia: University of Pennsylvania Press, 1988); Iris Marion Young, *Justice and the Politics of Difference* (Princeton: Princeton University Press, 1990); Martha Minow,

Making All the Difference: Inclusion, Exclusion, and American Law (Ithaca: Cornell University Press, 1990); Robert Murphy, *The Body Silent* (New York: Holt, 1987); Lennard J. Davis's *Enforcing Normalcy: Disability, Deafness, and the Body* (New York: Verso, 1995); and Joseph Shapiro, *No Pity: People with Disabilities Forging a New Civil Rights Movement* (New York: Times Books/Random House, 1993). Many theorists and historians come close to confronting disability as a cultural product, but they do not question the category, perhaps because disability is so widely naturalized in Western culture. This omission has motivated my own study. See, for example, Michel Foucault, *Birth of the Clinic: An Archaeology of Medical Perception*, trans. A. M. Sheridan-Smith (New York: Pantheon, 1973); Mary Douglas, *Purity and Danger: An Analysis of Concepts of Pollution and Taboo* (New York: Praeger, 1966); Geoffrey Galt Harpham, *On the Grotesque: Strategies of Contradiction in Art and Literature* (Princeton: Princeton University Press, 1982); and David Rothman, *The Discovery of the Asylum: Social Order and Disorder in the New Republic* (Boston: Little, Brown, 1971).

2. U.S. Congress, The Americans with Disabilities Act of 1989, 101st Cong., 1st sess., S. Res. 933 (Washington, DC: GPO, 1989), p. 6.

3. See Nora Groce's study of the prevalence of hereditary deafness on Martha's Vineyard (*Everyone Here Spoke Sign Language*).

4. Marcia Pearce Burgdorf and Robert Burgdorf Jr., "A History of Unequal Treatment: The Qualifications of Handicapped Persons as a 'Suspect Class' Under the Equal Protection Clause," *Santa Clara Lawyer* 15 (1975): 863.

5. My repeated use of the term "figure"is meant to indicate an important distinction between actual people with disabilities and the subject positions "disabled" and "able-bodied" that culture assigns and that must be negotiated in lives and relationships. As products of cultural representation, figures reveal attitudes and assumptions about disability that make up the ideological environment. As I suggest later, there is always a gap between the subjective experience and the cultural identity of having a disability, between any actual life and any imposed social category. From this gap arises the alienation and sense of oppression with which people labeled as different must contend. It should be clear that this study focuses on the representations of disability that yield stigmatized collective identities, not the histories of actual people who have physical disabilities.

6. This term was suggested in jest by my colleague, the sociologist Daryl Evans, in an informal talk given at the 1989 Society for Disability Studies Annual Conference in Denver.

7. Erving Goffman, *Stigma: Notes on the Management of Spoiled Identity* (Englewood Cliffs, N.J.: Prentice-Hall, 1963), p. 128.

8. Paul Robinson, "Responses to Leslie Fiedler," *Salmagundi* 57 (Fall 1982): 78. For an example of disability analyzed as an apolitical metaphor, see Peter Hays, *The Limping Hero: Grotesques in Literature* (New York: New York University Press, 1971).

9. Schutz is quoted in Ainlay et al., eds., *The Dilemma of Difference*, p. 20.

10. Ainlay et al., eds., *The Dilemma of Difference*, p. 20; Sander Gilman, *Difference*

and Pathology: Stereotypes of Sexuality, Race, and Madness (Ithaca: Cornell University Press, 1985), p. 16.

11. Marianna Torgovnick's discussion of Homer's Polyphemus as one of the earliest Western tropes of primitivist discourse is suggestive here (*Gone Primitive: Savage Intellects, Modern Lives* [Chicago: University of Chicago Press, 1990], p. 8). According to Torgovnick, Odysseus becomes a kind of founding father of ethnography by reading the Cyclops's otherness as uncivilized and savage. Grounded in physiognomy, Polyphemus's otherness is figured as the monstrous state of being cycloptic (cycloptic fetuses are always stillborn). Torgovnick does not note that Polyphemus's aberrant physical form, not simply his foreignness, determines his otherness. In fact, this visible physical stigma is perhaps the most salient feature of the story. Moreover, Polyphemus's treatment by Odysseus seems to be justified because the Cyclops is inhuman, and he is inhuman because he is physically different from Odysseus. I would add to Torgovnick's observation, then, that the representation of Polyphemus can also be read as an early and definitive instance of physical disability as a sign of inhumanness.

12. Because most disabilities in literature are necessarily manifest, I discuss here visible disabilities. However, hidden disabilities present somewhat different and in some ways more stressful social encounters. The person with the disability controls the exposure of the disability in order to avoid undue surprise. Furthermore, a nondisabled person may reveal prejudices or expectations before he or she is aware of the disability, making both people feel uncomfortable later. A hidden disability simply introduces more unpredictability into an encounter. Sometimes a person will actually announce a hidden disability to avoid this uncertainty. For a discussion of interactions between the disabled and nondisabled, see Fred Davis, "Deviance Disavowal: The Management of Strained Interaction by the Visibly Handicapped," *Social Problems* 9 (1961): 120–32.

13. Murphy, *The Body Silent*, chapters 4 and 5.

14. A term that has much currency in the disability rights movement brings this point home nicely: people who consider themselves to be nondisabled are often called TABs, an acronym that stands for the label "temporarily able-bodied."

15. Elaine Scarry, *The Body in Pain: The Making and Unmaking of the World* (New York: Oxford University Press, 1985), pp. 3–10.

16. The cultural propensity to further mark and bound such classifications testifies to their fluidity and socially constructed character. Miscegenation laws, legal definitions of slaves, laws that defined disability for economic assistance, gendered dress codes, and customs such as branding slaves, criminals, and paupers erect boundaries around social categories in order to maintain and enforce distinctions purported to inhere in the body. The yellow star and the scarlet letter are familiar socially mandated marks of deviance that witness the need to absolutely mark what is in fact biologically unstable.

17. The important exceptions to this generalized portrayal of disabled people's situations are the communities that arise from institutionalization. Like ethnic ghettoes, these communities are often sites of both solidarity and exclusion. Deaf schools and

their surrounding communities, based on common language, seem to function more like ethnic communities in building positive identities and self-concepts. Perhaps this is due to the difference between the profound isolation deaf signers experience in a speaking population and the contrasting opportunities available in a community of signers. For discussions of disability communities, see Irving Kenneth Zola, *Missing Pieces: A Chronicle of Living with a Disability* (Philadelphia: Temple University Press, 1982); Oliver Sacks, *Seeing Voices: A Journey into the World of the Deaf* (Berkeley: University of California Press, 1989); Tom Humphreys and Carol Paden, *Deaf in America: Voices from a Culture* (Cambridge: Harvard University Press, 1988).

18. Martin Norden's *The Cinema of Isolation* explores images of disability in film; cultural studies essays on disability are also collected in Lennard J. Davis, ed., *The Disability Studies Reader* (New York: Routledge, 1996). Davis's *Enforcing Normalcy* lays out a humanities-based theory of disability.

19. Hevey, *The Creatures That Time Forgot*, p. 53.

2. Theorizing Disability

1. See Patricia Vertinsky, "Exercise, Physical Capability, and the Eternally Wounded Woman in Late Nineteenth-Century North America," *Journal of Sport History* 14 (1):7; Thorstein Veblen, *The Theory of the Leisure Class* (1899; reprint, Boston: Houghton Mifflin, 1973); Jane Flax, *Thinking Fragments: Psychoanalysis, Feminism, and Postmodernism in the Contemporary West* (Berkeley: University of California Press, 1990), p. 136.

2. Aristotle, *Generation of Animals*, trans. A. L. Peck (Cambridge: Harvard University Press, 1944), Book II, p. 175 and Book IV, p. 401. For discussions of Aristotle's conflation of femaleness with monstrosity and deformity, see Maryanne Cline Horowitz, "Aristotle and Women," *Journal of the History of Biology* 9 (1976): 183–213; Nancy Tuana, *The Less Noble Sex: Scientific, Religious, and Philosophical Conceptions of Woman's Nature* (Bloomington: Indiana University Press, 1993); and Marie-Hélène Huet, *Monstrous Imagination* (Cambridge: Harvard University Press, 1993). Edwin Schur examines the assignment of deviance in *Labeling Women Deviant: Gender, Stigma, and Social Control* (Philadelphia: Temple University Press, 1983).

3. For discussions of the notion of woman as an inferior version of man, see Thomas Laquer, *Making Sex*, and Nancy Tuana, *The Less Noble Sex*. For a discussion of whiteness, see David Roediger, *The Wages of Whiteness* (New York: Verso, 1991) and Richard Dyer, *The Matter of Images: Essays on Representation* (New York: Routledge, 1993). For a seminal discussion of the normal-pathological dichotomy, see Georges Canguilhem, *The Normal and the Pathological*, trans. Carolyn R. Fawcett with Robert S. Cohen (New York: Zone Books, 1989).

4. Examples are Diane Price Herndl and Robyn Warhol, *Feminisms* (New Brunswick: Rutgers University Press, 1991); Marianne Hirsch and Evelyn Fox Keller, eds., *Conflicts in Feminism* (New York: Routledge, 1990). "Hyphenated feminism" is

used by Judith Grant, *Fundamental Feminism: Contesting the Core Concepts of Feminist Theory* (New York: Routledge, 1993), p. 3; Brigitta Boucht et al., *Postfeminism* (Esbo, Finland: Draken, 1991).

5. A good overview of the history of academic feminist theory is Elizabeth Weed, "Introduction: Terms of Reference," in Elizabeth Weed, ed., *Coming to Terms: Feminism, Theory, Politics* (New York: Routledge, 1989), pp. ix–xxxi. For discussion of these debates and bifurcations in feminism, see Linda Alcoff, "Cultural Feminism Versus Post-Structuralist Feminism: The Identity Crisis in Feminist Theory," *Signs* 13 (3): 405–36; Hester Eisenstein, *Contemporary Feminist Thought* (Boston: G. K. Hall, 1983); and Josephine Donovan, *Feminist Theory* (New York: Continuum, 1992). Early analyses of gender identity include Elizabeth V. Spelman, *Inessential Woman: Problems of Exclusion in Feminist Thought* (Boston: Beacon, 1988) and Monique Wittig, "The Straight Mind," *Feminist Issues* 1 (1): 101–10. Diana Fuss, *Essentially Speaking: Feminism, Nature, and Difference* (New York: Routledge, 1989) deconstructs the opposition of essentialism, often associated with cultural feminism, and constructionism, often associated with radical feminism. Judith Butler's *Gender Trouble: Feminism and the Subversion of Identity* (New York: Routledge, 1990) and *Bodies That Matter: On the Discursive Limits of "Sex"* (New York: Routledge, 1993) most fully articulates the constructionist approach to gender.

6. Feminist texts that announce themselves as postmodernist and materialist often take the positions I am outlining here; some examples are Susan Bordo, *Unbearable Weight: Feminism, Western Culture, and the Body* (Berkeley: University of California Press, 1993); Rosemary Hennessy, *Materialist Feminism and the Politics of Discourse* (New York: Routledge, 1993); Jennifer Wicke, "Celebrity Material: Materialist Feminism and the Culture of Celebrity," *South Atlantic Quarterly* 93 (4): 751–78; Judith Grant, *Fundamental Feminism*; Linda Nicholson, ed., *Feminism/Postmodernism* (New York: Routledge, 1990).

7. Most theorists of disability either naturalize it while protesting exclusion and oppression of disabled people, or adopt a strict social constructionist perspective to claim equality while asserting difference in order to establish identity. For an example of the former, see the collection of essays by Harold E. Yuker, ed., *Attitudes Toward Persons with Disabilities* (New York: Springer, 1988); an example of the latter can be found in Harlan Hahn, "Can Disability Be Beautiful?" *Social Policy* (Fall 1988): 26–31.

8. Eve Kosofsky Sedgwick, *Epistemology of the Closet* (Berkeley: University of California Press, 1990), p. 1.

9. For discussions of this problem, see Susan Bordo, "Feminism, Postmodernism, and Gender Skepticism," in *Unbearable Weight*, pp. 215–43; Judith Butler, *Bodies That Matter*; and Betsy Erkkila, "Ethnicity, Literary Theory, and the Grounds of Resistance," *American Quarterly* 47 (4): 563–94.

10. For an example, see Monique Wittig, "The Straight Mind."

11. For histories of civil rights legislation for people with disabilities, see Joseph Shapiro, *No Pity*; Claire Liachowitz, *Disability as a Social Construct*; and Richard

Scotch, *From Good Will to Civil Rights*. An anecdote illustrates that disabled people are only now gaining physical access: On September 6, 1995, the Modern Language Association headquarters in New York completed the building of a wheelchair ramp minutes before the arrival of a delegation of members who had been invited to discuss disability issues with the MLA's executive director. Although the MLA is a very progressive institution willing to recognize disability issues, apparently the fundamental problem of accessibility had never been addressed before. For more discussions of disability as a civil rights rather than as a pity issue, see Paul Longmore, "Conspicuous Contribution and American Cultural Dilemmas: Telethons, Virtue, and Community," forthcoming in David Mitchell and Sharon Snyder, eds., *Storylines and Lifelines: Narratives of Disability in the Humanities*. The problem of how to accommodate difference is addressed in many areas of feminist theory. Most often it appears as a critique of liberalism like the one later in this chapter. For a concise discussion of this problem, see the introduction and conclusion to Carole Pateman and Elizabeth Gross, eds., *Feminist Challenges: Social and Political Theory* (Boston: Northeastern University Press, 1986); also see, for example, Carole Pateman, *The Sexual Contract* (Stanford: Stanford University Press, 1988); Jean Bethke Elsthain, *Public Man, Private Woman: Women in Social and Political Thought* (Princeton: Princeton University Press, 1981); Iris Marion Young, *Justice and the Politics of Difference*; and Martha Minow, *Making All the Difference*.

12. Diana Fuss in *Essentially Speaking* examines this tension between constructionist and essentialist concepts of identity, concluding that to deconstruct identity is not to deny categories, but rather to expose their fictionality while using them to establish community. Benedict Anderson suggests the strategic aspect of such communities for political and psychological purposes in *Imagined Communities: Reflections on the Origin and Spread of Nationalism* (New York: Verso, 1991). I support here as well Judith Butler's subtle but significant point in *Bodies That Matter* that the social construction of the body does not simply overlay meaning on physical entities, but that culture actually creates bodies. Also see Susan Bordo, *Unbearable Weight*, quotation at p. 229.

13. This questioning of identity and focusing on difference has been analyzed using the feminist epistemological modes called perspectivism in Ellen Messer-Davidow, "The Philosophical Bases of Feminist Literary Criticism," *New Literary History: A Journal of Theory and Interpretation* 19 (1): 65–103; standpoint theory in Patricia Hill Collins, *Black Feminist Thought: Knowledge, Consciousness, and the Politics of Empowerment* (Boston: Unwin Hyman, 1990) and Bettina Aptheker, *Tapestries of Life: Women's Work, Women's Consciousness, and the Meaning of Daily Experience* (Amherst: University of Massachusetts Press, 1989); and positionality in Linda Alcoff, "Cultural Feminism Versus Post-Structuralist Feminism." However, standpoint theory has recently been criticized by Judith Grant in *Fundamental Feminism* as fragmenting the feminist communal project and risking a degeneration of feminism into individualism. Elizabeth Fox-Genovese also assails the tendency in recent feminist thought to sacri-

fice the benefits of community and shared culture for the sake of individuality in *Feminism Without Illusions* (Chapel Hill: University of North Carolina Press, 1991).

14. See Collins, *Black Feminist Thought,* and Rosemarie Garland Thomson, "Redrawing the Boundaries of Feminist Disability Studies," *Feminist Studies* 20 (Fall 1994): 583–95.

15. Nancy Mairs, "On Being a Cripple," in *Plaintext: Essays* (Tucson: University of Arizona Press, 1986), quotation at p. 90. For a discussion of my own concerns about focusing on pain and dysfunction in disability discourse, see Thomson, "Redrawing the Boundaries of Feminist Disability Studies," in which I reflect on Mairs's elaboration of the critical subgenre she calls "The Literature of Catastrophe."

16. Hahn's comment is quoted from a personal conversation. The anecdote about the wheelchair user is from Fred Davis, "Deviance Disavowal," p. 124. Michelle Fine and Adrienne Asch, "Disabled Women: Sexism without the Pedestal," in Mary Jo Deegan and Nancy A. Brooks, eds., *Women and Disability: The Double Handicap* (New Brunswick, N.J.: Transaction Books, 1985), pp. 6–22, quotation at p.12. Cheryl Marie Wade, "I Am Not One of the," *MS.* 11 (3): 57.

17. Anita Silvers, "Reconciling Equality to Difference: Caring (f)or Justice for People with Disabilities," *Hypatia* 10 (1). For a critique of the feminization of caring for the disabled, see Barbara Hillyer, *Feminism and Disability* (Norman: University of Oklahoma Press, 1993); for discussions of the ethic of care, see Nel Noddings, *Caring: A Feminine Approach to Ethics and Moral Education* (Berkeley: University of California Press, 1984) and Eva Feder Kittay and Diana T. Meyers, *Women and Moral Theory* (Totowa, N.J.: Rowman and Littlefield, 1987). Although cultural feminism tends to view motherhood as less oppressive than do early liberal feminists such as Shulamith Firestone (*The Dialectic of Sex: The Case for Feminist Revolution* [New York: Morrow, 1970]), motherhood nevertheless is most often cast as a choice, but this choice is denied to some women on the basis of cultural prejudices; see Michelle Fine and Adrienne Asch, eds., *Women with Disabilities: Essays in Psychology, Culture, and Politics* (Philadelphia: Temple University Press, 1988), pp. 12–23.

18. Regarding the feminist position on "defective" fetuses, a recent example that supports my point is the new Maryland abortion legislation, hailed in the March 4, 1991, issue of *Time* magazine as a "feminist victory," in which unconditional abortion is permitted until fetal viability, but after that point, only if a woman's health is endangered or if the fetus is "deformed" (p. 53). I am not suggesting abortion restrictions here; rather, I am questioning the myth of "free choice" regarding bearing congenitally disabled infants in a society in which attitudes about the disabled tend to be negative, oppressive, and unexamined. Disabled people simply need advocates who will examine the cultural ideology inherent in these rationales and policies. For discussions of the issue of disability in relation to abortion and reproductive rights, see Ruth Hubbard, "Who Should and Should Not Inhabit the World," in Ruth Hubbard, ed., *The Politics of Women's Biology* (New Brunswick, N.J.: Rutgers University Press, 1990); Marsha Saxton, "Born and Unborn: The Implications of Reproductive Technologies for People

with Disabilities," in Rita Arditti, Renate Duell Klein, and Shelley Minden, eds., *Test-Tube Women: What Future for Motherhood?* (Boston: Pandora, 1984), pp. 298–312; and Anne Finger, "Claiming All of Our Bodies: Reproductive Rights and Disability," in Arditti et al., eds., *Test-Tube Women*, pp. 281–96; Fine and Asch, eds., *Women with Disabilities*, esp. chapters 12 and 13; and Deborah Kaplan, "Disability Rights Perspectives on Reproductive Technologies and Public Policy," in Sherrill Cohen and Nadine Taub, eds., *Reproductive Laws for the 1990s* (Totowa, N.J.: Humana Press, 1989), pp. 241–47. For discussions of ageism in feminism, see Shulamit Reinharz, "Friends or Foes: Gerontological and Feminist Theory," *Women's Studies International Forum* 9 (5): 503–14; and Barbara McDonald and Cynthia Rich, *Look Me in the Eye: Old Women, Aging, and Ageism* (San Francisco: Spinsters, Ink., 1983).

19. Susan Bordo argues in a similar vein that the feminist search for equality has caused a flight from gender, and hence from the body, that often masquerades as "professionalism." Disabled women's inability to fit the standardized image of the "professional" often alienates them from feminists who enter the workplace on such terms. See Bordo, *Unbearable Weight*, pp. 229–33; for a discussion of this point, also see Fine and Asch, eds., *Women with Disabilities*, pp. 26–31.

20. Personal conversation, Society for Disability Studies Annual Meeting, June 1991, Denver, Colorado.

21. The philosopher Iris Marion Young argues for the construction of femininity as disability by asserting that cultural objectification inhibits women from using their bodies. "Women in a sexist society are physically handicapped," concludes Young in the essay "Throwing Like a Girl" (*Throwing Like a Girl and Other Essays in Feminist Philosophy and Social Theory* [Bloomington: Indiana University Press, 1990], p. 153). For discussions of foot binding, scarification, clitoridectomy, and corseting, see Mary Daly, *Gyn/ecology: The Metaethics of Radical Feminism* (Boston: Beacon, 1978) and Barbara Ehrenreich and Deirdre English, *For Her Own Good: 150 Years of the Experts' Advice to Women* (Garden City, NY: Anchor Books, 1979). For discussions of anorexia, hysteria, and agoraphobia, see Susan Bordo, *Unbearable Weight*; Kim Chernin, *The Hungry Self: Women, Eating, and Identity* (New York: Times Books, 1985) and *The Obsession: Reflections on the Tyranny of Slenderness* (New York: Harper & Row, 1981); and Susie Orbach, *Fat Is a Feminist Issue: The Anti-Diet Guide to Permanent Weight Loss* (New York: Paddington Press, 1978) and *Hunger Strike: The Anorectic's Struggle as a Metaphor for Our Age* (New York: Norton, 1986).

22. Susan Sontag, *Illness as Metaphor* (New York: Farrar, Straus, and Giroux, 1977). For cultural critiques of beauty standards, see Lois W. Banner, *American Beauty* (New York: Knopf, 1983); Robin Tolmach Lakoff and Raquel L. Scherr, *Face Value: The Politics of Beauty* (Boston: Routledge, 1984); Naomi Wolf, *The Beauty Myth: How Images of Beauty Are Used Against Women* (New York: Morrow, 1991); Sharon Romm, *The Changing Face of Beauty* (St. Louis: Mosby-Year Book, 1992); Rita Jackaway Freedman, *Beauty Bound* (Lexington, Mass.: Lexington Books, 1986); Susan Bordo, *Un-*

bearable Weight, esp. Part II; and Susan Faludi, *Backlash: The Undeclared War Against American Women* (New York: Crown, 1991).

23. This language comes from advertising for cosmetic surgery in *Newsweek* magazine, although it can be found in almost any of the many ads or articles in women's magazines. One is reminded here of Foucault's "docile bodies" described in *Discipline and Punish: The Birth of the Prison*, trans. Alan Sheridan (New York: Vintage, 1979), pp. 135–69. For discussions of cosmetic surgery, see Kathryn Pauly Morgan, "Women and the Knife: Cosmetic Surgery and the Colonization of Women's Bodies," *Hypatia* 6 (3): 25–53; Anne Balsamo, "On the Cutting Edge: Cosmetic Surgery and the Technological Production of the Gendered Body," *Camera Obscura* 28 (Jan. 1992): 207–36; and Kathy Davis, *Reshaping the Female Body: The Dilemma of Cosmetic Surgery* (New York: Routledge: 1995).

24. Mary Russo's *The Female Grotesque: Risk, Excess, and Modernity* (New York: Routledge, 1994) observes what she calls "the normalization of feminism," which involves "strategies of reassurance" that encourage feminists to focus on standard forms of femininity and avoid what she calls "the grotesque," which I might term the "abnormal."

25. Gilman, *Difference and Pathology*, p. 90.

26. On reevaluating and expanding stigma theory, see Ainlay et al., eds., *The Dilemma of Difference*; Robert Bogdan and Steven Taylor, "Toward a Sociology of Acceptance: The Other Side of the Study of Deviance," *Social Policy* 18 (2): 34–39; also Adrienne Asch and Michelle Fine, eds. "Moving Beyond Stigma," *Journal of Social Issues*, 44 (1); Simone de Beauvoir, *The Second Sex*, trans. H. M. Parshley (1952; reprint, New York: Vintage, 1974), p. xix.

27. Edward E. Jones et al., *Social Stigma: The Psychology of Marked Relationships* (New York: Freeman, 1984), pp. 8–9.

28. See Ainlay et al., eds., *The Dilemma of Difference*, p. 212.

29. Schutz is quoted in Ainlay et al., eds., *The Dilemma of Difference*, p. 20; Goffman, *Stigma*, p. 4.

30. Goffman, *Stigma*, quotation at p. 128. Because perception rather than actual physical characteristics governs stigmatization and distribution of power, many people seek to normalize their social status, either by disavowing potentially stigmatizing conditions by "passing" or by compensating for them in some way. Nevertheless, the psychological costs of passing are often isolation and a self-loathing denial, as Audre Lorde shows in *Sister Outsider* (Trumansburg, N.Y.: The Crossing Press, 1984). The familiar script of racial passing translates to disability; for example, Franklin Roosevelt escaped the marginalized status disability usually confers, because he had the resources to minimize his disability in public and also because he possessed virtually every other normate characteristic. See Hugh Gallagher, *FDR's Splendid Deception* (New York: Dodd Mead, 1985).

31. Julia Kristeva's psychoanalytical theory of abjection is conceptually similar to stigma theory and to this concept of dirt, but where Goffman and Douglas deal with

group dynamics and the construction of communal identity, Kristeva discusses the individual psyche. See Julia Kristeva, *Powers of Horror: An Essay on Abjection*, trans. Leon S. Roudiez (New York: Columbia University Press, 1982). Also see Ainlay et al., eds., *The Dilemma of Difference*, pp. 18–20, 101–103, and Jones, *Social Stigma*, p. 93; Douglas, *Purity and Danger: An Analysis of Concepts of Pollution and Taboo*, quotation at p. 35.

32. Whereas dirt is an anomaly, something that will not fit into established taxonomies, treacle, for example, is an ambiguity, fitting into two categories. Neither liquid nor solid, yet both at once, treacle is "an aberrant fluid," according to Douglas, who muses over Sartre's essay on stickiness (p. 38).

33. Immanuel Kant, "Critique of Judgement," in Hazard Adams, ed., *Critical Theory Since Plato* (New York: Harcourt Brace Jovanovich, 1971), p. 358. For an example of how this principle of impurity operates in encounters among ethnic groups, see Leonard Cassuto's discussion of Mary Rowland's captivity narrative in *The Inhuman Race* (New York: Columbia University Press, 1996).

34. Douglas, *Purity and Danger*, p. 40. Also see Jones, *Social Stigma*, p. 89.

35. Jones, *Social Stigma*, p. 302.

36. For discussions of the roles of institutions in enforcing dichotomous identities, see Deborah Stone, *The Disabled State*, and Paula Giddings, *When and Where I Enter: The Impact of Black Women on Race and Sex in America* (New York: Bantam, 1984). For an incisive literary treatment of the hybrid figure, consider the mulatto Joe Christmas in William Faulkner's *Light in August*.

37. Douglas, *Purity and Danger*, quotation at p. 39. For a discussion of eugenics in the United States, see Hubbard, "Who Should and Should Not Inhabit the World," in *The Politics of Women's Biology*, p. 181. Ronald Walters's views on eugenics are drawn from *The Anti-Slavery Appeal: American Abolitionism After 1830* (Baltimore: Johns Hopkins University Press, 1976), pp. 85–86. Historians of science and medicine have recently shown that the Nazi "racial hygiene" program was not a historical exception. Legitimated by eugenic ideology, the program to eliminate "lives not worth living" was approved and enacted by many highly regarded members of a scientific and intellectual community that extended well beyond the Nazi doctors and even German borders (see Robert Proctor, *Racial Hygiene: Medicine Under the Nazis* [Cambridge: Harvard University Press, 1988], p. 177). Extensive forced sterilization of "undesirables" began in 1933, and in 1939 the government issued a secret plan for killing physically and mentally disabled children, beginning with registration and "selection" of congenitally disabled newborns and the most "severely" or "incurably" disabled children and escalating to teenagers and nondisabled Jewish children by 1943, according to Proctor. The very gas chambers designed for killing disabled people were dismantled and shipped east to be used for the Jews and other ethnic groups in the notorious camps. For discussions of eugenics and racial hygiene, see also Hugh Gallagher, *By Trust Betrayed: Patients, Physicians, and the License to Kill in the Third Reich* (New York: Holt, 1989); Daniel J. Kevles, *In the Name of Eugenics: Genetics and the Uses of Human Heredity*

(Berkeley: University of California Press, 1985); and Mark H. Haller, *Eugenics: Hereditarian Attitudes in American Thought* (New Brunswick, N.J.: Rutgers University Press, 1984).

38. Douglas, *Purity and Danger*, quotation at p. 39. For Foucault's discussion of marginalization, see *Madness and Civilization: A History of Insanity in the Age of Reason*, trans. Richard Howard (New York: Pantheon, 1965) and *The Birth of the Clinic: An Archeology of Medical Perception*, trans. A. M. Sheridan-Smith (New York: Pantheon, 1973). Regarding "ugly laws," see Burgdorf, "A History of Unequal Treatment," p. 863.

39. For discussion of asylums and almshouses, see Rothman, *Discovery of the Asylum*, and Tom Compton, "A Brief History of Disability" (Berkeley: unpublished manuscript, 1989), p. 42. For histories of disability legislation, see Scotch, *From Good Will to Civil Rights*; Shapiro, *No Pity*; Marvin Lazerson, "The Origins of Special Education," in J. G. Chambers and William T. Hartman, eds., *Special Education Politics: Their History, Implementation, and Finance* (Philadelphia: Temple University Press, 1983), pp. 15–47; Wolf Wolfensberger, *The Origin and Nature of Our Institutional Models* (Syracuse: Human Policy Press, 1975); and Liachowitz, *Disability as a Social Construct*.

40. See Fine and Asch, eds., *Women with Disabilities*, pp. 9–12, for discussion of poverty and lack of education among the disabled. For accounts of deaf culture, see Harlan L. Lane, *When the Mind Hears: A History of the Deaf* (New York: Random House, 1984); Carol Paden and Tom Humphreys, *Deaf in America: Voices from a Culture*; and John Van Cleve and Barry Crouch, *A Place of Their Own: Creating the Deaf Community in America* (Washington, D.C.: Gallaudet University Press, 1989). For the effects of segregated education and institutionalization on the independent living movement, see Zola, *Missing Pieces*.

41. See the following discussions of disability in literature and film: Shari Thurer, "Disability and Monstrosity: A Look at Literary Distortions of Handicapping Conditions," *Rehabilitation Literature* 41 (1–2): 12–15; Douglas Biklin and Robert Bogdan, "Media Portrayals of Disabled People. A Study in Stereotypes," *Interracial Books for Children Bulletin* 8 (6) and (7): 4–9; Leonard Kriegel, "The Wolf in the Pit in the Zoo," *Social Policy* (Fall 1982): 16–23; Paul Longmore, "Screening Stereotypes: Images of Disabled People," *Social Policy* 16 (Summer 1985): 31–38; and Deborah Kent, "Disabled Women: Portraits in Fiction and Drama," in Alan Gartner and Tom Joe, eds., *Images of the Disabled, Disabling Images* (New York: Praeger, 1987); and Martin Norden, *The Cinema of Isolation*. For discussions of the monster in culture, see Jeffrey Cohen, ed., *Monster Theory: Reading Culture* (Minneapolis: University of Minnesota Press, 1996) and Marie Hélène Huet, *Monstrous Imagination*.

42. Nathaniel Hawthorne's story "The Birthmark" can be read as an exploration of culture's intolerance of anomaly and the danger that surrounds it. For discussions of Hawthorne's story in the context of bodily difference, see Diane Price Herndl, *Invalid Women: Figuring Feminine Illness in American Fiction and Culture, 1840–1940* (Chapel Hill: University of North Carolina Press, 1993) and Frances E. Mascia-Lees and Patricia Sharpe, "The Marked and the Un(re)marked: Tattoo and Gender in Theory and Nar-

rative," in Frances E. Mascia-Lees and Patricia Sharpe, eds., *Tattoo, Torture, Mutilation, and Adornment* (Albany: SUNY Press, 1992), pp. 145–70.

43. For discussions of social Darwinism and Lamarckian thought, see Richard Hofstadter, *Social Darwinism in American Thought* (Boston: Beacon, 1944) and Stephen Jay Gould, *The Mismeasure of Man* (New York: Norton, 1981). Regarding "just world" assumptions about disability, see Ainlay et al., eds., *The Dilemma of Difference*, pp. 33–34.

44. See Davis, "Deviance Disavowal," p. 124.

45. For Freud's delineation of "deformities of character," see "Some Character Types Met with in Psychoanalytic Work," in *Collected Papers*, vol. IV, trans. Joan Riviere (London: Hogarth, 1957), pp. 319–22. There are many studies about pathologizing difference, for example, Sander Gilman, *Difference and Pathology*. For a discussion of pathologizing disability, see Deborah Stone, *The Disabled State*.

46. Douglas, *Purity and Danger*, p. 40.

47. Thomas S. Kuhn, *The Structure of Scientific Revolutions* (Chicago: University of Chicago Press, 1992), p. 5.

48. Although M. M. Bakhtin does not explicitly associate the carnivalesque with disability in his privileging of the exceptional body (*The Dialogic Imagination*, trans. Caryl Emerson and Michael Holquist [Austin: Texas University Press, 1981], quotation at p. 159), it is worth noting that Bakhtin himself was disabled by a bone disease at the age of twenty-eight, leading to the amputation of his leg in 1938, at age forty-three, precisely when he was writing on Rabelais and the Middle Ages.

49. See, for example, Harpham, *On the Grotesque*; Peter Stallybrass and Allon White, *The Poetics and Politics of Transgression* (Ithaca: Cornell University Press, 1986); Mary Russo, *The Female Grotesque*; and Leonard Cassuto, *The Inhuman Race*.

50. Michel Foucault, *Discipline and Punish: The Birth of the Prison*, trans. Alan Sheridan (New York: Vintage, 1979), pp. 193, 135.

51. Foucault, *Madness and Civilization*, pp. 38 and 48; Michel Foucault, *Power/Knowledge: Selected Interviews and Other Writings, 1972–1977*, ed. and trans. Colin Gordon (New York: Pantheon, 1980), p. 166. Echoing Foucault's analysis of Europe, both David Rothman in *The Discovery of the Asylum* and Deborah Stone in *The Disabled State* lay out this process in the history of the United States.

52. Foucault, *Discipline and Punish*, p. 184.

53. Both Foucault and his American counterpart, David Rothman (in *The Discovery of the Asylum*), occasionally imply that disability is a natural state justifying indolence and confinement. Only chroniclers of the disabled category, like Deborah Stone (*The Disabled State*) and Tom Compton ("A Brief History of Disability") question this.

54. Goffman, *Stigma*, p. 128. For a discussion of the costuming of power, see Richard Sennett, *The Fall of Public Man* (New York: Knopf, 1977), pp. 65–72 and 161–74.

55. Foucault supports this hypothesis by noting that the writing of lives in premodern regimes involved a "heroization" that delineated the "individuality of the memorable man," while the modern marked individual is objectified (*Discipline and Punish*,

pp. 192–93). The phenomena of religious stigmata, an occurrence of functional disabilities and wounds like those of the crucified Christ, usually on the bodies of subsequently canonized saints, certainly testifies to a positive interpretation of bodily damage. St. Francis of Assisi displayed stigmatic wounds, which were always associated with ecstasy; and some Christians during the thirteenth century evidently actually maimed themselves in an effort to identify with Christ's sufferings, according to the *New Catholic Encyclopedia* (New York: McGraw-Hill, 1967, vol. 13, p. 711). Harlan Hahn draws from prehistorical archeological evidence through studies of the Middle Ages, concluding that in these premodern times, "the appearance of physical differences seemed to be associated with festiveness, sensuality, and entertainment rather than loss, repugnance, or personal tragedy" ("Can Disability Be Beautiful?" p. 31).

56. Murphy, *The Body Silent*, pp. 4, 116–17.

57. My understanding of the ideology of individualism is informed by Yehoshua Arieli, *Individualism and Nationalism in American Ideology* (Cambridge, Mass.: Center for Study of History of Liberty in America, 1964); Robert N. Bellah et al., *Habits of the Heart: Individualism and Commitment in American Life* (Berkeley: University of California Press, 1985); Gillian Brown, *Domestic Individualism: Imagining Self in Nineteenth Century America* (Berkeley: University of California Press, 1990); Wai Chee Dimock, *Empire for Liberty: Melville and the Poetics of Individualism* (Princeton: Princeton University Press, 1989); Jean Bethke Elsthain, *Public Man, Private Woman: Women in Social and Political Thought* (Princeton: Princeton University Press, 1981); Myra Jehlen, *American Incarnation: The Individual, the Nation, and the Continent* (Cambridge: Harvard University Press, 1986); C. B. MacPherson, *The Political Theory of Possessive Individualism: Hobbes to Locke* (Oxford: Clarendon, 1962); John W. Meyer, "Myths of Socialization and of Personality," in Thomas C. Heller et al., eds., *Reconstructing Individualism: Autonomy, Individuality, and Self in Western Thought* (Stanford: Stanford University Press, 1986); and Marvin Meyers, *The Jacksonian Persuasion: Politics and Belief* (New York: Vintage Press, 1957).

58. Ralph Waldo Emerson, "Self-Reliance," and "Fate," in *The Works of Ralph Waldo Emerson* (1847; reprint, New York: Tudor, 1938), vol. 1, p. 32; vol, 3, p. 8; David Leverenz, "The Politics of Emerson's Man-Making Words," *PMLA* 101 (1): 49.

59. Richard Selzer, *Mortal Lessons: Notes on the Art of Surgery* (New York: Simon & Schuster, 1987).

60. For a discussion of antinominianism, see Amy Schrager Lang, *Prophetic Woman: Anne Hutchinson and the Problem of Dissent in the Literature of New England* (Berkeley: University of California Press, 1987).

61. For a discussion of conformity and intolerance, see G. J. Barker-Benfield, *The Horrors of the Half-Known Life: Male Attitudes Toward Women and Sexuality in Nineteenth-Century America* (New York: Harper & Row, 1976). Alexis de Tocqueville's remarks come from *Democracy in America*, vol. 1 (1840: reprint, New York: Vintage Books, 1990), p. 267.

62. Barker Benfield, *The Horrors of the Half-Known Life*, p. 178; Siegfried Kracauer,

The Mass Ornament: Weimar Essays, trans. and ed. Thomas Y. Levin (Cambridge: Harvard University Press, 1995).

63. It is interesting to note that one of Ahab's literary descendants, Captain Falcon of Charles Johnson's *Middle Passage* (New York: Macmillan, 1990) is also a disabled figure who invites interpretation. In Falcon, Ahab's missing leg is transformed into foreshortened legs that render this embodiment of evil a demasculinized dwarf.

64. See MacPherson, *The Political Theory of Possessive Individualism*. Susan Sontag's *Illness as Metaphor* examines this assignment of blame, analyzing cultural meanings attributed to tuberculosis and cancer in the nineteenth and twentieth centuries. The concept of "fighting" cancer or other diseases is just one example of our tendency to imagine ourselves as bounded, autonomous individuals.

65. Wai Chee Dimock explores the personification of the nation in this sense, showing Melville's commitment to "the institution of the discrete, a faith in the self-contained and the self-sufficient" (*Empire for Liberty*, quotation at p. 111; also see especially pp. 26–30).

66. The alternative, less dramatic, and less compelling response of simply leaving the whale alone is suggested by the English captain of the *Samuel Enderby*, who has lost his arm in an encounter with Moby Dick.

67. F. O. Matthiessen suggested as early as 1941 that Ahab stood for a critique of individualism, but he links Ahab's behavior, not his body, to this assessment (*The American Renaissance* [New York: Oxford, 1941], p. 459).

68. For a discussion of Emerson's denial of care and dependence, see Joyce W. Warren, *American Narcissus: Individualism and Women in Nineteenth-Century American Fiction* (New Brunswick, N.J.: Rutgers University Press, 1984).

69. Tocqueville, *Democracy in America*, vol. 2, p. 34.

70. An interesting counternarrative of spiritual perfectibility in which the disabled figure is privileged appears in the case of Stowe's Eva and Dickens's Tiny Tim, where the physically vulnerable figure can attain spiritual perfection.

71. The problem of poverty in a society that equates work with virtue is explored by David Rothman in *The Discovery of the Asylum*, as well as by Frank Bowe in *Handicapping America: Barriers to Disabled People* (New York: Harper & Row, 1978), by Daniel Rodgers in *The Work Ethic in Industrial America, 1850–1920* (Chicago: University of Chicago Press, 1978), and by Deborah Stone in *The Disabled State*, all of which inform this discussion.

72. The concept of "disabled" was used as early as 1644 to designate soldiers compensated by law for war wounds. Legislation has always been clear about disabled soldiers, whose labor as warriors earned their compensation. The debate about who can legitimately be excused from the workforce still rages as questioning of the welfare system.

73. For discussions of the fellow-servant ruling see Lawrence M. Friedman and Jack Ladinsky, "Social Change and the Law of Industrial Accidents," *Columbia Law*

Review 67, no. 1 (January 1967): 55–65, and Brook Thomas, *Cross-Examinations of Law and Literature: Cooper, Hawthorne, Stowe, and Melville* (Cambridge: Cambridge University Press, 1987), pp. 164–82. It is interesting to note that Lemuel Shaw was Melville's brother-in-law.

74. By the latter part of the century the fellow-servant rule was legally weakened as industrial accidents increased dramatically and society began to recognize that the precedent was untenable and inequitable. Between 1910 and 1920, workmen's compensation statutes were becoming the rule, though according to Friedman and Ladinsky ("Social Change," pp. 60–70), the last state to institute such a law was Mississippi in 1948.

75. The history of public policy toward disability and its development as a political category is found in Deborah Stone, *The Disabled State* (pp. 1–117); Claire Liachowitz, *Disability as a Social Construct*; Tom Compton, "A Brief History of Disability"; and Richard Scotch, *From Good Will to Civil Rights*. Stone's linking of the disability category to a need-based rather than a work-based system is essential to my analysis. However, I question the concepts of ability and will, analyze the place of the ideology of work, and accept disability more fully as a social construction.

76. The poor-law precedence, which basically advocated institutionalization rather than direct aid as a form of public relief, was brought to colonial America and was the guiding principle of public welfare until the emergence of the welfare state around the turn of the century. Although poor-law policy effectively incarcerated and punished both disabled and nondisabled poor, it prevailed throughout the nineteenth century because of apprehensions that direct economic public aid would encourage idleness and compromise the motivation to work. The Jacksonian tendency to limit federal intervention and champion individual autonomy further discouraged revision of inherited poor-law policy. Only the glut of disabled Civil War veterans, the rise of private humanitarian efforts, and the movement into the Progressive Era finally rendered disability and other social problems issues appropriately addressed by the state rather than by families and locally. See J. Lenihan, "Disabled Americans: A History," *Performances* (Nov./Dec. 1976–Jan. 1977): 1–69, for an overview of American disability policy. For a discussion of the institutions that managed poverty, see David Rothman, *The Discovery of the Asylum*, and Michael B. Katz, *In the Shadow of the Poorhouse: A Social History of Welfare in America* (New York: Basic Books, 1986).

77. Stone, *The Disabled State*, pp. 91–99.

78. The modern welfare state's quantification of disability in order to administer economic aid uses formulas and charts to transform bodily conditions into percentages of ability that determine a person's eligibility for aid. These various public policy disability schedules locate disability exclusively in the body and presume an abstract notion of physical wholeness and ideal performance levels to which the "disabled" are compared. Certain physical states are then clinically evaluated as decreasing absolute able-bodiedness by a particular percentage. On one scale, for example, limb amputa-

tion translates as 70% reduction in ability to work, while amputation of the little finger at the distal joint reduces the capacity for labor by a single percentage point. What seems absurd here is the insistence that a precise mathematical relation can be posited between such complex, dynamic situations as bodily condition and ability to perform wage labor (see Stone, *The Disabled State*, pp. 107–17).

79. Rodgers, *The Work Ethic in Industrial America*, p. xi.

3. The Cultural Work of American Freak Shows, 1835–1940

1. Richard D. Altick, *The Shows of London* (Cambridge, Mass.: Belknap Press of Harvard University Press, 1978), pp. 272–73.

2. Bogdan, *Freak Show*.

3. The discussion here of monsters and the history of teratology draws from Dudley Wilson, *Signs and Portents: Monstrous Births from the Middle Ages to the Enlightenment* (London: Routledge, 1993); Josef Warkany, "Congenital Malformations in the Past," in T. V. N. Persaud, ed., *Problems of Birth Defects*, (Baltimore: University Park Press, 1977); Katharine Park and Lorraine Daston, "Unnatural Conceptions: The Study of Monsters in Sixteenth- and Seventeenth-Century France and England (*Past and Present* 92 [August 1981]: 20–54); John Block Friedman, *The Monstrous Races in Medieval Art and Thought* (Cambridge, Mass.: Harvard University Press, 1981); Mark V. Barrow, "A Brief History of Teratology," in Persaud, ed., *Problems of Birth Defects*; Howard Martin, *Victorian Grotesque* (London: Jupiter Books, 1977); and Huet, *Monstrous Imagination*.

4. Aristotle, *Nicomachean Ethics,* trans. Terence Irwin (Indianapolis: Hackett Publishing, 1985), pp. 36–44 and 49–52.

5. Friedman, *The Monstrous Races,* quotations at pp. 109 and 118.

6. Hevey, *The Creatures Time Forgot,* p. 53; on Robert Wadlow and Julia Pastrana, see Frederick Drimmer, *Born Different: Amazing Stories of Very Special People* (New York: Atheneum, 1988), p. 71.

7. Perhaps the fascination with freakishness has been redirected since contemporary culture proscribes the display of disabled people in the kinds of freak shows that took place prior to about 1940. Contemporary versions of the freak show might be anti-establishment entertainment, daytime talk shows, tabloid stories, disability telethons, televised surgical theater, geek shows, the popular writings of Oliver Sacks and Stephen Jay Gould, as well as recent academic inquiries into popular culture. See Rosemarie Garland Thomson, ed., *Freakery: Cultural Spectacles of the Extraordinary Body* (New York: New York University Press, 1996) and Cohen, ed., *Monster Theory*.

8. The discussion here draws from Neil Harris, *Humbug: The Art of P. T. Barnum* (Boston: Little, Brown, 1973); Gould, *The Mismeasure of Man*; Patricia Cline Cohen, *A Calculating People: The Spread of Numeracy in Early America* (Chicago: University of Chicago Press, 1982); Veblen, *The Theory of the Leisure Class*; John Tagg, *The Burden*

3. American Freak Shows 155

of Representation—Evidence, Truth, and Order: Essays on Photographies and Histories (London: Macmillan, 1988); and Bogdan, *Freak Show.*

9. For accounts of Joice Heth, see P. T. Barnum, *Struggles and Triumphs* (1869; reprint, New York: Arno Press, 1970); A. H. Saxton, *P. T. Barnum: The Legend and the Man* (New York: New York University Press, 1989); Harris, *Humbug,* pp. 20–26; and Bernth Lindfors, "P. T. Barnum and Africa," *Studies in Popular Culture* 7 (1984).

10. Thomas W. Laqueur notes a similar accumulation of physical details in Lynn Hunt, ed., "Bodies, Details, and the Humanitarian Narrative,"*The New Cultural History* (Berkeley: University of California Press, 1989), pp. 176–204.

11. Barnum, *Struggles and Triumphs,* p. 82.

12. My analysis of freak shows as cultural performances is influenced by Mary Ryan's reading of American parades as cultural texts in her essay "The American Parade: Representations of the Nineteenth-Century Social Order," in Hunt, ed., *The New Cultural History,* pp. 131–53.

13. John J. MacAloon, "Olympic Games and the Theory of Spectacle in Modern Times," in John J. MacAloon, ed., *Rite, Drama, Festival, Spectacle: Rehearsals Toward a Theory of Cultural Performance* (Philadelphia: Institute for the Study of Human Issues, 1984), p. 243.

14. Bernth Lindfors, "Circus Africans," *Journal of American Culture* 6 (2): 12.

15. I am elaborating here upon the central argument of Robert Bogdan's seminal study of the freak show: that the freak was created from disabled and nonwhite people. While I have highlighted the choreography between spectator and spectacle, Bogdan emphasizes the freak show as a form of entertainment in which the performers exercised autonomy and made choices. Bogdan's interpretation of consent is criticized by David Gerber, "Volition and Valorization: The 'Careers' of People Exhibited in Freak Shows," in Thomson, ed., *Freakery.*

16. Tagg, "A Means of Surveillance," in *The Burden of Representation,* p. 85; for discussion of photography as a disciplinary technology that constructed the worthy and the unworthy, see Allan Sekula, "The Body and the Archive," *October* 39 (Winter 1986): 3–64.

17. For a discussion and examples of freak portraits, see Michael Mitchell, *Monsters of the Gilded Age: The Photographs of Charles Eisenmann* (Toronto: Gage, 1979); freak photographs also appear in Philip B. Kunhardt, Jr., Philip B. Kunhardt III, and Peter W. Kunhardt, *P. T. Barnum: America's Greatest Showman* (New York: Knopf, 1995).

18. Susan Stewart, *On Longing: Narratives of the Miniature, the Gigantic, the Souvenir, the Collection* (Baltimore: Johns Hopkins University Press, 1984), p. 109. In *Freak Show,* Robert Bogdan stresses the show's construction of the freak by pointing out that many of the spectacles were counterfeited or created—like fake conjoined twins, wild men, or tattooed freaks. In fact, part of the attraction for the spectator was in determining whether or not the freaks were "authentic" (p. 8).

19. Lindfors, "Circus Africans," p. 10.

20. Massachusetts Historical Society, "The 'Aztec' Children," *M. H. S. Miscellany* 50 (Spring 1992): 1–3.

21. It is interesting to note that the science of eugenics, inaugurated by Darwin's cousin, Sir Francis Galton, developed during the second half of the nineteenth century and was based on Quetelet's work. The aim of eugenics, which was later implemented politically by the Nazis, was to scientifically "improve" or purify the race—in other words, to realize the ideal of the statistical, standardized Average Man. For a study of eugenics, see Proctor, *Racial Hygiene: Medicine Under the Nazis*, and Hubbard, *The Politics of Women's Biology*. For a discussion of the concept of the average man, see Stephen Stigler, *The History of Statistics: The Measurement of Uncertainty Before 1900* (Cambridge, MA: Belknap Press of Harvard University Press, 1986), pp. 169–72, and Theodore M. Porter, *The Rise of Statistical Thinking, 1820–1900* (Princeton: Princeton University Press, 1986), especially chapters 4 and 5. For a cultural critique of "statistical persons," see Mark Selzer, *Bodies and Machines* (New York: Routledge, 1992).

22. Henry Ward Beecher, *Lectures to Young Men, on Various Important Subjects,* (New York: J. B. Ford , 1873) p. 181. Although respectability was a problem for dime museums and later for circuses, Barnum almost surmounted the issue by appealing to the desire for education and middle-class values such as sentimentality and temperance. Barnum's American Museum was visited by all classes; his Tom Thumb was presented to Queen Victoria; and he was even supported by Henry Ward Beecher. See Bruce A. McConachie, "Museum, Theater and the Problem of Respectability for Mid-Century Urban Americans," in Ron Engle and Tice L. Miller, eds., *The American Stage: Social and Economic Issues from the Colonial Period to the Present* (New York: Cambridge University Press, 1993), pp. 65–80; Brooks McNamara, "'A Congress of Wonders:' The Rise and Fall of the Dime Museum," *ESQ* 20 (3): 216–32; Marcello Truzzi, "Circus and Side Shows," in Myron Matlaw, ed., *American Popular Entertainment* (Westport, Conn.: Greenwood Press, 1979), pp. 175–85; and James B. Twitchell, *Carnival Culture: The Trashing of Taste in America* (New York: Columbia University Press, 1992), pp. 57–65.

23. For discussions of the construction of racial others from this perspective, see Eric Lott, *Love and Theft: Blackface Minstrelsy and the American Working Class* (New York: Oxford University Press, 1993); and Roediger, *The Wages of Whiteness*.

24. In support of this point, Joan Burbick has suggested that the concept of the healthy body as a national responsibility acted out at the individual level was a response to the chaos and disruption of the nineteenth century's changing social order. See Joan Burbick, *Healing the Republic: The Language of Health and the Culture of Nationalism in Nineteenth-Century America* (New York: Cambridge University Press, 1994).

25. For a similar argument about blacks, see Lott, *Love and Theft*.

26. Foucault, *Discipline and Punish*, pp. 191–99; and Stephen Greenblatt, "Fiction and Friction," in Thomas C. Heller et al., eds., *Reconstructing Individualism: Autonomy, Individuality and the Self in Western Thought* (Stanford: Stanford University Press, 1986), pp. 30–52.

27. Howard M. Solomon, "Stigma and Western Culture: A Historical Approach," in Stephen Ainlay et al., eds., *The Dilemma of Difference: A Multidisciplinary View of Stigma* (New York: Plenum Press, 1986), pp. 59–76; for a discussion of the costuming of power, also see Richard Sennett, *The Fall of Public Man*, pp. 65–72 and 161–74.

28. Harris, *Humbug*, p. 218.

29. See especially Martin, *Victorian Grotesque*, and George M. Gould and Walter L. Pyle, *Anomalies and Curiosities of Medicine* (Philadelphia: W. B. Saunders, 1897) for discussions of the Victorian concern with curiosities.

30. Bogdan, *Freak Show*, pp. 108, 161–66.

31. Meyer, "Myths of Socialization and of Personality," p. 211.

32. On the nineteenth-century American identity crisis, see Barker-Benfield, *The Horrors of the Half-Known Life*.

33. An early American example of the interpretation of monsters for political purposes can be found in John Winthrop's 1638 journal entry, which notes that the banished Anne Hutchinson "was delivered of a monstrous birth" that he and the Massachusetts Bay Colony interpreted as a message from God signifying Hutchinson's "error in denying inherent righteousness" (in Nina Baym et al., eds., *Norton Anthology of American Literature*, 4th ed. [New York: Norton, 1994], p. 185); on the conflict between prodigies and science, see Michael P. Winship, "Prodigies, Puritanism, and the Perils of Natural Philosophy: The Example of Cotton Mather," *William and Mary Quarterly* (Jan. 1994): 92–105.

34. My argument here elaborates on the explanation for Barnum's popularity given by Neil Harris in *Humbug*.

35. Saxon, *P. T. Barnum*, illustration following p. 82., no. 12 of Currier and Ives series on Barnum's Gallery of Wonders, Shelburne Museum, Shelburne, Vermont.

36. Victor Turner, *The Forest of Symbols: Aspects of Ndembu Ritual* (Ithaca: Cornell University Press, 1967).

37. Barbara Ehrenreich and Deirdre English, *For Her Own Good: 150 Years of the Experts' Advice to Women*, p. 31; for a discussion of resistance to these experts' claim to authority over the body, see Burbick, *Healing the Republic*, esp. chapter 1.

38. Paul Starr, *The Social Transformation of American Medicine* (New York: Basic Books, 1982).

39. Accounts of Sartje Baartman's display appear in Altick, *The Shows of London*; Stephen Jay Gould, "The Hottentot Venus," *Natural History* 91 (10): 20–27; Stephen Jay Gould, *The Flamingo's Smile: Reflections in Natural History* (New York: Norton, 1985), pp. 302–05; Bernth Lindfors, " 'The Hottentot Venus' and Other African Attractions in Nineteenth-Century England" (*Australasian Drama Studies* 1 [2]); and Gilman, *Difference and Pathology*. Julia Pastrana's history of exhibition is found in Frederick Drimmer, *Very Special People* (New York: Amjon Press, 1983) and *Born Different*; Otto Hermann, *Fahrend Volk* (Signor Salterino, Leipez: J. J. Weber, 1895); A. E. W. Miles, "Julia Pastrana, the Bearded Lady" (*Proceedings of the Royal Society of Medicine* 67 [1974]: 160–64); J. Z. Laurence, "A Short Account of the Bearded and Hairy Fe-

male" (*Lancet* 2 [1857]: 48); Jan Bondeson and A. E. W. Miles, "Julia Pastrana, the Nondescript: An Example of Congenital, Generalized Hypertrichosis with Gingival Hyperplasia" (*American Journal of Medical Genetics* 47 [1993]: 198–212); Francis T. Buckland, "The Female Nondescript Julia Pastrana, and Exhibitions of Human Mummies, etc.," in *Curiosities of Natural History*, vol. 4 (London: Richard Bentley and Son, 1888); and J. Sokolov, "Julia Pastrana and Her Child" (*Lancet* 1 [1862]: 467–69).

40. Gould, "The Hottentot Venus," p. 20.

41. Lindfors, "Circus Africans," p. 9. Lindfors also reports that the most recent case he discovered of an African displayed in a cage was in 1906 in the monkey house of the Bronx Zoo, but as recently as 1938 an African described as "near like the ape as he is like the human" was still being shown in an American circus (p. 10). For another account of an African displayed at a zoo, see Phillips Verner Bradford and Harvey Blume, *Ota Benga: The Pygmy in the Zoo* (New York: St. Martin's Press, 1992).

42. Baartman's case illustrates that history is always too complex for simple judgments or even unambiguous narration. Altick recounts that alongside this exploitative fascination arose an indignant protest against her display, which closed the show temporarily. After she was officially interrogated for several hours regarding her understanding of the situation, however, it seemed clear that she willingly participated—as do most freaks—in order to receive half of the profits, and the case for banning the show had to be dropped (*The Shows of London*, p. 270). For an examination of the role of consent in such displays, see Gerber, "Volition and Valorization."

43. "Curious History of the Baboon Lady, Miss Julia Pastrana," pamphlet, Harvard Theater Collection, pp. 5–7.

44. Laurence, "A Short Account of the Bearded and Hairy Female," p. 48.

45. Ibid.

46. Buckland, *Curiosities of the Natural World*, pp. 46 and 42.

47. Both Robert Bogdan in *Freak Show* as well as Kathryn Park and Lorraine Daston in "Unnatural Conceptions" link the demise of the freak show to the medicalization of disability.

48. Leslie Fiedler, *Freaks: Myths and Images of the Secret Self* (New York: Simon and Schuster, 1978), p. 250.

49. Bogdan, *Freak Show*, p. 81.

50. "Hybrid Indian!," broadside no. 616156A, New York Public Library.

51. For an extended discussion of this issue, see Cassuto, *The Inhuman Race*.

52. Altick, *The Shows of London*, p. 272. In his essay on "The Hottentot Venus," Stephen Jay Gould reports actually being shown this specimen on a special tour he received in 1982. Along with Baartman's genitals were two other sets in jars labeled "*une negresse*" and "*une peruvienne*" as well as a specimen of the bound foot, severed at the knee, of a Chinese woman, and the preserved brain of scientist Paul Broca. Gould notes pointedly, "I found no brains of women, and neither Broca's penis nor any male genitalia grace the collection" (*The Flamingo's Smile*, p. 21).

53. For example, Francis Galton, the father of eugenics, writes in 1853 in *Narrative*

of an Explorer in Tropical South Africa about an African woman who had what he discreetly and euphemistically describes as "that gift of bounteous nature to this favored race" which, being "a scientific man," he proceeded enthusiastically to measure from a distance with his sextant and record. Galton terms the object of his interest "not only a Hottentot in figure, but in that respect a Venus among Hottentots." That Galton never directly states what "that respect" is, but only alludes to the Hottentot Venus, testifies to her enduring notoriety within scientific discourse as an icon of physical aberration (qtd. in Gould, *The Flamingo's Smile*, p. 303).

54. Gilman, *Difference and Pathology*, p. 89. Gilman goes on to show how medical discourse identified the white prostitute through a catalog of bodily stigmata ranging from foot and ear shape to a hearty appetite and accompanying fatness that both indicated and made inevitable her deviant sexuality (pp. 94–101).

55. For critiques of science's complicity in dominant power relations, see, for example, Evelyn Fox Keller, "Gender and Science" in Evelyn Fox Keller, ed., *Reflections on Gender and Science* (New Haven: Yale University Press, 1985), pp. 75–94; Hubbard, *The Politics of Women's Biology*; Foucault, *The Birth of the Clinic*; and Gould, *The Mismeasure of Man*.

56. Foucault, *Discipline and Punish*, p. 184.

57. Gould, *The Flamingo's Smile*, pp. 65–77.

58. I do not mean to suggest freak and specimen are the only roles for people with disabilities; my point is that medical and freak discourses informed the attribution of physical aberration. Physical disability has always been privatized and read as unfortunate or shameful, while disabled people in public have traditionally been beggars.

59. Gilman, *Difference and Pathology*, p. 216.

60. Elizabeth Grosz's, "Intolerable Ambiguity: Freaks as/at the Limit," in Thomson, ed., *Freakery*, discusses the intolerance of such situations as conjoined twins and hermaphroditism, which are universally surgically "corrected" today.

61. After moving from the public role of Superman to that of a "courageous" disabled person, the actor Christopher Reeve now advocates that his supporters petition Congress to appropriate money to "fix people like me" (*Good Housekeeping* [June 1996], p. 88).

62. Hubbard, *The Politics of Women's Biology*, pp. 179–198.

4. Benevolent Maternalism and the Disabled Women in Stowe, Davis, and Phelps

1. Harriet Beecher Stowe, *Uncle Tom's Cabin or Life Among the Lowly* (1852; reprint, New York: Penguin, 1981); Rebecca Harding Davis, *Life in the Iron Mills* (1861; reprint, New York: The Feminist Press at the City University of New York, 1972); Elizabeth Stuart Phelps, *The Silent Partner* (1871; reprint, New York: The Feminist Press, 1983). All future references are to these editions and will be cited parenthetically as *UTC*, *LIM*, and *SP* respectively.

Several critics have offered generic categorizations of this large and diverse body of fiction in order to reevaluate what had been grouped together as "sentimental," a term that until recently was dismissive and denigrating. See Nina Baym, *Woman's Fiction: A Guide to Novels By and About Women in America, 1820–1870* (Ithaca: Cornell University Press, 1978); Mary Kelley, "The Sentimentalists: Promise and Betrayal in the Home," *Signs: Journal of Women in Culture and Society* 4 (31): 434–46; Jane P. Tompkins, *Sensational Designs: The Cultural Work of American Fiction, 1790–1860* (New York: Oxford University Press, 1985); Shirley Samuels, ed., *The Culture of Sentiment: Race, Gender, and Sentimentality in Nineteenth-Century America* (New York: Oxford University Press, 1992); Karen Sanchez-Eppler, "Bodily Bonds: The Intersecting Rhetorics of Feminism and Abolition," *Representations* 24 (Fall 1988): 28–59; and Philip Fisher, *Hard Facts: Setting and Form in the American Novel* (New York: Oxford University Press, 1985). Other generic analyses of the novels discussed in this chapter include Robyn Warhol's argument for *Uncle Tom's Cabin* as realism, "Poetics and Persuasion: *Uncle Tom's Cabin* as a Realist Novel," *Essays in Literature* 13 (2): 283–98; Sharon Harris's delineation of *Life in the Iron Mills* as a forerunner of naturalism, "Rebecca Harding Davis: From Romance to Realism," *American Literary Realism* 21 (2): 4–20; and Frances Malpezzi's placement of *The Silent Partner* in the social gospel tradition ("*The Silent Partner*: A Feminist Sermon on the Social Gospel," *Studies in the Humanities* 13 (2): 103–10.

2. The disabled figure is a convention in sentimental and domestic fiction, particularly in Davis and Phelps. For example, Lois in Davis's *Margret Howth: A Story of To-Day* (1862; reprint, New York: The Feminist Press, 1990); Asenath in Phelps's "The Tenth of January" (in *The Silent Partner*); and the mother in Phelps's *Doctor Zay* (1882; reprint, New York: The Feminist Press, 1987) are disabled figures. Maria Cummins' *The Lamplighter* (Boston: Jewett, 1854) also has a disabled heroine. In the English tradition, of course, Dickens's numerous disabled characters play significant roles.

3. Paul Longmore, conversation with the author, San Francisco, 28 June 1994.

4. This coincidence of pity and repugnance is particularly clear with Davis's Deb Wolfe, whose disability has no apparent historical explanation. Like her literary precursor, Roger Chillingworth, the "misshapen scholar" whose marked body is the "unmistakable token" of his twisted soul, Deb's "deformed" body signifies her economic and social degradation (Nathaniel Hawthorne, *The Scarlet Letter: A Romance* [1850; reprint, New York: Bobbs-Merrill, 1963], pp. 59, 60).

5. For discussions of institutional oppression of and individual attitudes toward people with disabilities, see Yuker, ed., *Attitudes Toward Persons with Disabilities*; Fine and Asch, eds., *Women with Disabilities*; Goffman, *Stigma*; Burgdorf, "A History of Unequal Treatment;" and Fred Davis, "Deviance Disavowal."

6. For my purposes, it is important to distinguish between visible and invisible disabilities. The exterior of the body tends to be read as a trope for the interior or soul. For example, Stowe's Eva and Marie St. Clare gain much of their signifying power from the disparity between their perfect exteriors and their "disabled" interiors, although they

have very different meanings in the two characters. I examine only visible disabilities here because external marks and invisible disabilities affect readings differently. For a discussion of how invisible disabilities in nineteenth-century American women function in discourse, see Herndl, *Invalid Women*.

7. In this sense these authors practice a cultural feminism that anticipates feminist theorists such as Gilligan, *In a Different Voice*; Elsthain, *Public Man, Private Woman*; Sara Ruddick, "Maternal Thinking," *Feminist Studies* 6 (2): 342–67; and Fox-Genovese, *Feminism Without Illusions*. These theorists associate feminine socialization more with an ethic of responsibility and care than with individual rights and autonomy.

8. Harriet Beecher Stowe, in *The Key to Uncle Tom's Cabin* (London: 1853), suggests that the best mothering is elicited by disabled children: "If a mother has among her children," she writes, "one whom sickness has made blind, or deaf, or dumb, incapable of acquiring knowledge through the usual channels of communication, does she not seek to reach its darkened mind by modes of communication tenderer and more intimate than those which she uses with the stronger and more favored ones?" (p. 38).

Within the domestic ideology that John L. Thomas ("Romantic Reform in America, 1815–1865," *American Quarterly* 17 [Winter 1965]: 656–81) shows to be inseparable from evangelical Christianity, human suffering meant more than human sinning, and consolation was more important than condemnation. The lowly sufferer sustained by the venerated caretaker parallels the relation between humanity and a sympathetic, nurturing, feminized Christ figure, the opposite of the earlier Calvinist patriarchal God in whose angry hands all sinners writhed. Because, as Kathryn Sklar shows, the concept of salvation through good works was replacing the doctrine of predestination within Christian theology, having an object toward whom to direct Christian love was essential (*Catharine Beecher: A Study in American Domesticity* [New York: Norton, 1973], p. 13). The perfect beneficiary is this innocent, suffering disabled figure; the more repugnant the sufferer, the nobler the Christian who loves him. Moreover, the disabled women suggest the blind, lame, and leprous characters who are the chosen of Jesus. Charles Kokaska, et al., "Disabled People in the *Bible*," *Rehabilitation Literature* 45 (1–2): 20–21 finds 180 incidents of disability in the Bible, most of which occur in the New Testament in association with Jesus. *Uncle Tom's Cabin* alludes to the Bible's use of disabled figures as objects to be redeemed (like Stowe's slaves) when we hear that St. Clare's saintly mother says "if we want to give sight to the blind, we must be willing to do as Christ did,—call them to us and *put our hands on them*" (*UTC* 410). Thus, Stowe appropriates the New Testament's reversal of the social power structure by elevating the lowest to the highest position, echoing the Christian injunction that "the least of these" is the equal of Jesus.

9. Fisher, *Hard Facts*, p. 99.

10. Gillian Brown's exploration of "domestic individualism" also asserts that feminine domesticity and masculine individualism were not discrete ideologies, but were intertwined and mutually reinforcing cultural developments. While Brown shows that domesticity provided the site and legitimation for individualism, I suggest that the pub-

lic role of benevolent maternalism as it appears in these texts was a feminine persona for middle-class women that granted them the prestige of the liberal individual.

11. For discussions of middle-class women's economic production in the nineteenth century, see Nancy F. Cott, *The Bonds of Womanhood: "Woman's Sphere" in New England, 1780–1835* (New Haven: Yale University Press, 1977); Mary P. Ryan, *Empire of the Mother: American Writing About Domesticity, 1830–1860* (New York: Institute for Research in History and The Hawthorne Press, 1982); Rodgers, *The Work Ethic in Industrial America 1850–1920*; and Charlotte Perkins Gilman, *Women and Economics: A Study of the Economic Relation Between Women and Men* (1898; reprint, Buffalo, N.Y.: Prometheus Books, 1994). Sara M. Evans, in *Born for Liberty: A History of Women in America* (New York: The Free Press, 1989), points out that most American women in the nineteenth century did not have the economic means or the motivation to maintain the identity of a woman reformer. In spite of the small proportion of women for whom this ideal was within reach, the figure of maternal benevolence nevertheless exerted considerable social power and status because it was one of the dominant group's versions of womanhood.

12. See Carroll Smith-Rosenberg, *Disorderly Conduct: Visions of Gender in Victorian America* (New York: Oxford University Press, 1985).

13. Cott, *The Bonds of Womanhood*, p. 7.

14. Thomas L. Haskell, "Capitalism and the Origins of the Humanitarian Sensibility, Part 1," *American History Review* 90 (2): 339–61; Thomas L. Haskell, "Capitalism and the Origins of the Humanitarian Sensibility, Part 2," *American History Review* 90 (3): 547–66.

15. With this move, the authors evoke the continuously controversial problem of what responsibility government has to those unable to "earn a living." See Rothman, *Discovery of the Asylum*; see also Stone, *The Disabled State*. Stone studies disability history for an examination of the ambivalence with which the public sector treats indigence and disability in its attempt to differentiate between "deserving" and "undeserving" poor.

16. Silvers, in *Reconciling Equality to Difference: Caring (F)or Justice for People with Disabilities*, points out that in asymmetrical relationships between caregivers and care receivers, the risk of caregiving becoming oppressive is always present because the caregiver is an autonomous agent while the receiver of care is often unable to define the terms of the relationship.

17. The pattern of attempted rescue set up by these social reform novels somewhat replicates the earlier American tradition of the captivity narratives of the late seventeenth and early eighteenth centuries, in which white women were captured by Indians and rescued by heroic white men. This social myth, so necessary to authorize and legitimate Euro-American expansion, is revised interestingly in the fiction examined here. The gender roles are reversed so that the previous victims—white women—now become the rescuing hero(in)es, saving the new victims—the disabled women—from the threatening villains—dominant males. The effect of both kinds of narrative is to es-

tablish group identity and entitlement. For a gender-based discussion of captivity narratives, see Annette Kolodny, *The Land Before Her* (Chapel Hill: University of North Carolina Press, 1984).

18. It is interesting to note that the closer to white, Christian, and maternal the heroines are, the more beautiful their bodies become. The quadroon, Eliza, has a "finely moulded shape" and the "beauty" that is "so fatal an inheritance to a slave" (*UTC* 45, 54). The Quaker, Rachel Halliday, has "the beauty of old women," which is akin to "a ripe peach" and she is like a Venus who, instead of turning heads, keeps all going about their work "harmoniously" (*UTC* 215, 216, 223). The exception is the hypocritically Christian slaveholder, Marie St. Clare, who becomes "unlovely," "a yellow, faded sickly woman," and a bad mother as her early beauty is perverted by the selfishness of being waited upon by slaves (*UTC* 243). In contrast to the heroines' effortless and unadorned beauty, the vain and self-indulgent Marie is "gorgeously dressed" and wears "diamond bracelets" while all around her suffer (*UTC*, 275).

19. See Laqueur, *Making Sex*; Barbara Welter, "The Cult of True Womanhood: 1820–60," *American Quarterly* 18 (2): 151–74; Gerda Lerner, "The Lady and the Mill Girl: Changes in the Status of Women in the Age of Jackson," *Midcontinent American Studies Journal* 10 (1969): 5–15, quotation at p. 11.

I want to make a distinction here between Barbara Welter's often cited "Cult of True Womanhood" and what I mean by using Lerner's term, "the cult of the lady." While Welter emphasizes behavior and attitudes, I stress the class-bound effects of being a "lady" on the body itself, even as I acknowledge that these views of womanhood are not discrete. Thus, I focus upon physical restrictions to work and on the discourses that name the female body pathological as well as ugly.

20. For discussions of this process's socioeconomic effect on women see Lerner, "The Lady and the Mill Girl"; Richard D. Brown, *Modernization: The Transformation of American Life 1600–1865* (New York: Hill and Wang, 1976), especially chapters 6 and 7; Rodgers, *The Work Ethic in Industrial America 1850–1920*, especially chapter 7; Stuart Blumin, *The Emergence of the Middle Class: Social Experience in the American City, 1760–1900* (Cambridge: Cambridge University Press, 1989), especially pp. 179–91; and Veblen, *The Theory of the Leisure Class*, especially pp. 125–31.

For discussions on the impact of scientific and medical discourses on women, see Ehrenreich and English, *For Her Own Good*, especially chapters 3 and 4; Smith-Rosenberg, *Disorderly Conduct*, especially the chapters on hysterical women and on abortion; Judith Walzer Leavitt, ed., *Women and Health in America* (Madison: University of Wisconsin Press, 1984), especially part 1; Herndl, *Invalid Women*, especially chapter 1; Tuana, *The Less Noble Sex*; and Gould, *The Mismeasure of Man*, pp. 103–07. Martha Verbrugge, in *Able-Bodied Womanhood: Personal Health and Social Change in Nineteenth-Century Boston* (New York: Oxford University Press, 1988), examines the paradox created by the cult of invalidism and the demand that women be fit enough to manage domestic duties.

For discussions of the institution of female beauty and its relation to consumerism and leisure, see Banner, *American Beauty*, especially chapters 1–4; Wolf, *The Beauty Myth*; and Veblen, *Theory of the Leisure Class*.

21. Testimonies to this sense of bodily restriction and vulnerability abound; two of the most powerful are, of course, Charlotte Perkins Gilman's "The Yellow Wallpaper," *The New England Magazine* (January 1892); and Florence Nightingale's "Cassandra" (1928; reprinted in Ray Strachey, ed., *The Cause: A Short History of the Women's Movement in Great Britain* (London: Virago, 1978), pp. 395–418.

22. Gail Parker, *The Oven Birds: American Women on Womanhood, 1820–1920* (Garden City, N.J.: Anchor Books, 1972), p. 197.

23. Tillie Olsen, *Silences* (New York: Dell Publishing, 1965), pp. 117–18; Susan Coultrap-McQuin, *Doing Literary Business: American Women Writers in the Nineteenth Century* (Chapel Hill: University of North Carolina Press, 1990), p. 175.

24. Elizabeth Stuart Phelps, "Why Shall They Do It?" *Harpers* 36 (1886): 219; Carol Farley Kessler, *Elizabeth Stuart Phelps* (Boston: Twayne, 1982), p. 15.

25. By 1899, Thorstein Veblen had asserted that the market economy's demand that women display "conspicuous waste and conspicuous leisure" enforced female habits and dress that amounted to "voluntarily induced physical disability" (*Theory of the Leisure Class*, p. 127). Cultural discourse described the female body as inferior, frail, and limited—precisely the same way that it framed the physical characteristics of disabled people.

26. See Amy Schrager Lang, "Class and the Strategies of Sympathy," in Samuels, ed., *The Culture of Sentiment*. Lang argues that the dilemma of representing class in both *Life in the Iron Mills* and *Uncle Tom's Cabin* is solved by substituting gender, leaving art as the final subject of Davis's novel.

27. Sharon Harris ("Rebecca Harding Davis") suggests that the Korl woman is a revision of Deb. If one accepts that reading, it is interesting that the statue appears to correct Deb's disability, releasing the idealized version of Deb from the physical limitations of the real, disabled woman (*LIM* 19). I find evidence in the text to suggest that the Korl woman is a self-portrait of the feminized Hugh, who is described as a living version of the statue, "mad with hunger; stretching out his hands to the world" (*LIM* 45).

28. Gerda Lerner ("The Lady and the Mill Girl") shows that by 1840—shortly before Phelps's birth, when Davis was a small child, and when Stowe was 30—class stratification among women was firmly in place. This division is what Stowe apparently resists in both her attempt to unite women through maternal experience for social change and to nostalgically portray the classless home. In their novels, Davis and Phelps both accept a more hierarchical arrangement between the workers and their middle-class supporters, although the guilty defensiveness and hopelessness that permeate *Life in the Iron Mills* may reflect Davis's suspicion that the gap was unbridgeable. Lois Banner (*American Beauty*) and Naomi Wolf (*The Beauty Myth*) assert that by 1840 the major features and institutions of American beauty culture were also in place and were fueled by the growth of consumerism, the mass production of images, and the continuing emergence of the middle-class lady.

29. Lerner, "The Lady and the Mill Girl," p. 11.

30. See Banner, *American Beauty*, for a discussion of this economy.

31. *Godey's Lady's Book*, 1852, quoted in Banner, *American Beauty*, p. 10.

32. Phelps's repudiation of marriage in *The Silent Partner* contrasts with Stowe, who seemed to assume marriage as a natural element of benevolent maternalism. At the beginning of Phelps's novel, the indulged, frivolous Perley (reminiscent of the early Marie St. Clare) is engaged to her father's rich partner, Maverick Hayle, whom she rejects in order to set up something akin to a settlement house after meeting the spunky but oppressed mill girl, Sip Garth. Although Perley refuses marriage to devote herself to the mill workers, she is validated as a woman by the adoration of the Christian Stephen Garrick, a man "she might have loved" (*SP* 260). Her response to the imploring and awestruck suitor is "I have no time to think of love and marriage . . . That is a business, a trade, . . . I have too much else to do . . . I cannot spare the time for it" (*SP* 260). Both his love and her self-sacrifice constitute part of the beatification that renders her more like Eva than Marie in the end.

33. Burgdorf relates disability to social Darwinism ("A History of Unequal Treatment," p. 887); for a discussion of social Darwinism, see Richard Hofstadter, *Social Darwinism in American Thought*.

34. The strategy of disembodiment suggested by splitting off the physically disabled figures is similar to the self-imposed female "passionlessness" Nancy Cott identifies among nineteenth-century middle-class women as a response to their vulnerability and an alternative to being an object of male desire (*The Bonds of Womanhood*, p 239). The ideology of passionlessness offered women empowerment through self-control rather than sexual attractiveness. It also promised to release them from some distinctly feminine liabilities, such as unwanted pregnancy, sexual and physical subjection, and association with the carnal. Although Cott sees an ethic of self-control primarily in sexual terms, the disabled women illustrate female liabilities including slavery, wage labor, motherhood, marriage, and the role of the decorative woman.

35. Lerner, "The Lady and the Mill Girl," p. 14.

5. *Disabled Women as Powerful Women in Petry, Morrison, and Lorde*

1. Audre Lorde, *Zami: A New Spelling of My Name* (Freedom, Calif.: Crossing Press, 1982), p. 15. All future references are to this edition and will be given parenthetically in the text.

In *Writing a Woman's Life* (New York: Norton, 1988), Carolyn Heilbrun discusses the lack of language and narrative forms with which to analyze the lives of nontraditional women. Like Lorde's "third designation," Heilbrun's term, "ambiguous woman," allows one to appropriate the strengths of gender identity and reject the liabilities. Both terms attempt to affirm and amend the concept of womanhood.

2. Ann Petry, *The Street* (1946; reprint, Boston: Beacon, 1974); Toni Morrison, *The Bluest Eye* (New York: Washington Square Press, 1970); Toni Morrison, *Sula* (New

York: New American Library, 1973); Toni Morrison, *Song of Solomon* (New York: New American Library, 1977); Toni Morrison, *Tar Baby* (New York: New American Library, 1981); Toni Morrison, *Beloved* (New York: New American Library, 1987). All future references are to these editions and will be cited parenthetically as *Street, BE, Sula, SS, TB,* and *Beloved,* respectively.

3. In her essay "When We Dead Awaken: Writing as Revision" (in *On Lies, Secrets, and Silence* [New York: Norton, 1979]), Adrienne Rich defines "re-vision" as reading, writing, and interpreting women's lives "with fresh eyes." More than simply cultural history, literary criticism, or autobiographical writing, Rich's well-known feminist concept is "an act of survival" that enables women to refute the "self-destructiveness" inherent in conventional womanhood (p. 35). The African-American novels discussed here revise black female identity in precisely Rich's sense. However, this study complicates the notion of simple racial or gender identity, "re-visioning" it by highlighting the sociohistorical category "physically disabled."Each of these novels approaches the disability category only obliquely, unselfconsciously; none confronts the disabled identity directly. The relationships among the stigmatized identities of blackness, femaleness, and physical disability are never explicitly enunciated.

4. Some examples of physically disabled characters in other African-American women's writing are the protagonists in Harriet Wilson's *Our Nig; or Sketches from the Life of a Free Black* (1859; reprint, New York: Vintage Books, 1983) and Harriet Jacobs's *Incidents in the Life of A Slave Girl* (1861; reprint, Cambridge: Harvard University Press, 1987); Miss Thompson in Paule Marshall's *Brown Girl, Brownstones* (1959; reprint, Old Westbury, N.Y.: Feminist Press, 1981); Uncle Willie in Maya Angelou's *I Know Why The Caged Bird Sings* (Toronto: Bantam, 1969); the protagonist of Alice Walker's *Meridian* (New York: Pocket Books, 1976); and Milkman Dead—Morrison's only disabled male—from *Song of Solomon*. The prevalence of such figures is perhaps due more to historical accuracy—disability occurs more frequently under conditions of poverty and oppression—than to metaphorical intent.

5. These rhetorical figurations of disability roughly correspond to a broad historical shift in cultural sensibility that can be briefly characterized as follows: the rhetoric of sympathy assumes unity (expressed, for example, in millennialism), a cultural and cosmic principle that dominated nineteenth-century American thinking but was questioned by the secularized and naturalist aesthetic of the century's end. The modernist rhetoric of despair that displaced and mourned the loss of such faith yielded the grotesque, the antihero, and existential thinking. The postmodern rhetoric of difference no longer mourns unity, even though it grapples with multiplicity; it is the most congenial cultural mode in which disability is represented. The terms modern and postmodern are used here in Fredric Jameson's sense, as "cultural dominants" that can be resisted but not transcended ("Postmodernism, or the Cultural Logic of Late Capitalism," *New Left Review* 146 [July-Aug. 1984]: 53–92). The transition from one cultural dominant to the next would necessarily be perceptible not only in literature but also in politics.

6. This historical shift in interpretation of disability is suggested in several studies of

the history of disability legislation; see Scotch, *From Good Will to Civil Rights*; Stone, *The Disabled State*; Liachowitz, *Disability as a Social Construct*; and Shapiro, *No Pity*.

7. For example, Robert Bone in *The Negro Novel in America* (New Haven: Yale University Press, 1958) sees Petry's novel as a successor to *Native Son*. Addison Gayle, Jr., analyzes *The Street* as a naturalist novel in *The Way of the New World: The Black Novel in America* (New York: Anchor/Doubleday, 1975, pp. 192–97).

8. Definitions of True Womanhood and New Womanhood can be found in Barbara Welter's essay "The Cult of True Womanhood: 1820–1860," and in Smith-Rosenberg's *Disorderly Conduct*, pp. 245–96.

9. Sharon Harris explicates *Life in the Iron Mills* as the forerunner of the naturalist novel in "Rebecca Harding Davis: From Romance to Realism," *American Literary Realism* 21 (2): 4–20.

10. Deb and Lutie are parallel in this respect: their actions accomplish exactly the opposite of what was intended, defeating both women. For Mrs. Hedges there is no disparity between intention and effect.

11. Baym, *Women's Fiction*, pp. 11–12.

12. In *The Bonds of Womanhood*, Nancy Cott analyzes the nineteenth-century ideology of feminine "passionlessness" as a functional cultural reformulation of the belief in female carnality as weakness and moral turpitude. If passionlessness placed nineteenth-century women on a higher moral plane and increased their status and independence, it has now outlived its usefulness, tending to alienate women from their own sexuality.

13. Marjorie Pryse, in " 'Pattern Against the Sky': Deism and Motherhood in Ann Petry's *The Street*," in Marjorie Pryse and Hortense J. Spillers, eds., *Conjuring: Black Women, Fiction, and Literary Tradition* (Bloomington: Indiana University Press, 1985), pp. 116–31, explores the implications of Lutie's identification with the Ben Franklin script, analyzing the novel and Mrs. Hedges in terms of deism. Pryse also suggests that Lutie's actions and attitudes are self-defeating and notes how she might have used Mrs. Hedges and others as models of survival, but Pryse does not go on to elaborate Mrs. Hedges's potential for becoming the new heroine.

14. John Berger, *Ways of Seeing* (London: British Broadcasting Corporation, 1972), p. 47.

15. Wolfgang Kayser is quoted in Michael Steig, "Defining the Grotesque: An Attempt at Synthesis," *Journal of Aesthetics and Art Criticism* 29 (2): 253.

16. William Van O'Connor traces the grotesque as "an American genre" from the gothic Poe, through the naturalists Crane and Norris, to Faulkner and the southern writers who are read through his work, and finally to the absurdist modernists such as Nathanael West and Nelson Algren (*The Grotesque: An American Genre, and Other Essays* [Carbondale: Southern Illinois University Press, 1962]). I would argue that the canon of modernist alienation is to some extent self-perpetuating; it promotes the trope of the grotesque by—like any other canon—selecting and reinforcing representations that support its theses.

17. One typical example is Gilbert H. Muller's analysis of Flannery O'Connor's "grotesque" disabled characters: "the protagonist, possessing a physiognomy that parallels her distorted spirit, is completely alienated from the world" (*Nightmares and Visions: Flannery O'Connor and the Catholic Grotesque* [Athens: University of Georgia Press, 1972], p. 27). O'Connor's critics seem unable to go beyond this type of reading; the term "grotesque" prevents their seeing her work as perhaps an exploration of physical disability. An exception is Kathleen Patterson's perceptive exploration of O'Connor's work in terms of a politicized disability awareness ("Disability and Identity in Flannery O'Connor's Short Fiction" [unpublished manuscript, 1991]). Ann Carlton also goes "Beyond Gothic and Grotesque" in her feminist analysis of Carson McCullers, although she does not treat disability directly ("Beyond Gothic and Grotesque: A Feminist View of Three Female Characters of Carson McCullers," *Pembroke* 20 [1988]: 54–68).

18. For like-minded discussions of the grotesque, see Philip Thomson, *The Grotesque* (London: Methuen, 1972); Frances K. Barasch, "Introduction," in Thomas Wright, *A History of Caricature and Grotesque in Literature and Art* (1865; reprint, New York: Frederick Ungar, 1968); Harpham, *On the Grotesque* (quotations at pp. 30 and 11); Stallybrass and White, *The Poetics and Politics of Transgression*; Bahktin, *The Dialogic Imagination*; and Cassuto, *The Inhuman Race*. Like every other theorist I cite except Goffman, these theorists of the grotesque never make an explicit connection between their theories and actual disabled people. Although Harpham, for example, mentions "the various cripples and amputees" in Flannery O'Connor's fiction, he never explores the distinctions between fantastic and human grotesques. Considerations of disability as a social category are limited almost exclusively to scholarly works that announce themselves as disability studies. Also see Turner, *The Forest of Symbols*, quotation at p. 97.

19. I want to stress that this refiguration is different from the use of disability as a trope. These disabled figures are not metaphors; rather, their representation mediates both the life experience and the social identity of disability, potentially recasting its cultural meaning. Murphy's ethnography of disability as liminality (*The Body Silent*) focuses primarily on loss of role and status because this was his own experience of becoming disabled. However, Fine and Asch suggest that disabled women's rolelessness can be freeing (*Women with Disabilities*, pp. 1–31). In any case, women, particularly black women, often have less cultural capital to lose by becoming disabled than do previously normate white men such as Murphy.

20. Donna Haraway, "A Manifesto for Cyborgs: Science, Technology, and Socialist Feminism in the 1980s," *Socialist Review* 80: 67.

21. Identifications such as "powerful woman" and "disabled person," which I am calling oxymoronic here, function similarly to the hyphenated ethnic identities, such as African-American, that W. E. B. Du Bois famously notes express the "double-consciousness" of their bearers. See *The Souls of Black Folks* (1903; reprint, New York: New American Library, 1982), p. 45.

22. Haraway, "A Manifesto for Cyborgs," quotations at pp. 65, 91, 73, and 95. Although Haraway does not develop a connection between cyborgs and disabled people, she notes in passing when discussing computers that "paraplegics and other severely handicapped people can . . . have the most intense experiences of complex hybridization with other communication devices" (p. 97). Although she refers to prosthetic devices as "friendly selves," she does not go on to acknowledge that a wheelchair is a part of the self, or that disability brings together two ostensibly mutually exclusive states.

23. For a discussion of prosthesis as a cultural concept, see David Wills, *Prosthesis* (Stanford: Stanford University Press, 1995).

24. Claudia Tate, ed., *Black Women Writers at Work* (New York: Continuum, 1988), p. 129.

25. Susan Willis's essay historicizing Morrison's first four novels cursorily discusses "lack, deformity, and self-mutilation as figures for liberation" ("Eruptions of Funk: Historicizing Toni Morrison," in *Specifying: Black Women Writing the American Experience* [Madison: University of Wisconsin Press, 1987], p. 104). Although Willis's main argument concerns the novels' resistance to bourgeois culture, she recognizes a relation between disability and social otherness in Morrison's fiction, suggesting that self-mutilation redefines the individual as a "new and whole person, occupying a radically different social space" (p. 103). While my reading of disabled figures agrees with her brief explication, this study extends and focuses the analysis much further, treating disability as a socially constructed identity that complicates racial and gender categories, not simply as a physical condition.

26. Henry Louis Gates Jr., "The Blackness of Blackness: A Critique of the Sign and the Signifying Monkey," in Henry Louis Gates Jr., ed., *Black Literature and Literary Theory* (New York: Methuen, 1984), p. 287.

27. Asch and Fine, eds., "Disabled Women: Sexism without the Pedestal," *Journal of Sociology and Social Welfare* 8 (2): 233–48.

28. Denver, Baby Suggs's granddaughter and Beloved's sister, also is physically disabled, having become deaf for two years in a psychological refusal to hear the truth about her sister's death. I have chosen, however, not to include her in this analysis, although she conforms fairly well to the pattern, because her disability is temporary. Sethe, Denver's mother, whom I do include because of the scar on her back, also has a temporary disability that should be noted: she stutters from the time that her mother is hanged until she first sees Halle, her husband-to-be.

29. By encompassing formal aspects such as birthmarks and functional conditions such as mobility impairments in the single category of "disability," I do not mean to propose an equivalence among all physically stigmatized conditions, but to suggest instead the interrelated sociopolitical interpretations of these marks. I am asserting as well that Morrison's narratives frame femaleness, nonwhiteness, and disability not as natural, inherently limiting biological conditions, but as identities shaped by the physical, institutional, and social aspects of an unaccommodating environment.

30. Tate, *Black Women Writers at Work*, p. 128.

31. Goffman, *Stigma*, p. 1; Gates Jr., "The Blackness of Blackness," p. 300.

32. Tate, *Black Women Writers at Work*, p. 129.

33. I am grateful to Mae Henderson for having pointed out this detail about Sethe's mother to me.

34. Susan Stewart, *Nonsense: Aspects of Intertextuality in Folklore and Literature* (Baltimore: Johns Hopkins University Press, 1978), p. 21.

35. Ibid.

36. Pauline, like the other ideal servant and the respectable lady characters such as Ondine and Jadine Childs in *Tar Baby*, Helene Wright in *Sula*, and Ruth Dead in *Song of Solomon*, is excluded from mythic representation to the same degree that she accepts her values and definitions from the dominant order.

37. Stewart, *Nonsense*, p. 62.

38. Kriegel, "The Wolf in the Pit in the Zoo," p. 22; Marshall, *Brown Girl, Brownstones*, p. 28.

39. Tate, *Black Women Writers at Work*, p. 115.

40. Biddy Martin's essay "Lesbian Identity and Autobiographical Difference[s]" in Bella Brodzki and Celeste Schenck, eds., *Life/Lines: Theorizing Women's Autobiography* (Ithaca: Cornell University Press, 1988), pp. 77–103, makes similar claims for the iconoclastic potential of the lesbian perspective in autobiography, asserting that "[l]esbian autobiographical narratives are about remembering differently, outside the contours and narrative constraints of conventional models" (p. 85). Audre Lorde is quoted from *Sister Outsider*, p. 40.

41. This poststructuralist/feminist effort is, of course, similar to *l'Ecriture Feminine* produced by Helene Cixous (see, for example, "The Laugh of the Medusa," *Signs: Journal of Women in Culture and Society* 1 [1976]: 875–93). Lorde's attempt here, however, seems grounded more in material experience and less in linguistic theory than Cixous's writing the body. For an elaboration of Lorde's poetic theory see "Uses of the Erotic: the Erotic as Power" in *Sister Outsider* (pp. 53–59).

42. This articulation of self is remarkably consonant with the theories of psychologist Jean Baker Miller and her associates at Wellesley College's Stone Center, who assert that women tend to develop a sense of self through relation rather than differentiation (see Miller's *Towards a New Psychology of Women* [Boston: Beacon Press, 1976]). For discussions see also Judith Jordan et al., *Women's Growth in Connection: Writings from the Stone Center* (New York: Guilford, 1991) and Nancy Chodorow, *The Reproduction of Mothering: Psychoanalysis and the Sociology of Gender* (Berkeley: University of California Press, 1978).

43. Claudine Raynaud, " 'A Nutmeg Nestled Inside Its Covering of Mace': Audre Lorde's *Zami*," in Brodzki and Schenck, eds., *Life/Lines*, p. 226.

44. Lorde, *Sister Outsider*, p. 42.

45. Although gender and racial essentialism are now being questioned vigorously by theorists of both subjects, the occasional emphasis on difference to ground a positive-identity politics or nationalism is important politically for both movements. See my ear-

lier discussion of feminism in chapter 2 for an examination of the role of physical differences in political movements.

46. Jacobs, *Incidents in the Life of a Slave Girl*, p. 56.

47. Stowe's advocacy is fervently contested by such critics as James Baldwin in *Notes of a Native Son* (Boston: Beacon Press, 1953), pp. 13–23; and Hortense J. Spillers, "Changing the Letter: The Yokes, the Jokes of Discourse, or, Mrs. Stow, Mr. Reed," in Deborah E. McDowell and Arnold Rampersad, eds., *Slavery and the Literary Imagination: Selected Papers from the English Institute, 1987* (Baltimore: Johns Hopkins University Press, 1989), who claim that her portrayals of black people are negative, condescending, and self-serving.

48. Tate, *Black Women Writers at Work*, p. 129.

49. Lorde, *Sister Outsider*, p. 42.

50. Ibid., p. 112.

BIBLIOGRAPHY

• • • • •

Ainlay, Stephen, Gaylene Becker, and Lerita M. Coleman, eds. *The Dilemma of Difference: A Multidisciplinary View of Stigma*. New York: Plenum Press, 1986.

Alcoff, Linda. "Cultural Feminism Versus Post-Structuralist Feminism: The Identity Crisis in Feminist Theory." *Signs* 13, no. 3 (1988): 405–36.

Altick, Richard D. *The Shows of London*. Cambridge: The Belknap Press of Harvard University Press, 1978.

Anderson, Benedict. *Imagined Communities: Reflections on the Origin and Spread of Nationalism*. New York: Verso, 1991.

Angelou, Maya. *I Know Why the Caged Bird Sings*. Toronto: Bantam Books, 1969.

Appiah, Kwame Anthony. *In My Father's House*. New York: Oxford University Press, 1992.

Aptheker, Bettina. *Tapestries of Life: Women's Work, Women's Consciousness, and the Meaning of Daily Experience*. Amherst: University of Massachusetts Press, 1989.

Arieli, Yehoshua. *Individualism and Nationalism in American Ideology*. Cambridge, Mass.: Center for the Study of the History of Liberty in America, 1964.

Aristotle. *Generation of Animals*. Trans. A. L. Peck. Cambridge: Harvard University Press, 1944.

Aristotle. *Nicomachean Ethics*. Trans. Terence Irwin. Indianapolis: Hackett Publishing, 1985.

Aristotle. "The Poetics." In Hazard Adams, ed., *Critical Theory Since Plato*. New York: Harcourt Brace Jovanovich, 1971, pp. 48–66.

Asch, Adrienne and Michelle Fine, eds. "Moving Beyond Stigma." *Journal of Social Issues* 44, no. 1 (1988).

Bakhtin, Mikhail M. *The Dialogic Imagination*. Ed. Michael Holquist. Trans. Caryl Emerson and Michael Holquist. Austin: Texas University Press, 1981.

Baldwin, James. "Everybody's Protest Novel." In James Baldwin, *Notes of a Native Son*. Boston: Beacon Press, 1955, pp. 13–23.

Balsamo, Anne. "On the Cutting Edge: Cosmetic Surgery and the Technological Production of the Gendered Body." *Camera Obscura* 28 (Jan. 1992): 207–36.

Banner, Lois W. *American Beauty*. New York: Alfred A. Knopf, 1983.

_____. "Religious Benevolence as Social Control: A Critique of an Interpretation." *Journal of American History* 60, no. 1 (June 1973): 23–41.

Barasch, Frances K. "Introduction." In Thomas Wright, *A History of Caricature and Grotesque in Literature and Art.* 1865. Reprint, New York: Frederick Ungar, 1968.

Barker-Benfield, G. J. *The Horrors of the Half-Known Life: Male Attitudes Toward Women and Sexuality in Nineteenth-Century America.* New York: Harper & Row, 1976.

Barnum, P. T. *Struggles and Triumphs.* 1869. Reprint, New York: Arno Press, 1970.

Barrow, Mark V. "A Brief History of Teratology." In T. V. N. Persaud, ed., *Problems of Birth Defects.* Baltimore: University Park Press, 1977, pp. 18–28.

Baym, Nina, et al., eds. *Norton Anthology of American Literature.* 4th ed. New York: Norton, 1994.

_____. *Women's Fiction: A Guide to Novels by and about Women in America, 1820–1870.* Ithaca: Cornell University Press, 1978.

Baynton, Douglas C. "A Silent Exile on This Earth: The Metaphorical Construction of Deafness in the Nineteenth Century." *American Quarterly* 44, no. 2 (June 1992): 216–43.

de Beauvoir, Simone. *The Second Sex.* Trans. H. M. Parshley. 1952; reprint, New York: Vintage, 1974, p. xix.

Becker, Ernest. *The Denial of Death.* New York: The Free Press, 1973.

Beecher, Henry Ward. *Lectures to Young Men, on Various Important Subjects.* New York: J. B. Ford, 1873.

Bellah, Robert N., et al. *Habits of the Heart: Individualism and Commitment in American Life.* Berkeley: University of California Press, 1985.

Berger, John. *Ways of Seeing.* London: British Broadcasting Corporation, 1972.

Berger, Peter and Thomas Luchmann. *The Social Construction of Reality.* New York: Doubleday, 1966.

Biklin, Douglas and Lee Bailey, eds. *Rudely Stamp'd: Imaginal Disability and Prejudice.* Washington, D.C.: University Press of America, 1981.

Biklin, Douglas and Robert Bogdan. "Media Portrayals of Disabled People: A Study in Stereotypes." *Interracial Books for Children Bulletin* 8, nos. 6, 7 (1977): 4–9.

Blumin, Stuart. *The Emergence of the Middle Class: Social Experience in the American City, 1760–1900.* Cambridge: Cambridge University Press, 1989.

Bogdan, Robert. *Freak Show: Presenting Human Oddities for Amusement and Profit.* Chicago: University of Chicago Press, 1988.

Bogdan, Robert and Steven Taylor. "Toward a Sociology of Acceptance: The Other Side of the Study of Deviance." *Social Policy* 18, no.2 (Fall 1987): 34–39.

Bondeson, Jan and A. E. W. Miles. "Julia Pastrana, the Nondescript: An Example of Congenital, Generalized Hypertrichosis Terminalis with Gingival Hyperplasia." *American Journal of Medical Genetics* 47 (1993): 198–212.

Bone, Robert. *The Negro Novel in America.* New Haven: Yale University Press, 1958.

Bordo, Susan R. "The Body and the Reproduction of Femininity: A Feminist

Appropriation of Foucault." In Alison Jaggar and Susan Bordo, eds., *Gender/Body/ Knowledge: Feminist Reconstructions of Being and Knowing*. New Brunswick, N.J.: Rutgers University Press, 1989, pp. 13–31.

———. *Unbearable Weight: Feminism, Western Culture, and the Body*. Berkeley: University of California Press, 1993.

Boucht, Brigitta, et al. *Postfeminism*. Esbo, Finland: Draken, 1991.

Bowe, Frank. *Handicapping America: Barriers to Disabled People*. New York: Harper and Row, 1978.

Boydston, Jeanne, Mary Kelley, and Anne Margolis. *The Limits of Sisterhood: The Beecher Sisters on Women's Rights and Woman's Sphere*. Chapel Hill, N.C.: The University of North Carolina Press, 1988.

Bradford, Phillips Verner and Harvey Blume. *Ota Benga: The Pygmy in the Zoo*. New York: St. Martin's Press, 1992.

Brown, Gillian. *Domestic Individualism: Imagining Self in Nineteenth-Century America*. Berkeley: University of California Press, 1990.

Brown, Richard D. *Modernization: The Transformation of American Life 1600–1865*. New York: Hill and Wang, 1976.

Buckland, Francis T. "The Female Nondescript Julia Pastrana, and Exhibitions of Human Mummies, etc." In *Curiosities of Natural History*. vol. 4. London: Richard Bentley and Son, 1888.

Burbick, Joan. *Healing the Republic: The Language of Health and the Culture of Nationalism in Nineteenth-Century America*. New York: Cambridge University Press, 1994.

Burgdorf, Marcia Pearce and Robert Burgdorf, Jr. "A History of Unequal Treatment: The Qualifications of Handicapped Persons as a 'Suspect Class' Under the Equal Protection Clause." *Santa Clara Lawyer* 15 (1975): 855–910.

Butler, Judith. *Bodies That Matter: On the Discursive Limits of "Sex."* New York: Routledge, 1993.

———. *Gender Trouble: Feminism and the Subversion of Identity*. New York: Routledge, 1990.

Canguilhem, Georges. *The Normal and the Pathological*. Trans. Carolyn R. Fawcett with Robert S. Cohen. New York: Zone Books, 1989.

Carlton, Ann. "Beyond Gothic and Grotesque: A Feminist View of Three Female Characters of Carson McCullers." *Pembroke* 20 (1988): 54–68.

Cassuto, Leonard D. *The Inhuman Race: The Racial Grotesque in American Literature and Culture*. New York: Columbia University Press, 1996.

Chernin, Kim. *The Hungry Self: Women, Eating, and Identity*. New York: Times Books, 1985.

———. *The Obsession: Reflections on the Tyranny of Slenderness*. New York: Harper & Row, 1981.

Chodorow, Nancy. *The Reproduction of Mothering: Psychoanalysis and the Sociology of Gender*. Berkeley: University of California Press, 1978.

Cixous, Helene. "The Laugh of the Medusa." *Signs: Journal of Women in Culture and Society* 1 (1976): 875–93.

Cohen, Jeffrey Jerome, ed. *Monster Theory: Reading Culture.* Minneapolis: University of Minnesota Press, 1996.

Cohen, Patricia Cline. *A Calculating People: The Spread of Numeracy in Early America.* Chicago: University of Chicago Press, 1982.

Collins, Patricia Hill. *Black Feminist Thought: Knowledge, Consciousness, and the Politics of Empowerment.* Boston: Unwin Hyman, 1990.

Compton, Tom. "The Brief History of Disability." Berkeley, Cal.: unpublished manuscript, 1989.

Cott, Nancy F. *The Bonds of Womanhood: "Woman's Sphere" in New England, 1780–1835.* New Haven: Yale University Press, 1977.

Coultrap-McQuin, Susan. *Doing Literary Business: American Women Writers in the Nineteenth Century.* Chapel Hill, N.C.: University of North Carolina Press, 1990.

Cummins, Maria. *The Lamplighter.* Boston: Houghton, Osgood, 1879.

"Curious History of the Baboon Lady, Miss Julia Pastrana." Pamphlet. Cambridge: Harvard Theater Collection.

Daly, Mary. *Gyn/ecology: The Metaethics of Radical Feminism.* Boston: Beacon Press, 1978.

Davis, Fred. "Deviance Disavowal: The Management of Strained Interaction by the Visibly Handicapped." *Social Problems* 9 (1961): 120–32.

Davis, Kathy. *Reshaping the Female Body: The Dilemma of Cosmetic Surgery.* New York: Routledge, 1995.

Davis, Lennard J. *Enforcing Normalcy: Disability, Deafness, and the Body.* New York: Verso, 1995.

_____, ed. *The Disability Studies Reader.* New York: Routledge, 1996.

Davis, Rebecca Harding. *Life in the Iron Mills.* 1861. Reprint, New York: Feminist Press, 1972.

_____. *Margret Howth.* 1862. Reprint, New York: Feminist Press, 1990.

DeBord, Guy. *Society of the Spectacle.* Detroit: Black and Red, 1983.

Dimock, Wai Chee. *Empire for Liberty: Melville and the Poetics of Individualism.* Princeton: Princeton University Press, 1989.

Donovan, Josephine. *Feminist Theory.* New York: Continuum, 1992.

Douglas, Ann. *The Feminization of American Culture.* New York: Alfred A. Knopf, 1977.

Douglas, Mary. *Purity and Danger: An Analysis of Concepts of Pollution and Taboo.* New York: Praeger, 1966.

Drimmer, Frederick. *Born Different: Amazing Stories of Very Special People.* New York: Atheneum, 1988.

_____. *Very Special People.* New York: Amjon Press, 1983.

Du Bois, W. E. Burghardt. *The Souls of Black Folk.* 1903. Reprint, New York: New American Library, 1982.

Dyer, Richard. *The Matter of Images: Essays on Representation*. New York: Routledge, 1993.

Ehrenreich, Barbara and Deirdre English. *For Her Own Good: 150 Years of the Experts' Advice to Women*. Garden City, N.Y.: Anchor Books, 1979.

Eisenstein, Hester. *Contemporary Feminist Thought*. Boston: G. K. Hall, 1983.

Elshtain, Jean Bethke. *Public Man, Private Woman: Women in Social and Political Thought*. Princeton: Princeton University Press, 1981.

Emerson, Ralph Waldo. *The Works of Ralph Waldo Emerson*. Boston: Houghton Mifflin, 1865.

Erkkila, Betsy. "Ethnicity, Literary Theory, and the Grounds of Resistance." *American Quarterly* 47, no. 4 (Dec. 1995): 563–94.

Evans, Sara M. *Born for Liberty: A History of Women in America*. New York: The Free Press, 1989.

Faludi, Susan. *Backlash: The Undeclared War Against American Women*. New York: Crown, 1991.

Fiedler, Leslie. *Freaks: Myths and Images of the Secret Self*. New York: Simon and Schuster, 1978.

_____. *Love and Death in the American Novel*. New York: Criterion Books, 1960.

_____. "Pity and Fear." *Salmagundi* 57 (Fall 1982): 57–69.

Fine, Michelle and Adrienne Asch, eds. *Women with Disabilities: Essays in Psychology, Culture, and Politics*. Philadelphia: Temple University Press, 1988.

_____. "Disabled Women: Sexism without the Pedestal." *Journal of Sociology and Social Welfare* 8 (2): 233–48.

Finger, Anne. "Claiming All Our Bodies: Reproductive Rights and Disability." In Rita Arditti, Renate Duell Klein, and Shelley Minden, eds., *Test-Tube Women: What Future for Motherhood?* Boston: Pandora, 1984.

Finkelstein, Victor. *Attitudes and Disabled People: Issues for Discussion*. New York: World Rehabilitation Fund, 1980.

Firestone, Shulamith. *The Dialectic of Sex: The Case for Feminist Revolution*. New York: William Morrow, 1970.

Fisher, Philip. *Hard Facts: Setting and Form in the American Novel*. New York: Oxford University Press, 1985.

Foucault, Michel. *The Archaeology of Knowledge and the Discourse on Language*. Trans. Alan M. Sheridan-Smith. New York: Pantheon, 1972.

_____. *Birth of the Clinic: An Archaeology of Medical Perception*. Trans. Alan M. Sheridan-Smith. New York: Pantheon, 1973.

_____. *Discipline and Punish: The Birth of the Prison*. Trans. Alan M. Sheridan-Smith. New York: Vintage Books, 1979.

_____. *Madness and Civilization: A History of Insanity in the Age of Reason*. Trans. Richard Howard. New York: Pantheon, 1965.

_____. *Power/Knowledge: Selected Interviews and Other Writings*. Ed. and trans. Colin Gordon. New York: Pantheon, 1980.

Fox-Genovese, Elizabeth. *Feminism Without Illusions*. Chapel Hill: University of North California Press, 1991.

Freaks. Dir. Tod Browning. Metro-Goldwyn-Mayer, 1932.

Freedman, Rita Jackaway. *Beauty Bound*. Lexington, Mass.: Lexington Books, 1986.

Friedman, John Block. *The Monstrous Races in Medieval Art and Thought*. Cambridge: Harvard University Press, 1981.

Friedman, Lawrence M. and Jack Ladinsky. "Social Change and the Law of Industrial Accidents." *Columbia Law Review* 67, no. 1 (Jan. 1967): 50–81.

Freud, Sigmund. "Some Character Types Met with in Psycho-Analytic Work." In *Collected Papers* vol. 4. Trans. Joan Riviere. London: Hogarth, 1957, pp. 318–23.

Fuss, Diana. *Essentially Speaking: Feminism, Nature, and Difference*. New York: Routledge, 1989.

Gallagher, Hugh Gregory. *By Trust Betrayed: Patients, Physicians, and the License to Kill in the Third Reich*. New York: Holt, 1989.

_____. *FDR's Splendid Deception*. New York: Dodd Mead, 1985.

Gartner, Alan and Tom Joe, eds. *Images of the Disabled, Disabling Images*. New York: Praeger, 1987.

Gates, Henry Louis, Jr. "The Blackness of Blackness: A Critique of the Sign and the Signifying Monkey." In Henry Louis Gates, Jr., ed., *Black Literature and Literary Theory*. New York: Methuen, 1984, pp. 285–321.

Gayle, Addison, Jr. "The Black Rebel." In *The Way of the New World: The Black Novel in America*. New York: Anchor/Doubleday, 1975.

Gerber, David. "Volition and Valorization: The 'Careers' of People Exhibited in Freak Shows." In Rosemarie Garland Thomson, ed., *Freakery: Cultural Spectacles of the Extraordinary Body*. New York: New York University Press, 1996.

Giddings, Paula. *When and Where I Enter: The Impact of Black Women on Race and Sex in America*. New York: Bantam Books, 1984.

Gilligan, Carol. *In a Different Voice: Psychological Theory and Women's Development*. Cambridge: Harvard University Press, 1982.

Gilman, Charlotte Perkins. *Women and Economics*. 1898. Reprint, New York: Harper Torchbooks, 1966.

_____. "The Yellow Wallpaper." *New England Magazine* (Jan. 1892).

Gilman, Sander L. *Difference and Pathology: Stereotypes of Sexuality, Race, and Madness*. Ithaca: Cornell University Press, 1985.

Ginzberg, Lori D. *Women and the Work of Benevolence: Morality, Politics, and Class in the Nineteenth-Century United States*. New Haven: Yale University Press, 1990.

Goffman, Erving. *Stigma: Notes on the Management of Spoiled Identity*. Englewood Cliffs, N.J.: Prentice-Hall, 1963.

Gould, George M. and Walter L. Pyle. *Anomalies and Curiosities of Medicine*. Philadelphia: W. B. Saunders, 1897.

Gould, Stephen Jay. *The Flamingo's Smile: Reflections in Natural History*. New York: Norton, 1985.

_____. "The Hottentot Venus." *Natural History* 91, no. 10 (Oct. 1982): 20–27.

_____. *The Mismeasure of Man.* New York: Norton, 1981.

Grant, Judith. *Fundamental Feminism: Contesting the Core Concepts of Feminist Theory.* New York: Routledge, 1993.

Greenblatt, Stephen. "Fiction and Friction." In Thomas C. Heller et al., eds., *Reconstructing Individualism: Autonomy, Individuality and Self in Western Thought.* Stanford: Stanford University Press, 1986, pp. 30–52.

Groce, Nora. *Everyone Here Spoke Sign Language: Hereditary Deafness on Martha's Vineyard.* Cambridge: Harvard University Press, 1985.

Grosz, Elizabeth. "Intolerable Ambiguity: Freaks as/at the Limit." In Rosemarie Garland Thomson, ed., *Freakery: Cultural Spectacles of the Extraordinary Body.* New York: New York University Press, 1996.

Hahn, Harlan. "Can Disability Be Beautiful?" *Social Policy* (Fall 1988): 26–31.

Haller, Mark H. *Eugenics: Hereditarian Attitudes in American Thought.* New Brunswick, N.J.: Rutgers University Press, 1984.

Haraway, Donna. "A Manifesto for Cyborgs: Science, Technology, and Socialist Feminism in the 1980s." *Socialist Review* 80 (1985): 65–107.

Harpham, Geoffrey Galt. *On the Grotesque: Strategies of Contradiction in Art and Literature.* Princeton: Princeton University Press, 1982.

Harris, Neil. *Humbug: The Art of P. T. Barnum.* Boston: Little, Brown, 1973.

Harris, Sharon M. *Rebecca Harding Davis and American Realism.* Philadelphia: Pennsylvania University Press, 1991.

_____. "Rebecca Harding Davis: From Romance to Realism." *American Literary Realism* 21, no. 2 (Winter 1989): 4–20.

Haskell, Thomas L. "Capitalism and the Origins of the Humanitarian Sensibility, Part 1." *American History Review* 90, no. 2 (April 1985): 339–61.

_____. "Capitalism and the Origins of the Humanitarian Sensibility, Part 2." *American History Review* 90, no. 3 (June 1985): 547–66.

Hawthorne, Nathaniel. *The Scarlet Letter: A Romance.* 1850. Reprint, New York: Bobbs-Merrill, 1963.

Hays, Peter L. *The Limping Hero: Grotesques in Literature.* New York: New York University Press, 1971.

Heilbrun, Carolyn. *Writing a Woman's Life.* New York: Norton, 1988.

Hennessy, Rosemary. *Materialist Feminism and the Politics of Discourse.* New York: Routledge, 1993.

Hermann, Otto W. *Fahrend Volk.* Signor Salterino, Leipzig: Weber, 1895.

Hevey, David. *The Creatures Time Forgot: Photography and Disability Imagery.* London: Routledge, 1992.

Herndl, Diane Price. *Invalid Women: Figuring Illness in American Fiction and Culture, 1840–1940.* Chapel Hill: University of North Carolina Press, 1993.

_____ and Robyn Warhol. *Feminisms.* New Brunswick, N.J.: Rutgers University Press, 1991.

Hillyer, Barbara. *Feminism and Disability*. Norman, Okla.: University of Oklahoma Press, 1993.

Hirsch, Marianne and Evelyn Fox Keller, eds. *Conflicts in Feminism*. New York: Routledge, 1990.

Hofstadter, Richard. *Social Darwinism in American Thought*. Boston: Beacon Press, 1944.

hooks, bell. *Ain't I A Woman: Black Women and Feminism*. Boston: South End Press, 1981.

Horowitz, Maryanne Cline. "Aristotle and Women." *Journal of the History of Biology* 9 (1976): 183–213.

Hubbard, Ruth. "Who Should and Should Not Inhabit the World." In Ruth Hubbard, ed., *The Politics of Women's Biology*. New Brunswick, N.J.: Rutgers University Press, 1990, pp. 179–98.

Huet, Marie-Hélène. *Monstrous Imagination*. Cambridge: Harvard University Press, 1993.

Hurston, Zora Neale. *Their Eyes Were Watching God*. Chicago: University of Illinois Press, 1978.

Jacobs, Harriet. *Incidents in the Life of a Slave Girl*. 1861. Reprint, Cambridge: Harvard University Press, 1987.

Jameson, Fredric. "Postmodernism, or The Cultural Logic of Late Capitalism." *New Left Review* 146 (July-Aug. 1984): 53–92.

Jehlen, Myra. *American Incarnation: The Individual, the Nation, and the Continent*. Cambridge: Harvard University Press, 1986.

Johnson, Charles. *Middle Passage*. New York: MacMillan, 1990.

Johnson, James Weldon. *The Autobiography of an Ex-Coloured Man*. New York: Alfred A. Knopf, 1927.

Jones, Edward E., et al. *Social Stigma: The Psychology of Marked Relationships*. New York: Freeman, 1984.

Jordan, Judith, et al. *Women's Growth in Connection: Writings from the Stone Center*. New York: Guilford, 1991.

Kant, Immanuel. "Critique of Judgement." In Hazard Adams, ed., *Critical Theory Since Plato*. New York: Harcourt Brace, 1971, pp. 379–99.

Kaplan, Deborah. "Disability Rights: Perspectives on Reproductive Technologies and Public Policy." In Sherrie Cohen and Nadine Taub, eds., *Reproductive Laws for the 1990s*. Totowa, N.J.: Humanities Press, 1989, pp. 241–47.

Kaplan, E. Ann. "Is the Gaze Male?" In Ann Snitow, Christine Stansell, and Sharon Thompson, eds., *Powers of Desire: The Politics of Sexuality*. New York: Monthly Review Press, 1983, pp. 309–25.

Katz, Michael B. *In the Shadow of the Poorhouse: A Social History of Welfare in America*. New York: Basic Books, 1986.

Keller, Evelyn Fox. "Gender and Science." In Evelyn Fox Keller, ed., *Reflections on Gender and Science*. New Haven: Yale University Press, 1985, pp. 75–94.

Kelley, Mary. *Private Woman, Public Stage: Literary Domesticity in Nineteenth-Century America*. New York: Oxford University Press, 1984.

_____. "The Sentimentalists: Promise and Betrayal in the Home." *Signs: Journal of Women in Culture and Society* 4, no. 31 (1979): 434–46.

Kent, Deborah. "In Search of a Heroine: Images of Women with Disabilities in Fiction and Drama." In Asch and Fine, eds., *Women with Disabilities*, pp. 90–110.

Kessler, Carol Farley. *Elizabeth Stuart Phelps*. Boston: Twayne, 1982.

Kevles, Daniel J. *In the Name of Eugenics: Genetics and the Uses of Human Heredity*. Berkeley: University of California Press, 1985.

Kittay, Eva Feder and Diana T. Meyers. *Women and Moral Theory*. Totowa, N.J.: Rowman and Littlefield, 1987.

Kokaska, Charles, et al. "Disabled People in the Bible." *Rehabilitation Literature* 45, no. 1–2 (1984): 20–21.

Kolodny, Annette. *The Land Before Her*. Chapel Hill: University of North Carolina Press, 1985.

Kracauer, Siegfried. *The Mass Ornament: Weimar Essays*. Trans. and ed. Thomas Y. Levin. Cambridge: Harvard University Press, 1995.

Kriegel, Leonard. "Uncle Tom and Tiny Tim: Some Reflections on the Cripple as Negro." *The American Scholar* 38, no. 3 (Summer 1969): 412–30.

_____. "The Wolf in the Pit in the Zoo." *Social Policy* (Fall 1982): 16–23.

Kristeva, Julia. *Powers of Horror: An Essay on Abjection*. Trans. Leon S. Roudiez. New York: Columbia University Press, 1982.

Kuhn, Thomas S. *The Structure of Scientific Revolutions*. Chicago: University of Chicago Press, 1992.

Kunhardt, Philip B., Jr., Philip B. Kunhardt III, and Peter W. Kunhardt. *P. T. Barnum: America's Greatest Showman*. New York: Alfred A. Knopf, 1995.

Lakoff, Robin Tolmach and Raquel L. Scherr. *Face Value: The Politics of Beauty*. Boston: Routledge, 1984.

Lane, Harlan. *When the Mind Hears: A History of the Deaf*. New York: Random House, 1984.

Lang, Amy Schrager. "Class and the Strategies of Sympathy." In Shirley Samuels, ed., *The Culture of Sentiment: Race, Gender, and Sentimentality in Nineteenth-Century America*. New York: Oxford University Press, 1992.

_____. *Prophetic Woman: Anne Hutchinson and the Problem of Dissent in the Literature of New England*. Berkeley: University of California Press, 1987.

Laqueur, Thomas W. "Bodies, Details, and the Humanitarian Narrative." In Lynn Hunt, ed., *The New Cultural History*. Berkeley: California University Press, 1989.

_____. *Making Sex: Body and Gender from the Greeks to Freud*. Cambridge: Harvard University Press, 1990.

Laurence, J. Z. "A Short Account of the Bearded and Hairy Female." *Lancet* 2 (1857): 48.

Lazerson, Marvin. "The Origins of Special Education." In J. G. Chambers and William T. Hartman, eds., *Special Education Politics: Their History, Implementation, and Finance*. Philadelphia: Temple University Press, 1983, pp. 15–47.

Leavitt, Judith Walzer, ed. *Women and Health in America*. Madison: University of Wisconsin Press, 1984.

Lenihan, J. "Disabled Americans: A History." *Performances* (Nov./Dec. 1976–Jan. 1977): 1–69.

Lerner, Gerda. "The Lady and the Mill Girl: Changes in the Status of Women in the Age of Jackson." *Midcontinent American Studies Journal* 10 (1969): 5–15.

Lerner, Melvin. *The Belief in a Just World*. New York: Plenum, 1980.

Leverenz, David. "The Politics of Emerson's Man-Making Words." *PMLA* 101, no. 1 (Jan. 1986): 49.

Liachowitz, Claire H. *Disability as a Social Construct: Legislative Roots*. Philadelphia: Pennsylvania University Press, 1988.

Lindfors, Bernth. "Circus Africans." *Journal of American Culture* 6, no. 2 (1983): 9–14.

———. "'The Hottentot Venus' and Other African Attractions in Nineteenth-Century England." *Australasian Drama Studies* 1, no. 2 (1983): 82–104.

———. "P. T. Barnum and Africa." *Studies in Popular Culture* 7 (1984): 18–25.

Longmore, Paul K. "Conspicuous Contribution and American Cultural Dilemmas: Telethons, Virtue, and Community." In David Mitchell, and Sharon Snyder, eds., *Storylines and Lifelines: Narratives of Disability in the Humanities*. Forthcoming.

———. "A Note on Language and the Social Identification of Disabled People." *American Behavioral Scientist* 28, no. 3 (Jan.–Feb. 1985): 419–23.

———. "Screening Stereotypes: Images of Disabled People." *Social Policy* 16 (Summer 1985): 31–38.

Lorde, Audre. *Sister Outsider*. Trumansburg, N.Y.: The Crossing Press, 1984.

———. *Zami: A New Spelling of My Name*. Freedom, Calif.: The Crossing Press, 1982.

Lott, Eric. *Love and Theft: Blackface Minstrelsy and the American Working Class*. New York: Oxford University Press, 1993.

Lukács, Georg. *The Meaning of Contemporary Realism*. Trans. John and Necke Mander. London: Merlin, 1963.

MacAloon, John J. "Olympic Games and the Theory of Spectacle in Modern Times." In John J. MacAloon, ed., *Rite, Drama, Festival, Spectacle: Rehearsals Toward a Theory of Cultural Performance*. Philadelphia: Institute for the Study of Human Issues, 1984, pp. 241–80.

MacPherson, C. B. *The Political Theory of Possessive Individualism: Hobbes to Locke*. Oxford: Clarendon, 1962.

Mairs, Nancy. "On Being a Cripple." In Nancy Mairs, *Plaintext: Essays*. Tucson, Ariz.: University of Arizona Press, 1986, pp. 9–21.

Malpezzi, Frances. "*The Silent Partner*: A Feminist Sermon on the Social Gospel." *Studies in the Humanities* 13, no. 2 (Dec. 1986): 103–10.

Marshall, Paule. *Brown Girl, Brownstones*. Old Westbury, N.Y.: The Feminist Press, 1981.

_____. *Praisesong for the Widow*. New York: Dutton, 1983.

Martin, Biddy. "Lesbian Identity and Autobiographical Difference[s]." In Bella Brodzki and Celeste Schenck, eds., *Life/Lines: Theorizing Women's Autobiography*. Ithaca: Cornell University Press, 1988, pp. 77–103.

Martin, Howard. *Victorian Grotesque*. London: Jupiter Books, 1977.

Mascia-Lees, Frances E. and Patricia Sharpe. "The Marked and the Un(re)marked: Tattoo and Gender in Theory and Narrative." In Frances E. Mascia-Lees and Patricia Sharpe, eds., *Tattoo, Torture, Mutilation, and Adornment*. Albany: SUNY Press, 1992, pp. 145–70.

Massachusetts Historical Society. "The 'Aztec Children.' " *M. H. S. Miscellany* 50 (Spring 1992): 1–3.

Mathiessen, F. O. *The American Renaissance*. New York: Oxford University Press, 1941.

McConachie, Bruce A. "Museum Theater and the Problem of Respectability for Mid-Century Urban Americans." In Ron Engle and Tice L. Miller, eds., *The American Stage: Social and Economic Issues from the Colonial Period to the Present*. New York: Cambridge University Press, 1993, pp. 65–80.

McDonald, Barbara with Cynthia Rich. *Look Me in the Eye: Old Women, Aging, and Ageism*. San Francisco: Spinsters, Ink, 1983.

McNamara, Brooks. "'A Congress of Wonders': The Rise and Fall of the Dime Museum." *ESQ* 20, no. 3 (1974): 216–32.

Melville, Herman. *Moby Dick*. 1851. Reprint, New York: Bobbs-Merrill, 1964.

Messer-Davidow, Ellen. "The Philosophical Bases of Feminist Literary Criticism." *New Literary History: A Journal of Theory and Interpretation* 19, no. 1 (Autumn 1987): 65–103.

Meyer, John W. "Myths of Socialization and of Personality." In Thomas C. Heller et al., eds., *Reconstructing Individualism: Autonomy, Individuality, and Self in Western Thought*. Stanford. Stanford University Press, 1986, pp. 208–21.

Meyers, Marvin. *The Jacksonian Persuasion: Politics and Belief*. New York: Vintage, 1957.

Miles, A. E. W. "Julia Pastrana: The Bearded Lady." *Proceedings of the Royal Society of Medicine* 67 (1974): 160–64.

Miller, Jean Baker. *Towards a New Psychology of Women*. Boston: Beacon Press, 1976.

Minow, Martha. *Making All the Difference: Inclusion, Exclusion, and American Law*. Ithaca: Cornell University Press, 1990.

Mitchell, Michael. *Monsters of the Gilded Age: The Photographs of Charles Eisenmann*. Toronto: Gage, 1979.

Morgan, Kathryn Pauly. "Women and the Knife: Cosmetic Surgery and the Colonization of Women's Bodies." *Hypatia* 6, no. 3 (Fall 1991): 25–53.

Morrison, Toni. *Beloved*. New York: New American Library, 1987.

_____. *The Bluest Eye*. New York: Washington Square Press, 1970.

_____. *Playing in the Dark: Whiteness and the Literary Imagination*. Cambridge: Harvard University Press, 1992.

_____. *Song of Solomon*. New York: New American Library, 1977.

_____. *Sula*. New York: New American Library, 1973.

_____. *Tar Baby*. New York: New American Library, 1981.

Mudrick, Nancy. "Disabled Women." *Society* 20, no. 3 (March/April 1983): 52–55.

Muller, Gilbert H. *Nightmares and Visions: Flannery O'Connor and the Catholic Grotesque*. Athens: University of Georgia Press, 1972.

Murphy, Robert. *The Body Silent*. New York: Holt, 1987.

Nicholson, Linda J. *Feminism/Postmodernism*. New York: Routledge, 1990.

Nightingale, Florence. "Cassandra." 1928. Reprinted in Ray Strachey, ed., *The Cause: A Short History of the Women's Movement in Great Britain*. London: Virago, 1978, pp. 395–418.

Noddings, Nel. *Caring: A Feminine Approach to Ethics and Moral Education*. Berkeley: University of California Press, 1984.

Norden, Martin. *The Cinema of Isolation: A History of Physical Disability in the Movies*. New Brunswick, N.J.: Rutgers University Press, 1994.

Olsen, Tillie. *Silences*. New York: Dell, 1965.

Orbach, Susie. *Fat Is a Feminist Issue: The Anti-Diet Guide to Permanent Weight Loss*. New York: Paddington Press, 1978.

_____. *Hunger Strike: The Anorectic's Struggle as a Metaphor for Our Age*. New York: Norton, 1986.

Paden, Carol and Tom Humphreys. *Deaf in America: Voices from a Culture*. Cambridge: Harvard University Press, 1988.

Pare, Ambroise. *On Monsters and Marvels*. 1573. Trans. Janis Pallister. Reprint, Chicago: University of Chicago Press, 1982.

Park, Katherine and Lorraine Daston. "Unnatural Conceptions: The Study of Monsters in Sixteenth- and Seventeenth-Century France and England." *Past and Present* 92 (Aug. 1981): 20–54.

Parker, Gail. *The Oven Birds: American Women on Womanhood, 1820–1920*. Garden City, N.Y.: Anchor Books, 1972.

Pateman, Carole. *The Sexual Contract*. Stanford: Stanford University Press, 1988.

_____ and Elizabeth Gross, eds. *Feminist Challenges: Social and Political Theory*. Boston: Northeastern University Press, 1986.

Patterson, Kathleen. "Disability and Identity in Flannery O'Connor's Short Fiction." Unpublished manuscript, 1991.

Petry, Ann. *The Street*. 1946. Reprint, Boston: Beacon Press, 1974.

Phelps, Elizabeth S. *Doctor Zay*. 1882. Reprint, New York: The Feminist Press, 1987.

_____. *The Silent Partner*. 1871. Reprint, New York: The Feminist Press, 1983.

_____. "The Tenth of January." In Elizabeth S. Phelps, *The Silent Partner*. 1871. New York: The Feminist Press, 1983.

_____. "Why Shall They Do It?" *Harpers* 36 (1886): 218–23.

Porter, Theodore M. *The Rise of Statistical Thinking, 1820–1900*. Princeton: Princeton University Press, 1986.

Proctor, Robert. *Racial Hygiene: Medicine Under the Nazis*. Cambridge: Harvard University Press, 1988.

Pryse, Marjorie. "'Pattern Against the Sky': Deism and Motherhood in Ann Petry's *The Street*." In Marjorie Pryse and Hortense J. Spillers, eds., *Conjuring: Black Women, Fiction, and Literary Tradition*. Bloomington: Indiana University Press, 1985, pp. 116–31.

Raynaud, Claudine. "'A Nutmeg Nestled Inside Its Covering of Mace': Audre Lorde's *Zami*." In Bella Brodzki and Celeste Schenck, eds., *Life/lines: Theorizing Women's Autobiography*. Ithaca: Cornell University Press, 1988, pp. 221–42.

Reinharz, Shulamit. "Friends or Foes: Gerontological and Feminist Theory." *Women's Studies International Forum* 9, no. 5 (1986): 503–14.

Rich, Adrienne. "When We Dead Awaken." In Adrienne Rich, *On Lies, Secrets, and Silence*. New York: Norton, 1979.

Robinson, Paul. "Responses to Leslie Fiedler." *Salmagundi* 57 (Fall 1982): 74–78.

Rodgers, Daniel T. *The Work Ethic in Industrial America, 1850–1920*. Chicago: University of Chicago Press, 1978.

Roediger, David. *The Wages of Whiteness*. New York: Verso, 1991.

Romm, Sharon. *The Changing Face of Beauty*. St. Louis: Mosby-Year Book, 1992.

Roth, William. "Handicap as a Social Construct." *Society* 20, no. 3 (March/April 1983): 56–61.

Rothman, David. *The Discovery of the Asylum: Social Order and Disorder in the New Republic*. Boston: Little Brown, 1971.

Ruddick, Sara. "Maternal Thinking." *Feminist Studies* 6, no. 2 (Summer 1980): 342–67.

Russo, Mary. *The Female Grotesque: Risk, Excess, and Modernity*. New York: Routledge, 1994.

Ryan, Mary. "The American Parade: Representations of the Nineteenth-Century Social Order." In Lynn Hunt, ed., *The New Cultural History*. Berkeley: University of California Press, 1989, pp. 131–53.

———. *Empire of the Mother: American Writing About Domesticity, 1830–1860*. New York: Institute for Research in History and The Hawthorne Press, 1982.

Sacks, Oliver. *Seeing Voices: A Journey into the World of the Deaf*. Berkeley: University of California Press, 1989.

Samuels, Shirley, ed. *The Culture of Sentiment: Race, Gender, and Sentimentality in Nineteenth-Century America*. New York: Oxford University Press, 1992.

Sanchez-Eppler, Karen. "Bodily Bonds: The Intersecting Rhetorics of Feminism and Abolition." *Representations* 24 (Fall 1988): 28–59.

Saxton, A. H. *P. T. Barnum: The Legend and the Man*. New York: New York University Press, 1989.

Saxton, Marsha. "Born and Unborn: The Implications of Reproductive Technologies for People with Disabilities." In Rita Arditti, Renate Duell Klein, and Shelley

Minden, eds., *Test-Tube Women: What Future for Motherhood?* Boston: Pandora, 1984, pp. 298–312.

———. "Prenatal Screening and Discriminatory Attitudes about Disability." *Gene Watch* (Jan.-Feb. 1987): 8–10.

Scarry, Elaine. *The Body in Pain: The Making and Unmaking of the World.* New York: Oxford University Press, 1985.

Schur, Edwin M. *Labeling Women Deviant: Gender, Stigma, and Social Control.* Philadelphia: Temple University Press, 1983.

Scotch, Richard K. *From Good Will to Civil Rights: Transforming Federal Disability Policy.* Philadelphia: Temple University Press, 1984.

Scott, Joan Wallach. "Deconstructing Equality-Versus-Difference: or, The Uses of Poststructuralist Theory for Feminism." *Feminist Studies* 14, no. 1 (Spring 1988): 33–50.

Sedgwick, Eve Kosofsky. *Epistemology of the Closet.* Berkeley: University of California Press, 1990.

Sekula, Allan. "The Body and the Archive." *October* 39 (Winter 1986): 3–64.

Selzer, Mark. *Bodies and Machines.* New York: Routledge, 1992.

Selzer, Richard. *Mortal Lessons: Notes on the Art of Surgery.* New York: Simon and Schuster, 1987.

Sennett, Richard. *The Fall of Public Man.* New York: Alfred A. Knopf, 1977.

Shapiro, Joseph. *No Pity: People with Disabilities Forging a New Civil Rights Movement.* New York: Times Books/Random House, 1993.

Silvers, Anita. "Reconciling Equality to Difference: Caring (f)or Justice for People with Disabilities." *Hypatia* 10, no. 1 (Winter 1995): 30–55.

Sklar, Kathryn Kish. *Catharine Beecher: A Study in American Domesticity.* New York: Norton, 1973.

Smith, Sidonie. *Subjectivity, Identity, and the Body: Women's Autobiographical Practices in the Twentieth Century.* Bloomington: Indiana University Press, 1993.

Smith-Rosenberg, Carroll. *Disorderly Conduct: Visions of Gender in Victorian America.* New York: Oxford University Press, 1985.

——— and Charles Rosenberg. "The Female Animal: Medical and Biological Views of Woman and Her Role in Nineteenth-Century America." In Judith Leavitt Walzer, ed., *Women and Health in America.* Madison: University of Wisconsin Press, 1984, pp. 12–27.

Sokolov, J. "Julia Pastrana and Her Child." *Lancet* 1 (1862): 467–69.

Solomon, Howard M. "Stigma and Western Culture: A Historical Approach." In Stephen Ainlay et al., eds., *The Dilemma of Difference: A Multidisciplinary View of Stigma.* New York: Plenum, 1986, pp. 59–76.

Sontag, Susan. *Illness as Metaphor.* New York: Farrar, Straus and Giroux, 1977.

Spelman, Elizabeth V. *Inessential Woman: Problems of Exclusion in Feminist Thought.* Boston: Beacon Press, 1988.

Spillers, Hortense J. "Changing the Letter: The Yokes, the Jokes of Discourse, or, Mrs.

Stow, Mr. Reed." In Deborah E. McDowell and Arnold Rampersad, eds., *Slavery and the Literary Imagination: Selected Papers from the English Institute, 1987.* Baltimore: Johns Hopkins University Press, 1989, pp.25–61.

Stallybrass, Peter and Allon White. *The Poetics and Politics of Transgression.* Ithaca: Cornell University Press, 1986.

Starr, Paul. *Social Transformation of American Medicine.* New York: Basic Books, 1982.

Steig, Michael. "Defining the Grotesque: An Attempt at Synthesis." *Journal of Aesthetics and Art Criticism* 29, no.2 (Winter 1970): 253–60.

Stewart, Susan. *Nonsense: Aspects of Intertextuality in Folklore and Literature.* Baltimore: Johns Hopkins University Press, 1978.

_____. *On Longing: Narratives of the Miniature, the Gigantic, the Souvenir, the Collection.* Baltimore: Johns Hopkins University Press, 1984.

Stigler, Stephen M. *The History of Statistics: The Measurement of Uncertainty Before 1900.* Cambridge: Belknap Press of Harvard University Press, 1986.

"Stigmatization." *New Catholic Encyclopedia.* vol. 13. New York: McGraw Hill, 1967, pp. 711–12.

Stone, Deborah A. *The Disabled State.* Philadelphia: Temple University Press, 1984.

Stowe, Harriet Beecher. *The Key to Uncle Tom's Cabin.* London: 1853.

_____. *Uncle Tom's Cabin or, Life Among the Lowly.* 1852. Reprint, New York: Penguin, 1981.

Tagg, John. "A Means of Surveillance: The Photograph as Evidence in Law." In John Tagg, *The Burden of Representation: Evidence, Truth, and Order.* London: Macmillan, 1988, pp. 66–102.

Tate, Claudia, ed. *Black Women Writers at Work.* New York: Continuum, 1988.

Thomas, Brook. *Cross Examinations of Law and Literature: Cooper, Hawthorne, Stowe, and Melville.* Cambridge: Cambridge University Press, 1987.

Thomas, John L. "Romantic Reform in America, 1815–1865." *American Quarterly* 17 (Winter 1965): 656–81.

Thomson, Rosemarie Garland, ed. *Freakery: Cultural Spectacles of the Extraordinary Body.* New York: New York University Press, 1996.

_____. "Redrawing the Boundaries of Feminist Disability Studies." *Feminist Studies* 20 (Fall 1994): 583–95.

Thomson, Philip. *The Grotesque.* London: Methuen, 1972.

Thurer, Shari. "Disability and Monstrosity: A Look at Literary Distortions of Handicapping Conditions." *Rehabilitation Literature* 41, no. 1–2 (1980): 12–15.

Tocqueville, Alexis de. *Democracy in America.* vols. I and II. 1840, 1862. Reprint, New York: Vintage Books, 1990.

Tompkins, Jane. *Sensational Designs: The Cultural Work of American Fiction, 1790–1860.* New York: Oxford University Press, 1985.

Torgovnick, Marianna. *Gone Primitive: Savage Intellects, Modern Lives.* Chicago: University of Chicago Press, 1990.

Truzzi, Marcello. "Circus and Side Shows." In Myron Matlaw, ed., *American Popular Entertainment*. Westport, Conn.: Greenwood Press, 1979, pp. 175–85.

Tuana, Nancy. *The Less Noble Sex: Scientific, Religious, and Philosophical Conceptions of Woman's Nature*. Bloomington: Indiana University Press, 1993.

Turner, Victor. *The Forest of Symbols: Aspects of Ndembu Ritual*. Ithaca: Cornell University Press, 1967.

Twitchell, James B. *Carnival Culture: The Trashing of Taste in America*. New York: Columbia University Press, 1992.

U.S. Senate. 1989. *The Americans with Disabilities Act of 1989*. 101st Cong., 1st sess., S. Res. 933.

Van Cleve, John and Barry Crouch. *A Place of Their Own: Creating the Deaf Community in America*. Washington, D.C.: Gallaudet University Press, 1989.

Van O'Connor, William. *The Grotesque: An American Genre and Other Essays*. Carbondale, Ill.: Southern Illinois University Press, 1962.

Veblen, Thorstein. *The Theory of the Leisure Class*. 1899. Reprint, Boston: Houghton Mifflin, 1973.

Verbrugge, Martha. *Able-Bodied Womanhood: Personal Health and Social Change in Nineteenth-Century Boston*. New York: Oxford University Press, 1988.

Vertinsky, Patricia. "Exercise, Physical Capability, and the Eternally Wounded Woman in Late Nineteenth-Century North America." *Journal of Sport History* 14, no. 1 (1987): 7.

Wade, Cheryl Marie. "I Am Not One of the." *MS.* 11, no. 3 (Nov./Dec. 1991): 57.

Walker, Alice. *The Color Purple*. New York: Washington Square Press, 1982.

———. *Meridian*. New York: Pocket Books, 1976.

Walters, Ronald G. *American Reformers, 1815–1860*. New York: Hill and Wang, 1978.

———. *The Antislavery Appeal: American Abolitionism After 1830*. Baltimore: Johns Hopkins University Press, 1976.

Warhol, Robyn R. "Poetics and Persuasion: *Uncle Tom's Cabin* as a Realist Novel." *Essays in Literature* 13, no. 2 (Fall 1988): 283–98.

Warkany, Josef. "Congenital Malformations in the Past." In T. V. N. Persaud, ed., *Problems of Birth Defects*. Baltimore: University Park Press, 1977, pp. 5–17.

Warren, Joyce W. *American Narcissis: Individualism and Women in Nineteenth-Century American Fiction*. New Brunswick, N.J.: Rutgers University Press, 1984.

Weed, Elizabeth. "Introduction: Terms of Reference." In Elizabeth Weed, ed., *Coming to Terms: Feminism, Theory, Politics*. New York: Routledge, 1989, pp. ix–xxxi.

Weinberg, Nancy. "Another Perspective: Attitudes of People with Disabilities." In Harold E. Yuker, eds., *Attitudes Toward Persons with Disabilities*. New York: Springer, 1988, pp. 141–53.

Welter, Barbara. "The Cult of True Womanhood: 1820–60." *American Quarterly* 18, no. 2 (1966): 151–74.

Wicke, Jennifer. "Celebrity Material: Materialist Feminism and the Culture of Celebrity." *South Atlantic Quarterly* 93, no.4 (Fall 1994): 751–78.

Willis, Susan. "Eruptions of Funk: Historicizing Toni Morrison." In *Specifying: Black Women Writing the American Experience*. Madison: University of Wisconsin Press, 1987, pp. 83–109.

Wilson, Dudley. *Signs and Portents: Monstrous Births from the Middle Ages to the Enlightenment*. London: Routledge, 1993.

Wilson, Harriet E. *Our Nig; or, Sketches From the Life of a Free Black*. 1859. Reprint, New York: Vintage, 1983.

Winship, Michael P. "Prodigies, Puritanism, and the Perils of Natural Philosophy: The Example of Cotton Mather." *William and Mary Quarterly* (Jan. 1994): 92–105.

Wittig, Monique. "The Straight Mind." *Feminist Issues* 1, no. 1 (Summer 1980): 101–10.

Wolf, Naomi. *The Beauty Myth: How Images of Beauty Are Used Against Women*. New York: William Morrow, 1991.

Wolfensberger, Wolf. *The Origin and Nature of Our Institutional Models*. Syracuse, N.Y.: Human Policy Press, 1975.

Woloch, Nancy. *Women and the American Experience*. New York: Alfred A. Knopf, 1984.

Wood, Ann Douglas. "The Fashionable Diseases: Women's Complaints and Their Treatment in Nineteenth-Century America." In Judith Walzer Leavitt, ed., *Women and Health in America*. Madison: University of Wisconsin Press, 1984, pp. 222–38.

Wright, Beatrice. "Attitudes and the Fundamental Negative Bias: Conditions and Corrections." In Harold Yuker, ed., *Attitudes Toward Persons with Disabilities*. New York: Springer, 1988, pp. 3–21.

Young, Iris Marion. *Justice and the Politics of Difference*. Princeton: Princeton University Press, 1990.

_____. *Throwing Like a Girl and Other Essays in Feminist Philosophy and Social Theory*. Bloomington: Indiana University Press, 1990.

Yuker, Harold E., ed. *Attitudes Toward Persons with Disabilities*. New York: Springer, 1988.

Zola, Irving Kenneth. *Missing Pieces: A Chronicle of Living with Disability*. Philadelphia: Temple University Press, 1982.

INDEX

• • • • •